An Introduction to
Danish Culture

ALSO BY NORMAN BERDICHEVSKY

Nations, Language and Citizenship (2004)

An Introduction to Danish Culture

Norman Berdichevsky

McFarland & Company, Inc., Publishers
Jefferson, North Carolina, and London

LIBRARY OF CONGRESS CATALOGUING-IN-PUBLICATION DATA

Berdichevsky, Norman, 1943–
    An introduction to Danish culture / Norman Berdichevsky.
        p.   cm.
    Includes bibliographical references and index.

    ISBN 978-0-7864-6401-2
    softcover : 50# alkaline paper ∞

    1. Denmark — History.   2. Denmark — Biography.
    3. Denmark — Civilization.   I. Title.
    DL109.B47 2011
    948.9 — dc23   2011033863

BRITISH LIBRARY CATALOGUING DATA ARE AVAILABLE

Front cover images © 2011 Shutterstock

Manufactured in the United States of America

*McFarland & Company, Inc., Publishers
    Box 611, Jefferson, North Carolina 28640
    www.mcfarlandpub.com*

Table of Contents

Preface

This book, a guide to Danish society, culture and history, is intended to fill a gap in the English language literature on Denmark. For many American, British and other readers the Scandinavian countries are too often grouped together and simplified by stereotypes, silly jokes and clichés almost all dealing with socialism, cradle-to-grave security, football, pornography, Hamlet, cattle and beer. Much of the English language literature on Denmark is well outdated, considers the country to be a model of the European social welfare state or presents a tedious compendium of kings and battles. Denmark's contribution to science, engineering, seafaring, shipping, exploration, literature, philosophy, music, art, the theatre, the cinema, dance, sports, agriculture, and architecture — and its record on human rights, democratic institutions, and humanistic traditions — deserve to be much more widely known.

My initial acquaintance with Denmark came from meeting Bente Elisabeth, a Danish volunteer, at the Kibbutz in Israel (Sasa) where I lived in 1963–64. She was one of many Danish volunteers in the early '60s who felt a natural sympathy for Israel because of what had happened in Europe during the Holocaust and their support for the Kibbutz idea. I immediately felt a positive inclination towards the Scandinavian way of life — its healthier approach to social relations, love of the outdoors, rejection of the hard-sell American approach to commercial success, anti-militarism, modesty and anti-snobbery. I had seen two Danish films at the old Thalia movie theater on Broadway and 95th Street and they had made an enormous impression on me — Dreyer's *Ordet* (*The Word*) and *Ditte — Menneskebarn* (*Ditte — Child of Humanity*) based on the book by the great proletarian writer Martin Andersen Nexø. They intrigued me: how did these writers — much like Hans Christian Andersen — use the tiny canvas of their small country and "minor language" (about the same number of speakers as Hebrew) to paint such a great universal work?

My friendship with Bente led to marriage and a continued involvement with Danish culture, eventually leading me to complete my education (Ph.D. from the University of Wisconsin in geography), six years' residence in Denmark and a continued family connection. Along the way, I was fortunate to make the acquaintance and good fellowship of fellow geographers with common interests in Denmark, including Kenneth Olwig and his wife Karen (Fog) Olwig, at the University of Wisconsin, who imbued me with a love of the Danish language; Prof. Robert Newcomb, editor of *Kulturgeografi* and, for many years, head of the Department of Geography at Aarhus Universitet; the "grand old man" of research on Scandinavia in the U.K., Prof. W. R. Mead, my colleagues at Aarhus Katedralskole (which recently celebrated its 800th anniversary!), where I taught geography from 1980 to 1983, Jens Enemark, Erik Johannesen, and Knud Haaning Christensen, who helped me to appreciate the diverse attributes of Denmark's geographical character and who were congenial and very helpful at making me feel at home in the classroom. I also wish to express appreciation to Liz Kennedy, external relations and marketing manager of the International Boundaries research unit of Durham University, for permission to use their excellent map of the 1920 boundary change between Denmark and Germany.

Thanks also to distinguished British historian Professor Sir Martin Gilbert and Lars Hedegaard of Trykkefrihedsselskabet for their personal interest in my efforts to write a cultural guide to Denmark; Anna-Marie Eastwood of the Anglo-Danish Society in London; Henrik Becker-Christensen and Jørgen Kühl of the Institute for Border Research in Aabenraa; the ministers on duty at the Danish Seamen's Churches in Brooklyn and New Orleans and elsewhere who do so much to make Danes abroad feel at home; to Mr. Wesley D. Stewart, counselor of the American Embassy for Public Affairs in Copenhagen; and Ms. Lynne Carter, executive vice president of the American-Scandinavian Foundation for their encouragement over the years to do more to increase mutual understanding between the United States, Great Britain and Denmark.

I have also written the book as a small testimonial to my deep sense of gratitude towards the Danish people for their conduct during World War II and especially for the aid and comfort they provided to their Jewish fellow citizens.

My book is based primarily on Danish language sources. It is designed both for a general readership of tourists, travelers, students, business people, NGOs and government agencies and for the many persons living abroad who are of Danish heritage. It is an inside look at the best of what Denmark and the Danes have achieved.

Special thanks and appreciation of her invaluable assistance and devotion are due to my wife, Raquel, who once again helped me through the hurdles of computer manipulations, proofreading and frequent encouragement. I also wish to acknowledge the long friendship of Søren and his wife Lone from Humlebæk, generous hosts who always make me welcome on a visit to Denmark and require that I stop by to see them. Last but not least in this dedication to "Great Danes" is Randi Breslin, a dear friend, who continues to keep Danish culture and "det store koldebord" alive in Spain.

Chapter 1

The Rise and Fall of the Danish Sea State

Before the innovation of the railroad in the early 19th century, it was much easier and faster to travel across Denmark by sea, skirting the many islands rather than to march or ride overland, only to eventually have to stop at the land's edge, reload and transfer to a waiting boat or ship, if one was ready and available. For a thousand years, the Danish kingdom, located between the Baltic and the North Seas, has consisted of parts of the European mainland (the peninsula of Jutland bordering Germany) and hundreds of small islands. Until 1654, it also included the region known as "Skåne" (today part of Southern Sweden). To cross Danish territory meant having to use a variety of both land and sea means of transportation.

Ferry traffic across the "Belts" and between the many islands and Jutland were unable to offer any kind of regularly scheduled service due to the uncertainties of the weather and tides. There were no timetables. Privately run ferry connections were maintained by merchants and ship-builders who owned sailboats of every description as well as fishermen in their rowboats. Nevertheless, the king, the navy and post office employed a "standing fleet" of ferry craft at the most important crossing points. These were the Little Belt ("Lillebælt") between the island of Fünen and Jutland peninsula, the Great Belt ("Storebælt") between the islands of Fünen and Zealand and "the Sound" (Sundet) separating Zealand and Skåne. Until 1658, Copenhagen was centrally placed between what was then called "Eastern Denmark" (present-day Skåne) and "Western Denmark" (Jutland and the island of Fünen).

Today, major bridges cross all of these ancient ferry locations and one can drive by private automobile and truck or sit in a train and travel all across Danish territory without getting out of one's seat. This seems so natural to us but it was beyond the reach all but a fantastic dreamer for centuries when the Danish Sea State depended on ferry traffic to ensure the unity of the kingdom.

During much of the 19th century, Denmark was in a race with time to provide regularly scheduled ferry service between the many islands and Jutland in order to keep up with the fast pace made by railroad traffic. Trains provided much more rapid transportation overland but could not link the Danish realm together because of the various "belts." Rail service became very efficient within Jutland, Fünen and Zealand, but in each case, the trains had to stop at the water's edge. A reliable ferry service was still needed. In good weather and with a prevailing wind, the Great Belt could be crossed in three hours, but in stormy weather, the trip could take up to ten times longer. The wise would normally prefer to postpone the voyage until the weather was favorable. Even the much smaller Little Belt was a serious barrier.

Rapid progress was initiated when Denmark copied a brilliant innovation first deployed by engineers in Scotland to provide ferries with built-in railroad tracks on their decks to allow trains to simply "board" the vessel and then roll off on to the waiting tracks of the land connection at the ferry's destination. These railroad ferries were subsequently improved and refined in Denmark, making the country a world leader in ferryboat technology.

The first steamship used as a ferry, the *Caledonia*, was purchased in England in 1819. It was only 30 meters long but its regular power source freed from reliance on the wind and tides enabled it to offer the beginning of regularly scheduled ferry service in sailings between Kiel in Northern Germany and Copenhagen. In 1828, the Danish Post Office used its first steamship, the *Mercurius*, as a ferryboat over the Great Belt. Danish engineers began to use the railway ferry idea imported from Scotland in the 1850s. These ships with their inbuilt railway tracks and movable decks adjusted the height of the gangway to the water level in the harbor, allowing rapid continuous rail connections to all parts of Denmark. No longer did passengers and freight have to be transferred and reloaded to new modes of transport.

By 1872, the *Littlebelt*, bought in England, was acquired to begin regular ferry service between Fredericia in Jutland and Middlefart on Fünen and became an immediate success. The first water bottleneck had fallen to technology. The *Littlebelt* was provided with passenger cabins and carried freight

A stamp depicting a Danish ferry.

and mail as well. Subsequent ferries built in Denmark were equipped with greatly improved innovations such as powerful underwater screws at the rear of the boat to drive it forward instead of paddlewheels mounted on the boat's side. This allowed for much greater speed and stability. During the latter half of the 19th century, new Danish ferries eliminated the other bottlenecks by crossing the Great Belt, the Sound and smaller bodies of water in the Limfjord (body of water in Northern Jutland) and the "Storstrømmen" (the sea passage between the islands of Lolland-Falster and Zealand).

Most of the ferry service was taken over by the Danish State Railways (DSB) and integrated into a national train network. The length of the rail tracks on board the ferries grew considerably and later developments included multiple decks to carry automobiles and trucks. Gasoline and diesel motors replaced coal-driven steam boilers. Ferry service was extended to Germany from the island of Falster to connect with the German railways leading to Berlin. Passenger comfort was prioritized as well and dozens of modern ferries were designed and built by engineers. By the 1930s, the Danish shipbuilding firm B & W (Burmeister & Wain) had become the leading manufacturer of top-class diesel-driven ferries.

Further improvements in the construction of screws and complicated gears promoted greater stability and were so impressive that when the Danish freighter *Sealandia* visited London just before the outbreak of World War I, the First Lord of the Admiralty, Sir Winston Churchill, exclaimed, "We are used to the Danes being masters in agriculture but that we should also learn from them about seamanship is a great surprise."

By the mid–1920s, many modern ferries were an integral part of the Danish transportation network and gave the country a distinct image in the world as a ferry-connected "sea state." Pressure from the automobile owners' lobby (FDM) to provide more ferries with special decks to accommodate cars met with limited success. DSB could only accept a limited number of cars on their ferries and would not devote funds to construct ferries that did not give first priority to rail traffic.

Private car ownership in Denmark was limited in the 1930s but even the wealthiest car owners had to contend with the fact that their mobility was limited by the country's unique geography and that their usage of the ferries was tied to the railway timetable. FDM financed the construction of its own specially built ferry in 1929, the car-friendly *Heimdal,* to carry traffic over the Great Belt. The anti-automobile mindset of the government only changed with the onset of the Great Depression when it decided to institute a series of major public works projects to help to create employment and stimulate the economy.

The result was a huge program of bridge building. These new bridges would accommodate both rail and automobile traffic. A new modern bridge over the Little Belt was completed in 1935, followed by those linking Lolland-Falster with Zealand in 1937 and several others between the minor islands and fjords in North Jutland. Danish public opinion had been encouraged to believe in the possibility of ultimately uniting the entire country into one economic unit and transportation system by bridging the Great Belt.

World War II witnessed the confiscation of many Danish ferries by the occupying German troops who needed them for the transportation of troops and war materiel. One of the great sabotage actions of the Danish underground was the sinking of the ferry *Danmark* between Gedser on the island of Falster and Warnemünde in Germany, thus greatly disrupting communi-

A map of Denmark showing the primary bridges.

cations and supply of the German forces in Denmark and forcing them to make greater use of the railroads, themselves subject to mounting and effective Danish sabotage actions.

The hard winter of 1947–48 gave further impetus to the vision of ultimately "bridging" the entire country. Once or twice a century extreme cold weather has caused the belts to become frozen with ice. One such event in 1658 enabled Swedish troops to avoid the powerful Danish fleet and attack Denmark "from the rear" by sending an army over the ice. In 1947, a powerful icebreaker, the *Holger Danske*, was set in to work, continually clearing the ice in order to allow normal ferryboat traffic and permit the trains and ferry connections to operate. This situation was of great concern to both the public and the authorities who realized that apart from the economic damage, the reliance on rail-ferry traffic could put the country at a great security risk. No doubt after Denmark joined NATO in 1949, military strategists were concerned how to ensure that the Russians would never be able to repeat the ice-crossing tactic of the Swedish army in 1658.

Danish shipbuilding firms were kept busy in the 1950s, racing to keep up with the demand to restore normal ferry traffic that had been disrupted as a result of the war and the loss of so many ships. The Danish ferries constructed in the 1960s made further technological advances, providing greater stability, and the use of radar made them much safer. Comfort levels in the lounges and cafeterias were built according to the principles of "Danish design," making them luxurious by foreign standards. The great rise in living standards and the growing desire for foreign travel shifted perspectives and made politicians respond to the public's growing love affair with the automobile. The idea of building a bridge across the Great Belt was now a foregone conclusion.

In the meantime, tastes were also changing, creating additional pressure for a Great Belt bridge to do away with the longer ferry routes. In 1970, the longest ferry routes from Aalborg and Aarhus in Northern Jutland directly to Copenhagen were ended. These all-sea routes (20–24 hours of sailing time) involved the need to spend a night on the ferry deck in shared cabins in uncomfortable conditions without private showers and toilets. Such connections were no longer acceptable by the public even if they offered a marginally cheaper fare than the much faster rail ferries. Equally unappealing was the ferry route between Aarhus in Jutland and Helsingborg in Sweden in spite of the promise of duty-free liquor and other products.

The decision to build a Great Belt Bridge was made in 1986 and given further dramatic impetus by a series of ferry disasters — the capsizing of the *Herald of Free Enterprise* at Zeebrügge off the Belgian coast in 1986, fire aboard the *Skaggerak Star* between Norway and Denmark in 1990, and the sinking of the *Estonia* in the Baltic Sea in 1994. Each one of these incidents led to the adoption of much greater safety demands and the withdrawal from service of older ferries that could not be modernized. Ferry traffic had also become very expensive due to the great rise in oil prices. All these events increased public support for the Great Belt bridge idea. There was also the simple fact of arithmetic — the number of passengers and amount of freight that can be carried across the Belts and the Sound in one hour is much greater via trucks and cars than aboard rail ferries.

After several false starts, a new state-owned company, *A/S Storbælts-forbindelsen,* was legally established in 1987 to go full speed ahead on construction of a bridge with both a railway link and a motorway. The railway link was partly a tunnel connecting Zealand to the tiny island of Sprogø. This 8 km (5 miles) of bored railway tunnel is second in length only to the rail tunnel under the English Channel. The bridge was built in two sections. The western branch connects Sprogø and Fünen. It was built between 1989 and 1993. It is a low-level bridge of pre-stressed concrete sections running 6.6 km (4 miles) long, the longest in Europe.

The Eastern section between Zealand and Sprogø is a suspension bridge and allows ships to pass underneath it up to a height of 65 meters. It has a single span of 1.6 km (one mile). The roadway part of the bridges was opened in 1998. The total cost of the project was an astronomical 25 billion kroner (more than all the previous bridges combined). Journey time between East and West Denmark was reduced by more than an hour and the country was effectively tied together by a land link for the first time in history. It also sounded the death knell for much of the ferry traffic across the Great Belt.

The final piece in the jigsaw puzzle was the bridge across the Sound connecting Copenhagen with southern Sweden. Like the Great Belt connection, the Sound Bridge consists of a motorway and a railway and has a submerged tunnel section. It is 15.9 km (just under 10 miles) long from coast to coast. It was inaugurated in July 2000 and trains can cross it at the phenomenal speed of 200 km per hour (120 mph). All the bottlenecks of the Belts that had first fallen to the rail ferry in the 19th century were finally vanquished by the new bridges and overland traffic now flows unimpeded. Smaller, specially built ferries, some driven by hydrofoil air-cushions, still cross the Great Belt and ply the smaller islands, but the ferries have seen the end of their glory days.

Nostalgic fans of the ferries are organized in several clubs and lament the passing of what was an indelible part of the Danish way of life and the country's human geography for generations. Many of them have been shocked and saddened by recent revelations that a number of older Danish ferries that were sold or given as aid to poor countries such as Bangladesh and India have been scrapped for their metal. This is an emotional wound for all those Danes who grew up with the ferries and loved them.

Chapter 2

Danish Wind Power

The Danes live in a wind-rich environment. This is particularly so along the west coast of Jutland and in the Kattegat and Skaggerak seas between the Danish islands and the Swedish and Norwegian coasts, where storms have wrecked many ships. It is a rich irony and testimony to Danish innovation that the country has turned what once was a hazard of nature into a valuable source of energy, technical creativity and economic wealth. According to recent statistics from 2007, wind power in Denmark accounted for 19.7 percent of electricity production and 24.1 percent of capacity, a significantly higher proportion than in any other country.

In Denmark, the humble windmill has yielded to thousands of 230-foot wind turbines sporting 130-foot blades harnessing winds both onshore and offshore. Sixty percent of the world's modern windmills are produced there. Denmark has taken the lead in the development of turbine design based on renewable sources of energy featuring the humble windmill. Although the modern windmills appear to be nothing more than simple propellers set on a long pole, within them lies the story of amazing progress that has made its mark on the public mind and political scene in Denmark, a country that lacks both oil and coal.

The development of windmill technology has to do with size, modern turbine design and lightweight materials. The tallest towers are 70 meters (230 feet) high with rotor blades 40 meters (131 feet) long, two or three times the height of the old-style traditional windmills and the length of their blades. New units that are 100 meters (328 feet) high are already in operation. The reason is simple: wind velocities increase with altitude. Those with the tallest towers are the most effective.

For generations, windmills formed an attractive part of the rural landscape and fulfilled an economically useful function in Denmark. Grinding grain into flour was one of the most necessary farm operations and the first step in producing the delightful breads and pastries for which Denmark achieved well-deserved fame. Historically, windmills were occasionally the sites of important gatherings and battles, the most famous being at Dybbøl near Sønderborg on the island of Als where Danish troops heroically held out and made a "last stand" in the disastrous 1864 war when both Prussia and Austria invaded Denmark and seized the strategic provinces of Schleswig-Holstein.

Considering this idyllic background of colorful old windmills, it is a surprise to many tourists to see the large number of ultra-modern windmills, as identical as bowling pins, that now dot the landscape. Danish industry turns out close to 2,000 Danish windmills a year, of which approximately 1,200 are sold for export. The major wind-power nations are Denmark, the Netherlands, Germany, Spain, the United States and China, all of which are turning increasingly to wind turbines as the cleanest form of energy. Wind-power generation results in no emissions of carbon dioxide. In Denmark wind energy now accounts for close to 20 percent of electricity consumption, a remarkable achievement considering that the average for the rest of Europe currently lies at only 2.5 percent. The "unknown factor" of the wind's variability, however, is a drawback and explains the discrepancy of the varying estimates from year to year of the amount of reliable energy production accounted for by wind power. Danish energy plans envision that wind power will reach close to a third of total energy generation in 2014!

New windmills are expensive, fixed facilities. They cannot easily be relocated. Their effectiveness will depend on the successful calculation of the best location of sites. The hope is that Denmark can keep its leading position in wind-power technology by developing expertise in offshore turbines. On average, a coastal location is windier than an inland site by at least 20 percent, making it possible to produce much more electricity than inland. Several offshore "wind-farms," consisting of rows of dozens of windmills between 14 and 20 kilometers (about 8.5 to 12.5 miles) in length, can be seen along the coasts of the North Sea and the Danish Straits. In offshore turbines, Denmark has the best chance of maintaining its technological lead in the next generation of megawatt-class windmills.

Moving them would be incredibly expensive and wasteful. They must be carefully sited whether on land or offshore to take maximum advantage of meteorological conditions that ensure a steady flow of wind. The energy they generate loses power over distance. There are critics who find them ugly and claim that they "spoil the landscape." In spite of what you may think (if you haven't examined a modern one closely), and the assumption that this cleanest form of energy has no drawbacks, they do produce pollution of one sort— noise. The bigger the propeller blades, the noisier they are. Wind energy is an advancing technology and improvements in just the last few years have more than halved the weight of Danish windmills and the noise they produce. Most remarkably, their energy output has increased by a factor of one hundred times in the last 15 years.

Suggestions to "camouflage" the windmills are highly impractical. If they are located to blend in with the surroundings, too many obstacles interfere with the flow of wind. They also have a problem of "wear and tear" with an estimated lifespan of only 20 years. Long-term planning is essential to guarantee the best possible integration of the windmills with the surrounding landscape and environment. Very tall height presents possible dangers to aviation and therefore the authorities rightly demand prominent markings to guarantee safety.

Wind power in Denmark is currently based on the presence of approximately 4,000 wind turbines with a maximum capacity. The newest large wind turbines, where properly sited, are competitive in price with traditional coal and oil-powered energy plants. The most economical sites for the construction of wind turbines are still on land; however, land-based windmills still have a number of disadvantages including restrictions in areas devoted to housing and nature preservation.

The government intends to continue its promotion of employment and export opportunities by continued research and development in support of the Danish wind turbine industry, today the largest in the world, with a turnover of more than 6 billion Danish kroner, of which exports will soon reach approximately 75 percent. The number of jobs in the sector stands at well over 10,000.

The size of modern wind turbines is a new challenge for local authorities. The present environmental and planning guidelines lag behind the technology and must be rewritten in order to locate new large wind turbines without violating environmental restrictions. There are still many excellent sites in Denmark, but choosing and using them requires a great deal of planning. Because of the noise, nobody wants to live near a windmill, although in practice everyone is in favor of clean energy. This is the major political problem to be solved since Danes are experts at using democratic tactics through their political parties to either delay or hinder "obnoxious facilities" that they don't want in their neighborhoods.

Svend Sigaard, the chief executive of operations of Vestas, the largest manufacturer of windmills in Denmark, located on the island of Langeland, was one of the keynote speakers at "Renewables 2004," a roundtable conference on renewable energy sources held in Bonn, Germany, in which more than 60 finance ministers and 2,500 delegates from 150 different countries participated. Sigaard stressed the fact that the wind industry is now competitive with nuclear power and fossil fuels due to the industry's cost reduction by 70–80 percent within the past 30 years, a truly amazing achievement. He had this to say about this development and the role he expects Vestas to play:

> I am convinced the renewable power industry will continue to develop more cost-efficient technologies. For wind power solutions, Vestas has the aim of reducing the cost per kilowatt hour from 3 to 5 percent annually on average. Stable renewable energy policies with clear target settings in Germany, Spain and Denmark, along with visionary policies from the EU, strong public support — and a lot of work from the industry — have formed the basis of the remarkable development of wind energy up till today.

This development has attracted considerable attention because of the recent instability in the oil-producing states in the Middle East. It is no secret that Europe feels particularly vulnerable to conflict in the area and that nuclear energy, which once had the support of both politicians and much of the public, has lost much ground and was until quite recently being phased out in those nations that previously had set long-term goals for its expansion, such as Sweden and Germany.

Sigaard emphasized this geopolitical instability in his talk and urged all the participating ministers to put more reliance on renewable energy sources by clearly stating that "unless we change direction in our energy choices now, we will continue to be at the mercy of volatile, unpredictable oil and gas prices and imports from potentially unstable regions of the world."

Usually, economic pricing of energy sources ignores health and environmental costs that are paid for by society in the form of hazards and illness, especially respiratory problems, work accidents, pollution of the environment and detrimental climate change (global warming). These costs make wind power even more attractive than traditional fossil

A modern Vestas wind turbine V90 3MW Nacelle. Photo courtesy of Vestas Wind Systems A/S.

fuels. Research studies have concluded that wind power has the lowest external costs of all energy technologies — approx 0.1 eurocent/kilowatt hour compared to 4–7 euro-cents/kilowatt hour for coal in Denmark.

Denmark has become the hub of global wind-power development. It has assembled a core inventory of knowledge and information embodied in the Danish Wind Industries Association, where manufacturers, suppliers and research and educational institutions combine expertise, innovation and advanced technology.

The Association's vision is to strengthen Denmark's position as the wind power hub — the leading global wind-power center of advanced technology, a highly qualified work force and intelligent energy system solutions. It believes that this technology is the strongest weapon in the intense competition with multinational companies, and in order for Denmark to achieve its goals, it needs political backing from the government. The Association estimates that by the year 2020, the international windmill market will grow to 82 billion euros and that Danish industry should be able to continue its astounding lead of approximately 40 percent market share.

The modern windmill industry has grown from being a provider of small-size mills sold to private household customers into a far more professional market of very large-size units for which the utility companies are now the natural customers. In other words, the industry previously sold "wind turbines" whereas now they deliver "power plants." What have been the drastic changes that produced this revolution? After all, wind power has been known and used to drive sailboats and windmills for thousands of years. Basically, wind turbines are built to catch the wind's kinetic (motion) energy. So why do the modern ones have only three blades? We have all seen the old ones from Western movies or Don Quixote's famous joust. They had four wide blades clothed in fabric.

The modern mills use turbines that effectively drive the aerodynamically designed blades to maximize wind force and minimize drag. The energy content of the wind at great heights would rip apart an old windmill's blades. Physicists will tell you that the energy content of the wind varies with the *cube of the wind speed* (i.e., doubling the wind speed increases the force eight times). It is no wonder that wind turbine manufacturers have to certify that their turbines are built to withstand extreme winds that occur, say, during 10 minutes every 50 years.

In spite of all the achievements, a word to the wise is in order. Apart from wind-driven turbines, the remainder of Danish electricity today (close to 80 percent) is still produced from imported coal. There are too few hours of sunshine on an annual basis to justify development of solar energy. Denmark has no nuclear reactors or raging rivers to power massive dams and this means that, at the moment, the Danes produce more carbon dioxide per kilo-watt-hour than the supposedly environmentally hostile Americans, where, thanks to nuclear energy, hydroelectricity and solar energy, only about 55 percent of electricity comes from coal.

The outlook for Denmark's future in the field of energy, however, is still bright and the answer is "blowing in the wind."

Chapter 3

Bornholm: Denmark's Easternmost Baltic Reach

Bornholm is distinctive in many of its customs, traditions, regional dialect, architecture, climate, geology and landscape, all of which differ from the rest of the country. It is warmer, less rainy and still heavily forested. Its underlying granite has also resulted in more angular surface features than the rounded hills and gently rolling terrain of much of the rest of Denmark. The granite rock has provided the raw material for many Danish sculptors. Farmsteads are more dispersed in Bornholm and not grouped together in small villages. The distribution of churches also follows this pattern. In the rest of Denmark they are mostly found in the centers of towns and villages rather than spread out across the countryside.

Called the "Pearl of the Baltic," Bornholm lies about 100 miles from Copenhagen but only about 25 miles southeast of southern Sweden. Anyone glancing at the map without much knowledge of Scandinavian history would therefore be likely to ask why this island is Danish rather than Swedish. The answer also explains why the Danish capital is at the extreme eastern end of the Danish realm, a seemingly strange, peripheral place for administering the rest of the country.

In the past, Bornholm's outlying location from Denmark proper proved problematical. Bornholmers have always resented what they consider to be the view of most Danes that their island was of little value and too remote. While Denmark was spared any major fighting or bombing during World War II, Bornholm was chosen for target practice by German V-1 rocket scientists. Multiple rocket launches were sent from Peenemunde on the German Baltic coast 200 miles away. Thanks to the alertness of the Danish police, news of the test was smuggled out to the Allies. The islanders' very different experience of the war was most apparent on May 5, 1945, a date that all other Danes regard as their liberation day, after five years of German occupation.

There were noisy celebrations and jubilation everywhere in the country but no attention was paid to the fate of Bornholm, where German troops refused to surrender the island to the Russians. The result was three additional days of intense bombing by the Soviet air force and an occupation by Russian troops that lasted until April 1946.

The Mysterious Round Churches: Their Function and Location

A truly unique feature of Bornholm is the four imposing round medieval churches. It has always been assumed until quite recently that they were constructed sometime in the twelfth century and served a defensive purpose for the population to seek refuge from the nearly continuous raids by Slavonic pirates from the island of Rugen off the German coast. There still remain questions regarding their origin and architecture, unlike any other churches found in Denmark. New evidence stemming from the precise geographical coordinates of their locations has presented a controversy and doubts concerning the previous theory of their origin. What has excited attention is their exact location relative to one another, to the geography of Bornholm and to the nearby islet of Christiansø (12.5 miles northeast of Bornholm). Several new theories have linked the four round churches to medieval religious order of the Knights Templar. The locations of the four churches of Osterlars, Nylars, Olsker, and Nyker demonstrate a complex and very beautiful pattern of landscape geometry incorporating three-, four-, five-, six- and seven-sided figures. These geometric patterns are supposedly also found among a number of churches in Rennes le Chateau in southern France, also linked to the Templars.

Østerlars Kirke on Bornholm, Denmark, from the south.

Bornholm's Fishing Wealth

In Denmark proper, farming and fishing were two distinct occupations, but the great fishing wealth in the waters around Bornholm resulted in a seasonal shift by farmers to become full-time fishermen during the fall, between mid–August and early October. Salmon, cod and herring are sources of nutritional wealth and even today, the island provides almost the entire supply of fish for McDonald's restaurants in Europe. For those who love traditional smoked fish, Bornholm is a paradise and all the work of salting, skinning and smoking is still done by hand.

Archaeologists have uncovered a wealth of treasures including buried coins of Russian and Arab origin that reveal a profitable trade in which Bornholm played a major role as the midpoint between the oldest Viking center in Hedeby, in south Jutland, and the great Russian rivers, as well as between Germany and Sweden. The clerical scholar, Adam of Bremen, referred to Bornholm as the "great harbor of Denmark." More evidence of the island's prosperity has been found on the rune stones, with their chiseled inscriptions. The Bornholm rune stones refer only to Christian saints, indicating that Christianity came to the island only after the disappearance of old pagan beliefs. Several of them indicate that Bornholm and the Swedish province of Skåne became part of the Danish kingdom in the late 10th century, after Harold Blåtand (Bluetooth) had "won all of Denmark."

The herring population of the Baltic virtually exploded in the 14th and 15th centuries and brought with it great prosperity. It also attracted many foreigners, especially Germans from the Hanseatic city states. The Church also took advantage of this increased wealth from fishing to build chapels in favored coves and bays from where the boats were launched. The golden age of fishing brought with it the threat of piracy long after it disappeared elsewhere in northern Europe. Local authority was insufficient to stop organized attacks, blackmail, arson and plunder carried out by pirates in cahoots with merchants from Lübeck and other Hanseatic cities. The pirates burned and looted Bornholm's major cities of Neksø and Aakirkeby. Not until 1512 was the king in Copenhagen sufficiently motivated to defend the island to send a fleet to ward off further attacks. The Swedes, ever ready to lend a hand to weaken Danish authority, aided the pirates.

The Danish-Swedish Rivalry and Its Outcome for Bornholm

Until the peace of Roskilde in 1658, southern Sweden (Skåne), containing the major cities of Malmø and Lund, had been the easternmost part of the Danish kingdom for centuries. Denmark once exercised total control of the exit and entry to the Baltic Sea. All shipping had to pass through Øresund (the narrow strait separating Sweden and Denmark) and pay tolls to the Danes.

For a brief period, Denmark was a major naval power and even ruled Estonia on the eastern shore of the Baltic.

Sweden and Denmark fought several wars for control of the Baltic and the status of Skåne (chapter 30). A Swedish victory in 1645 resulted in a major change of the map. Denmark ceded to Sweden the islands of Gotland and Øsel, Bornholm, two large Norwegian border provinces, and Halland — a large part of what is today southern Sweden. The occupying Swedish force, however, was driven off the island by Bornholmers who refused to accept the treaty. Further Danish attempts to win back these lost possessions resulted in an even greater loss in 1658. In this disastrous 1658 war, the Øresund froze over, allowing Swedish forces to attack Denmark on foot. This allowed the Swedes to outmaneuver the Danish fleet, causing panic in Copenhagen. Faced with the threat of total defeat by Sweden, Danish King Frederick III willingly signed a treaty relinquishing all Danish territories east of Øresund, including Bornholm.

Although the island was still protected and accessible only by sea, the Swedes willingly withdrew from their siege of Copenhagen in return for a guarantee of permanent control over Skåne rather than continue the war as the ice began to melt. After some strenuous negotiations the Danes accepted a humiliating peace (Treaty of Roskilde, 1658) that permanently ceded all of Skåne including Bornholm to Sweden. Nevertheless, a revolt and the assassination of a Swedish governor made the Swedes reconsider that it was not worth the effort. They saw an opportunity to throw a bone to the Danes to assuage their pride. The Bornholmers petitioned Danish King Frederick III to accept them back into the Danish kingdom on condition that the island would never be ceded again (Treaty of Copenhagen, 1660).

In the ensuing three centuries, Skåne was gradually "Swedified." From 1676 to 1679, a bitter guerrilla uprising attempted to oust the Swedes from the newly conquered region but was unsuccessful. The Danish-minded inhabitants of Skåne could not repeat the successful resistance of the Bornholmers. For two centuries, Danish nationalists continued to dream of recovering "eastern Denmark," but by the mid–19th century Sweden had clearly achieved military superiority and suppressed any lingering resistance in Skåne. As late as 1854, a Swedish law prohibited the import of Danish books that might recall Skåne's Danish past.

The World War II Experience and Bornholm's Most Famous Son

Bornholmers consider themselves fortunate in having escaped the Iron Curtain. The island actually lies east of the Polish port city of Stettin, one of the boundaries of Eastern Europe (Trieste in Italy was the other), cited by Winston Churchill in his famous Iron Curtain speech in 1946. When Soviet troops ultimately were withdrawn from Bornholm, many of them returned home with tales of capitalist Denmark as an affluent paradise. The Bornholmers' experience with Russian communism is all the more ironic because its greatest literary figure, Martin Andersen Nexø, perhaps second only to Hans Christian Andersen in fame and the number of books sold, devoted his career to the struggle on behalf of the working class and was hailed by the Soviet Union as a great author of international stature.

Although born in Copenhagen, Nexø moved to Bornholm as a young child and worked as a shepherd and shoemaker's apprentice under the most appalling conditions. He became a teacher and then writer. He was an ardent admirer of the USSR, even after a visit there in 1923. His works reflect the struggle of the Danish working class to achieve dignity and some have been made into powerful films such as *Pelle the Conqueror* (*Pelle Erobreren*) and *Ditte, the Daughter of Man* (*Ditte menneskebarn*). In 1949, upon Denmark's admission to NATO, Nexø left Denmark to settle in East Germany until his death in 1954.

Tourist Paradise Today

The island's 228 square miles of heaths, fertile fields, forests and lakes are contained within a 68-mile coastline of dramatically steep cliffs and white, sandy beaches. Also known as the Sunshine Island and the Wild Cherry Island, Bornholm offers vacationers hiking and biking trails and three golf courses as well as museums, quaint old churches and galleries. The island can be reached by two ferries (a two-and-a-half hour trip) and a catamaran (80-minute voyage) from Copenhagen. The completion of the Øresund bridge linking southern Sweden with Copenhagen and faster ferry connections have renewed Denmark's ties to Skåne. Denmark has also granted generous subsidies to lighten the burden of travelers to Bornholm's outlying location. Danes planning to live or work in Bornholm are no longer burdened by excessive transportation costs. Tourists too can now enjoy easier access to what was once Denmark's "remote, far-eastern" island.

Chapter 4

The Faroe Islands: An Ancient Nordic North Atlantic Outpost

The 18 Faroe Islands (Faeroe is an older alternative spelling) located about half way between Iceland and Norway but lying closest to several of the Scottish Shetland Islands, total only 540 square miles. The terrain is mostly treeless, rugged and rocky, consisting of geologic layers of basalt lava with the coasts marked by steep cliffs. After fishing, sheepherding has been the mainstay of the islands' economy. Their climate is marked by windy, cloudy and cool conditions throughout the year with over 260 rainy days annually. Sunny days are rare, for the islands lie in the path of frequent depressions moving northeastwards.

These islands were an important stepping stone in Viking expansion across the North Atlantic. Due to an accident of history they have been politically tied to Denmark. Jutland, the islands of Funen, and Zealand are the Danish kingdom familiar to all European and American tourists but there are two other very unequal parts: the great ice-covered land mass of Greenland (50 times larger than Denmark proper) and the tiny, rugged Faroe Islands. Both Greenland and the Faroes have their own flag, banknotes, postage stamps, language and traditions.

Whale Hunting Brings the Faroese into the World Spotlight

The people of the Faroes have for centuries been in the forefront of the whaling nations and this has put them in the spotlight of ecology-minded "green" activists. This is perhaps one of the most dramatic examples of a proud and distinctive people who have lived by their wits and traditions for more than a thousand years. They constitute one of the oldest and most homogeneous societies that will not bow to the dictates of globalization, although the open-ing of a McDonald's fast-food site in Tórshavn, the capital and largest city, has demonstrated that the islands cannot turn their backs on the larger world.

The whale hunt known as the Grindadrap takes place in the summer months and makes use of modern technology such as echo-sounders, power boats and radios. The method of the hunt, however, is strictly traditional and has provoked great consternation among opponents of whaling. The whales are driven by the boats toward the islands' shores from which hunters wade out to drive hooks into the whale's head, pulling them to the shore where they are dispatched by deft use of a 7-inch-long knife used to sever the animal's carotid artery and jugular vein.

By tradition, the meat and the blubber are handed out free of charge to local inhabitants after the first choice of meat is given to those who actually did the slaughtering. Critics term such practices barbaric and claim that much of the meat is wasted while the diet is unhealthy. Responding to worldwide criticism, Faroese spokesmen claim that their traditions are hallowed by time and that their methods do not lead to over-exploitation of the pilot whale population in the area.

Nevertheless, it is admitted that whale meat contains high amounts of mercury as well as DDT and other dangerous substances. Although Denmark is a member of the European Union both Greenland and the Faroes enjoy a special autonomous status and do not fall within the scope of EU directives and regulations.

The Faroes and Greenland as Danish Colonies

Both Greenland (population 55,000) and the Faroes (population 50,000) enjoy home rule today, a special self-governing status that put an end to hun-dreds of years of direct colonial rule from Copenhagen. Only foreign affairs and defense remain completely under the control of the government in Copen-hagen and both the Faroes and Greenland have a fixed quota of two seats each in the Danish parliament (Folketing).

How did the Danes get to Greenland and the Faroes? They didn't! Labrador, Newfoundland, Greenland, the Shetland and Orkney Islands off the coasts of Scotland and both the Faroes and Iceland were discovered and settled during the westward exploration of Viking seafarers (Eric the Red and Leif the Lucky) who sailed mostly from Norway. Danish control of the North Atlantic and the acquisition of the Faroes, Iceland and Greenland was the result of Denmark's absorption of Norway following the notorious Black Death epidemic (1349–51) when one-third of the population died, which made its continued independence unviable. For centuries, Norway and these North Atlantic "stepping stones" to America were under Danish rule as were the West Indian islands that were later (1917) sold to the United States to become the American Virgin Islands.

History and Cultural Individuality

Irish monks probably first settled the islands sometime in the early sixth century, and introduced sheep and oats as the principal livestock and cereal crop. The Faroese today are overwhelmingly the descendants of this Irish-Scandinavian mixture, known as "Norse-Gaels." The very name of the islands is the Faroese term for "sheep islands." Later on, about 650 A.D., Vikings replaced the early Irish settlers, bringing the Old Norse language to the islands from which modern Faroese evolved. It is believed that the first settlers came from Norwegian settlements in the Shetland and Orkney islands off the coast of Western Scotland.

According to the *Færeyinga Saga*, emigrants from Norway left their home-land for the Faroes to escape the tyranny of Harald I at the end of the 9th century. Early in the 11th century, the Norwegian monarchy established its control of the islands and introduced Christianity. From 1380 under a joint union with Norway, Denmark gradually assumed more control of the settlers and finally brought them under direct colonial rule. With the Reformation and the establishment of the Danish Lutheran state church in Denmark in 1538, both Norway and the Faroes were more firmly subject to Danish cultural influences.

When the union between Denmark and Norway was dissolved as a result of the Treaty of Kiel in 1814, Denmark retained possession of the Faroe Islands. Ironically, both Greenland and the Faroes should have gone to Sweden along with Norway but the Swedish negotiator was not aware of the historical settlement of the islands and Sweden had no interest in administering these remote possessions out in the North Atlantic.

In June 1944, the American and British bases in Greenland and the Faroes were aware that a break in the stormy weather pattern that had prevailed for the previous few days would make the chances for a successful D-Day landing more likely, an advantage they had over the German defenders on the Normandy beaches who were not expecting an attack in stormy weather.

The islands are well served today by air and sea, fast ferries, and the recent development of under-ocean tunnels, causeways and bridges interconnecting six of the largest islands in the northeast. The seven smallest islands have only one village each! Much like Iceland, the economy of the Faroe

Islands is totally dependent on fishing and the processing of fish products. Much of the population lives in dispersed villages and educational opportunities are limited. Most young people go on to study in Denmark to get a higher education if they have any interest and ambition for a career in the professions. Recently, some diversification of the workforce has occurred to develop an information technology industry. The population is characterized by an age pyramid that is heavily skewed to over-represent a largely middle-aged and elderly population.

The Faroes are "The Sheep Islands."

The Faroese language is descended from Old Norse, brought by the first settlers from Norway. The authorities replaced it with Danish for use in schools, churches and official documents after the success of the Reformation in 1538 but the local population continued to speak it at home and in their daily lives even though the language did not have a standard orthography and was not used in written documents. All poems and folktales were handed down orally until well into the 19th century. A strong musical and "chain" dance tradition of pagan origin was also preserved.

World War II and the Independence Referendum

In the Faroes, national consciousness had been growing and received a huge boost with the granting of independence to Norway by Sweden in 1905. A Faroese Independence Party was established, gained increasing support among the youth, and by 1918 had become the largest party represented in the local assembly (Lagting). Opposing it stood the Union Party in favor of a continued association with Denmark, claiming that with such a small population, the islands would not be able to successfully support an independent state.

Through the two decades between the end of World War I and the occupation of Denmark by Germany in April 1940, more and more Danish laws were replaced by new legislation of the Lagting. Minor irritations occurred at official ceremonies when independence-minded Faroese hoisted the Faroese flag when official etiquette demanded the use of the Danish flag (the Dannebrog).

It was during World War II that a break was made with Denmark as a result of the German occupation and the strategic importance of Greenland and the Faroes emerged. The two remote island communities played decisive roles both in the battle for the Atlantic and the Allied invasion of occupied Europe, although few were aware of this on April 9, 1940, when Denmark surrendered. Many Danes looked in astonishment and disbelief at the abject surrender of its armed forces within four hours of the German invasion. The surrender left the Danish dependencies of Iceland, Greenland and the Faroes in a lurch.

It lay only in the power of thousands of Danish seamen and the Danish diplomatic corps abroad to continue the fight. Many Danish crews and captains of scores of fishing vessels and cargo ships sought to reach American and British ports or remain in Greenland and the Faroes rather than return to an occupied Denmark. Denmark's ambassador in Washington, Henrik Kauffmann, refused to heed his government's orders and publicly announced that he would represent "Free Denmark," explaining that the king and the government had been coerced. He offered the American government the right to construct, maintain and operate landing fields, seaplane facilities and radio and meteorological installations in Greenland.

Within a few days of Denmark's surrender, British troops occupied the Faroes. The Faroese did not object beyond an initial formal protest to the immediate occupation of the islands by the British. All locally owned and operated ships flew the Faroese flag to distinguish them from the vessels of occupied Denmark. In this way, the desire for independence was further stimulated. Relations between the occupying British forces and the local population were very good and the economy enormously stimulated by the demand for the islands' fish products in wartime. The Icelandic declaration of independence from Denmark in 1944 further fueled similar demands in the Faroes. However, the British wisely counseled patience until a Free Denmark was reestablished.

Post–World War II Era

In 1945, the Danish government recognized that a majority of the Faroese might wish to declare the islands independent and agreed to recognize this decision but also strongly advised the people that they would enjoy full autonomous rights and cultural expression in the future if they chose to continue their association with Denmark. A referendum was held with the confusing results that 33 percent voted for full independence, 32 percent for continued union, 3 percent submitted blank ballots and the remainder abstained. The Danish government declared that it would not accept such ambiguous results as a binding expression of the will for independence, the Lagting was dissolved and in a subsequent election, a clear majority emerged favoring continued union.

The war convinced most Faroese and many Greenlanders that the paternalistic authorities in Copenhagen did not "always know best" and gave them the first real taste of deciding things for themselves. An act granting full self-government was approved by the Lagting in March 1948, granting the Faroes a special status within the Danish kingdom. In all matters concerning the Faroes alone, the Lagting has sovereign legislative powers and the Faroese flag was recognized as co-equal with the Danish. Faroese is today the language of instruction in schools but the two most prominent Faroese writers and the only ones to win recognition on the world stage, William Heinesen and Jørgen-Fritz Jacobsen, wrote in Danish.

The Faroese have accepted their status and role as part of the Danish kingdom. It is noteworthy that the present queen, Margrethe II, makes it a priority to visit the Faroes annually and has studied the language so that she is conversant in Faroese. She dresses in Faroese folk costumes and participates in local festivals during her stay. More than a dozen Faroese and Danish postage stamps picture the monarch in typical Faroese folk costume. In this way, she has helped strengthen and personify the ties between the two peoples. The Faroese are today proud of their status of equality as a fellow Nordic nation along with Denmark, Norway, Sweden, Iceland and Finland.

Chapter 5

"Arctic Denmark": Greenland Yesterday and Today

Denmark and Greenland could not be more different from one another. Geologically, climatically, biologically, and culturally, Greenland is much more similar to North America than Europe. The native Inuit peoples (formerly called Eskimos) of Greenland and northern Canada are related and speak closely related languages. Greenland's interior ice cap, which covers the greater part of the island, measures up to 3,000 meters (10,000 feet) in thickness. Underneath, lies the Greenland Shield, a mass of ancient hard rock, mainly gneisses and granite.

Danes occasionally like to tease foreigners, especially Americans, who are notoriously deficient in geographical knowledge, by asking the question "What is the largest country in Europe?" and then aggressively responding, "Why, Denmark, of course!" Although Greenland has been an autonomous part of the Danish kingdom since 1953, it is roughly fifty times the size of Denmark proper. However, Greenlanders opted out of membership in the European Union in 1982 shortly after Denmark joined, thus stressing that although part of the same country officially, Greenlanders wish to preserve much that is uniquely their own.

Lying mostly north of the Arctic Circle, Greenland (Greenlandic: *Kalaallit Nunaat*; Danish: Grønland) is an island that enjoys home rule, a special self-governing status that put an end to hundreds of years of direct colonial rule from Copenhagen. In a referendum in 1979, Greenlanders voted to manage their own internal matters. Only foreign affairs and defense remain completely under the control of the government in Copenhagen. Like the Faroes, Greenland has a fixed quota of two seats in the Danish parliament (Folketing). Local executive power is held by a seven-member body, the Landsstyre.

Agriculture has hardly been possible, even on the tiny coastal belt in the southwest, although it is believed that when the first Viking settlers arrived in the 11th century, the warmer climate prevailing then made agriculture and sheep grazing possible on a considerably greater scale than in more recent times. The main livelihood has always been fishing and hunting whales, seals, reindeer, polar bears and musk-ox. Most townspeople work in public services. There is limited tourism during the summer season for the hardy outdoor types from Denmark, but it is quite expensive. All who have been there will tell you that the spectacular scenery makes it well worth it.

Greenlanders, numbering only 55,000 and many of them of mixed race, now increasingly demand to make full use of their rights and opted out of the European Economic Community to ensure that access to traditional fishing (primarily cod, shrimp and salmon) and hunting grounds as well its mineral wealth are protected. Denmark is still Greenland's largest trading partner and receives much of the island's catch of fish, as well as hides and skins. The Greenlanders are primarily Inuit and mixed-European, especially Danish-Norwegian. The overwhelming majority of the population is located on the narrow southwestern coastal fringe.

In 1721 the Danes revisited Greenland and founded their own Cape of Good Hope colony (Godthaab, or Nuuk, the capital). Originally motivated to find the descendants of the original Viking settlers and convert the "heathen," monarchs subsequently dreamt of a Danish empire stretching across the North Atlantic to the Caribbean.

Many Greenlanders are critical today of Denmark's former commercial policies that exploited the island's resources when still a colony. Whale oil for use as a lubricant in the textile industry and in streetlamp lighting was an important raw material that enabled Danish capitalism, commerce and industrialization to make great strides.

The local Inuit, who had only hunted whales for consumption, were brought into the modern industrial world economy and encouraged to kill as many as possible in exchange for modern consumer goods, especially tobacco and alcohol. Europeans brought venereal disease and alcohol, causing havoc among the Inuit. What had been a largely egalitarian society became a class-divided one with better and more successful whalers encouraged to invest in new equipment and boats.

Glacier pictured on Greenland stamp

"Border Conflict" with Norway

The KGH (initials in Danish for den Kongelige Grøndlandske Handel — the Royal Greenland Trade — a government monopoly) dominated all trade with the local population as a "company store" arrangement. The KGH stores became the most important factor in the lives of the native Inuit people and brought about a concentration of the population in their vicinity. Almost all administrative, health, educational and social work was carried out by Danes who typically came for a period of a few years and then returned home. Although Danes are not proud of their past colonial treatment of the Greenlanders, few feel that Denmark deserves continued criticism. Most reject the idea that Greenland should dissolve its union with Denmark.

When Norway finally re-established its independence (from Sweden) in 1905, claims were made to regain at least part of Greenland. This simmering dispute later erupted into the most serious "border conflict" among the Scandinavian states in the 20th century. In May 1921, Denmark declared the entire island of Greenland "Danish territory." Norway insisted that this violated its traditional hunting and fishing rights along the east coast and argued that prior discovery by Norwegians entitled it to claim at least part of the island. The issue was finally decided, in Denmark's favor, by the Permanent Court of International Justice at the Hague in 1933. The United States had also promised to support Denmark's claim in 1917 when it purchased the Danish West Indies (today's Virgin Islands) and relinquished its own claim to Northern Greenland based on the explorations of Robert E. Peary.

During World War II a decisive break was made with the Danes as a result of the German occupation of Denmark, and the strategic importance of Greenland emerged. Greenland played key roles both in the battle for the Atlantic and the Allied invasion of occupied Europe, although few were aware of this on April 9, 1940, when Denmark surrendered. American air bases in Greenland were vital in the struggle against German submarines preying on Allied convoys of supplies to Britain and Russia.

D-Day Landings

Joint Danish-Greenlander sled patrols drove off expeditions of German radio technicians and meteorologists attempting to gain vital weather information. A "Free Denmark" in Greenland and the Faeroes raised the spirits of Danes at home and won the support of Danish ambassadors, including Henrik Kauffman, Danish ambassador to the United States, who signed a treaty authorizing the U.S. to defend Greenland from the Germans. The government in Copenhagen officially declared that Kauffmann was acting illegally (after the war he was decorated for having defied orders; see also chapter 27), but most significantly the local authorities in Greenland voted to follow him and not instructions from Copenhagen.

Greenland was vital for the protection of Allied convoys and for early meteorological reporting, the secret to the successful D-Day landings on June 6, 1944, when the Germans, without such facilities, were unaware that the stormy weather in the North Sea that made an invasion unlikely, had abated.

Postwar Greenland

The war convinced many Greenlanders that the paternalistic authorities in Copenhagen did not "always know best" and gave them the first real taste of deciding things for themselves. The result was the formation of a new political force determined to win a measure of autonomy and end the long relationship of a remote colony that simply supplied raw materials to the mother country.

In May 1947, Denmark requested a formal agreement with the United States over the use of bases in Greenland. Arduous negotiations culminated in April 1951, providing for Danish control of the chief U.S. naval station in Greenland and for the establishment of jointly operated defense areas. Later, the U.S. Air Force, operating under the NATO command, built a huge airbase in Thule in the far north.

This was the most important advanced early-warning station for possible Soviet missile strikes against the United States. Demands for autonomy were gradually met by a new Danish constitution in May 1953, when Greenland became "an integral part of the Danish monarchy" and obtained representation in the Folketing.

An irritant in relations between Greenlanders and Danes for generations has been the inequality in standards of living, education and wages. Although the Danes have always prided themselves on the absence of great gaps between the "haves" and the "have-nots" and maintain one of the highest tax burdens in the Western world, designed to provide welfare benefits, it has not been possible to enforce a formal equality with its former colony. In order to entice Danes to live and work in Greenland, it has been necessary to offer much higher salaries than the state can afford to pay Greenlanders.

Many Danes believe that even with much goodwill, there are sharp differences in outlook, sense of responsibility and "mentality" with Greenlanders that are difficult to overcome. It is a story that has also occurred elsewhere — the transition from a hunting and gathering economy to an industrialized and bureaucratic society. Greenlanders are still dependent on (and resentful of) so many Danes who continue to be needed in such sensitive areas as education.

Debate and doubt still cause unrest among Greenlanders that while their language has been recognized, there is little to read in it and that "home-rule" is a nice name but they are still poor, distant third-world cousins. They question what is authentically Greenlandic in their society where the same Danish-style administration, education, legal and penal systems, health services, political system and social welfare policies characterize everyone's daily existence. Many have had great difficulties in making the transition from what was the universal traditional form of accommodations in Greenland, single-family dwellings at ground level, to multistory apartment blocks.

The best-selling novel by Danish author Peter Hoeg, *Smilla's Sense of Snow*, dramatically exploits the native Greenlanders' skills at survival and understanding of the arctic environment. The book was made into a film that received mixed reviews for its acting and plot but universal praise for its beautiful photography of the Greenland environment. Smilla is a mixed Inuit-Danish girl living in Copenhagen who has not forgotten the traditional skills learned as a child in Greenland.

Her "sense" for snow and ice are critical in the unfolding of the mystery. The Copenhagen detectives simply judge a boy's death as an accident. He must have slipped on the snow and fallen from the roof to his death, but Smilla's sense of snow make her doubt this explanation. The book and film reawakened the interest of many Danes in Greenland, part of their own country yet still distant and so totally different.

Chapter 6

How the Danish West Indies Became the U.S. Virgin Islands

For close to 260 years, Denmark maintained a colonial presence in the Caribbean. The American Virgin Islands are a favorite tourist spot for Caribbean cruises. Its status as a Danish possession was long considered an anomaly but repeated American attempts to purchase the islands from the end of the Civil War until just prior to American entry into World War I proved elusive.

Alone of all the Nordic countries, Denmark aspired to become a great maritime power with a colonial empire extending into the tropics. The three islands that today are known as the American Virgin Islands, St. Thomas, St. Croix and St. John (called Sankt Thomas, Sankt Croix and Sankt Jan in Danish), were acquired by a Denmark anxious to obtain precious metals, spices, sugar, tobacco, rum, cotton, indigo, ginger, cacao and coffee. No other colonial outpost in the New World proved so hospitable and advantageous for Jews. They played a major role in stimulating trade during the era of sailing ships and contributed greatly to the islands' development.

Few Danes had been enticed to settle in the West Indies voluntarily. The Danish colonies were nevertheless handicapped in spite of a well developed merchant fleet by the scarcity of manpower at its disposal. Settlers to farm new lands or even administrators to manage the colonies were in short supply. Danish rule was limited to a few forts, plantations and trading posts. Similar footholds in Africa and off the coast of India were given up as simply too remote, dangerous and unpromising.

Danish King Frederik III gave his approval for a permanent Danish settlement on Sankt Thomas in 1655. The Danes managed to make their few acquisitions due to the already heated rivalry between France, England, Spain and Holland, all of which were overextended and not willing to bother wasting resources in any attempt to expel them. The Spaniards regarded the Danish intrusion as illegal since they had claimed the entire region for themselves while the North European powers saw the arrival of the Danes primarily as a diversion that might distract the Spaniards further. In 1755, all three islands came under direct Danish rule instead of through the offices of the West India Company and were treated as overseas colonies.

Jewish Contribution to the Islands' Prosperity

For Jewish tourists, there is an extra added attraction in visiting the Virgin Islands. There are historic synagogues, cemeteries and active Jewish communities. The former Danish West Indies, sold to the United States in 1917, has had a fascinating and little known Jewish presence to the point that in the 1830s some visitors coined the expression that the islands should properly be called "The Jewish West Indies." A good deal of the technical expertise for the establishment of the sugar industry was due to Sephardic Jews of Spanish and Portuguese origin who had been driven out of Northeastern Brazil when the Portuguese retook the region. Eventually, the sugar industry became quite important for Denmark where distilleries turned it into rum.

Many Sephardic Jews, who had already been granted full equality by the Dutch in their possessions of Curaçao, Aruba and Dutch Guiana (Suriname), were active in establishing the sugar industry and served as administrators, bankers, and merchants, and helped established markets for tropical products. By 1820, the islands' population totaled 40,000; about 10 percent white, 20 percent "free coloreds" and 70 percent black slaves. It is estimated that the Jewish population of the islands constituted almost half the white population of Sankt Thomas in the period 1820–30 when the community established a beautiful synagogue with a sand-covered floor (the renowned *Beraka veShalom veGemilut Hasadim).* The free white population was divided among English, Scottish, Irish, Danish, Dutch, French and Sephardi settlers.

Every free inhabitant of the Danish possessions in the Caribbean had to belong to a religious community. Thus, the entire Jewish population was organized and they were accorded full citizenship. All male children celebrated their bar mitzvah and all marriages were performed according to the Orthodox Sephardic rite during the greater part of the 19th century.

By 1837, the port of Charlotte Amalie on Sankt Thomas had become the second largest city in the Danish "Empire," second only to Copenhagen. This was largely due to its important crossroads position as a transit harbor. This role was gradually reduced with the construction of larger and faster steamships sailing on established routes between Europe, Latin America, the Caribbean ports or southern United States. Jewish prominence in the Dutch and Danish islands was due to their linguistic abilities, expertise in trade, cultivation of sugar, and distilling of rum.

Many Sephardic Jews of the Danish West Indies eventually immigrated to the United States and became eminently successful. Among the prominent Sephardic Jews who were born in the Danish West Indies were Judah Benjamin (born on Sankt Croix, although at the time of his birth it was under temporary British occupation) who became the Secretary of State of the Confederacy; and David Levi Yulee (after whom Levy County in Florida is named), who helped engineer the annexation of Florida and became the first Jew to serve in the U.S. Senate; the French impressionist painter Camille Pissaro; and the renowned physician, Jacob Mendes da Costa (all born on Sankt Thomas).

The growth of the port of New Orleans and the development of Florida provided two powerful magnets that attracted many Jews of the small West Indian islands. The lure of the powerful United States and the growth of its own shipping, sugar industry, relations with Cuba and the promise of building a Panama Canal for the newer, much larger, and faster steamships all pointed to economic decline for the Danish West Indies and the eventual drift away from the islands of the Sephardic element. The economy of the islands had come to depend on slave labor and was thus directly damaged by a slave revolt in 1848.

Slavery was brought to an end in 1848 under the threat of a general uprising that would have necessitated the sending of a major expeditionary force had it not been for a far-seeing governor, Peter von Scholten (1784–1854), who convinced the white planters they could not expect Copenhagen to save their estates. The islands were becoming more of a handicap than an asset and their importance as a port for the trans-shipment and re-supply of sailing ships was in sharp decline. With the decline in trade, the economic underpinning of the Jewish merchants was weakened. This was due in large part to the growing traffic of much faster ships with a much larger cargo-carrying capacity, thus making it more convenient to sail directly between major ports and avoid many stops at the smaller islands to take on provisions or fuel.

Denmark's disastrous defeat in the 1864 against Prussia and Austria made the Caribbean islands seem like a needless worry to Danish politicians who feared that they would become involved in the naval rivalries of the United States, Britain, Spain and Germany. A major hurricane in 1867 caused extensive damage and a cholera epidemic made it clear to any potential "buyer" of the islands (i.e., the United States) that major economic investment was necessary to deal with these problems, rebuild facilities and improve health and education standards. Another uprising by the island's poorest ex-slaves in 1878 had to be put down by armed plantation owners and Danish military forces. These events were a sharp setback for most of the Jewish community who had looked forward to transfer of sovereignty to the United States and as a result, emigration accelerated.

Sale of the Islands to the United States

At a New Year's Eve festivity at the White House in 1865, President Lincoln warmly addressed the Danish ambassador Valdamar Rassløff. Shortly thereafter, Secretary of State Seward spoke to him and made it clear that the United States was interested in purchasing the islands. Since the ambassador had no direct instructions to negotiate, he requested time to communicate with his government. He also reminded Seward that the islands' population was content with Danish rule. The government, and even more, King Christian IX, were not happy at the news of the American initiative even though it promised economic relief. In reality, both the government and king felt that there was no need to rush and that time would be their ally and only help to increase the price. In this, they were mistaken.

In Denmark, only a few mercantile and manufacturing interests in the sugar, tobacco and rum industries centered in Copenhagen and Flensborg were determined to exercise their political influence to maintain Danish possession of the islands. A few Jews in Denmark were also involved in the distillery industry first in rum and later in the typically Scandinavian "snaps" product known as Aquavit, flavored with caraway, anise, coriander, or citrus rind (chapter 13).

First Round

Interest quickly waned following the assassination of President Lincoln on April 14, 1865. Seward had been seriously wounded in the attempt and took months to recover. Instructions were given to the Danish ambassador in the United States to ask the Americans what price they had in mind. The Danish negotiators hinted that $25 million would be acceptable as a fair price. Seward became coy at this stage and expressed the wish to actually visit the islands to personally examine their condition before any further negotiations could take place.

He returned from an inspection trip only to become embroiled in a crisis over Reconstruction which led to an impeachment trial against the new president, Andrew Johnson. Moreover, Congress was in a sullen mood and had already expressed indignation over the purchase of Alaska from Russia that Seward had engineered for the "astronomical" price of $7,000,000! Paying more than three times that amount as the Danes had requested would be scandalous. The intended sale fell through in 1867 and interest lapsed for another thirty years.

The speculation in Europe and concern in America over secret negotiations of a possible sale of the Danish West Indies was given added credence by the growth of German naval power and by its acquisition in 1890 of the island of Helgoland, lying about 70 kilometers (44 miles) off the west coast of Slesvig. Ironically Helgoland had originally been under the Danish crown until seized by Great Britain following the Napoleonic wars in 1815. The British made a costly mistake in exchanging it for the German-controlled island of Zanzibar in East Africa. The prospect of a German naval base in the Caribbean allowing ships to operate freely in the Western hemisphere (and before the completion of the Panama Canal) was sufficient to raise deep suspicions in American naval circles at the turn of the century.

The decisive American victory in the Spanish-American War in 1898 made Denmark apprehensive that any attempt to sell the West Indian islands to Germany would be strongly opposed by the United States, which was now vitally interested in a potential Caribbean base. At the time of the first proposed sale in 1865–67, Germany had not been a major sea power or become a united empire. By 1914, Germany had become a major maritime nation and great sea power rivaling Great Britain with a submarine fleet that would grow substantially.

Disappointment in the failure of the first sales proposal was greater in Denmark than in the islands themselves. An ever increasing amount of the islands' trade was directed towards the United States and the prospect of building the Panama Canal increased the potential advantages to be enjoyed by a closer association with the United States. Denmark's administrative costs in maintaining its tropical possessions were also an increasing burden. Several Danish journalists who visited the islands returned with reports of corrupt officials and a growing budgetary deficit. The islands were portrayed as a lazy tropical backwater where extravagant planters who had grown rich under slavery lived amidst an impoverished and illiterate black and mulatto population that was distant from Danish culture and the Danish language. Most of the islanders except those of pure Danish stock communicated with each other in English. It was significant that not a single Danish monarch had ever thought it worthwhile to visit the West Indies.

Second Round

The time was thus ripe for a renewed interest in a sale and a number of events converged to make this a likely eventuality in 1902. The well meaning King Oscar II of Sweden on a visit to Berlin even raised the idea of an exchange in which Germany would acquire one or more of the islands in return for the lost Danish province of North Slesvig. Whereas high-ranking German naval officers were positively disposed to the idea, the more influential and powerful German General Staff was unwilling to consider any loss of the strategic province astride a possible invasion corridor from the North. There was also the delicate foreign policy question of the American Monroe Doctrine. Did it only oppose any forceful attempt to acquire or reacquire European colonial possessions in the Western Hemisphere or did it also include the legal sale from one European power to another?

Henrik Calving, an unscrupulous reporter for the Copenhagen newspaper *Politiken*, used his knowledge of the islands from previous trips to exploit growing tension over the issue of Cuba and the looming Spanish-American War. He saw the opportunity to become a private agent to "facilitate" the sale of the islands and charge an exorbitant commission. While in Cuba in 1895, he let himself be "interviewed" by American journalists and fabricated a story based on so-called contacts that the German government was actively trying to acquire the islands. He also spread rumors that Denmark might grant independence to its colonies and that the British might try to seize them by appealing to the black and mulatto English-speaking majority. The ploy was sufficient to awaken interest in the purchase of the islands. Calving managed to gain interviews with Republican Senator Henry Cabot Lodge, resulting in the promotion of the idea of buying the islands from Denmark as an important plank in the Republic Party Convention of 1896. The Republicans victory seemed to assure that the sale would go through but another rival speculator, Niels Grøn, entered the picture and muddied the waters for all sides.

Grøn was one of several prominent businessmen who had established good relations with important sugar growers who were convinced that only by avoiding American import duties could the islands' sugar production be assured a permanent and profitable market, especially after both Cuba and Puerto Rico had become American protectorates. When two scoundrels could play such a game, there has to be room for a third! Into this imbroglio now entered a former Danish naval officer who had a shady past, the writer of boys' adventure books and the hyphened triple name of Walter Christmas-Dirkinck-Holmfeld.

Mr. Christmas, as he came to be known, acted as a double agent, traveling first to Germany where he made important connections with German naval circles and shipbuilding interests, including the Hamburg-America Line. He offered his service to buy up land in the less populated island of St. John which had several outstanding but undeveloped natural harbors. He was farseeing enough to argue in that in a generation or two, Germany would desperately need a base in the Caribbean in the eventuality of war with the United States. As a Dane, he could legally buy the land and secretly transfer it to German nationals who would slowly settle on the island and be able to help a German fleet. He tried unsuccessfully to convince the Danish administration of the islands to allow him to make such purchases. When this failed, he made an about-face and managed to reach President McKinley of the new Democrat administration in 1900 and Secretary of State John Hay, to whom he audaciously revealed his knowledge of the "German plot" to acquire St. John. He generously offered his services in helping the Americans reach an agreement with the Danish government to pay the debts owed by the islands' planters.

Hay believed him enough to ask an American diplomatic envoy, Henry White, to accompany Mr. Christmas to Copenhagen to enquire about Danish willingness to sell all three islands to the United States and how much they wanted for them. Through the good offices of Mr. Christmas, the price asked by the Danish government was $5,000,000. Although Christmas had no diplomatic status, the Danish government had begun to work through him until news leaked out and reached Niels Grøn, who spilled the beans to the American press. News of the scandal embarrassed King Christian IX. The king legitimately scolded ministers who had been involved in the negotiations. The machinations of these Danes to bribe American officials in order to facilitate the sale resulted in demands for a Congressional investigation. In spite of the bad publicity, both sides realized that a sale would still be in their long-term interests. A way had to be found so that on the Danish side, the king and government could demonstrate to the public that they were not simply selling Denmark's "birthright." The Danes included a demand that all subjects would be offered American citizenship, debts to American creditors would be settled and a just price would be paid. Secretary of State Hay had proposed $3,500,000, less than the $5,000,000 offered in 1867 when the Americans had proposed to buy only two of the islands. In the meantime, impending elections in 1901 in Denmark also made the political parties nervous. A shift towards the liberals and the left resulted in a new government less amenable to a sale. Moreover, the great Danish "East Asia" Shipping Company, ØK, entered the fray and opposed the sale with the claim that a future Panama Canal would greatly increase the economic and strategic importance of the Danish West Indies.

Finally, after approval by the Americans, holding fast to their $3.5 million offer, and granting the requests for citizenship and annulment of debts, the Danish side was given a deadline of January 24, 1902, to confirm the sale. It was passed by the lower house of the Danish parliament by a huge majority (88 to 7 with 6 abstentions). To speed things up, no referendum of the islanders' wishes was solicited. All that needed approval was the vote of the Danish upper house. Here, opposition was considerably stronger due to the right wing parties' more conservative stance and dislike of the egalitarian American society. Several elderly members of the chamber, who had been appointed by the king and resided in Jutland, and for whom the trip to Copenhagen was difficult, were afforded special aid to travel and take part in the vote. It ended in a tie, 32 to 32 and one abstention! Negotiations ended, leaving behind a bad taste in everyone's mouth.

The years following the failure of the 1902 negotiations witnessed some improvements in the islands' economy with more varied cultivation of cotton, sisal, lemons and animal husbandry. Regular steamship connections between Denmark and the islands were fostered by ØK and the opening of the Panama Canal in 1914 brought the promise of increased commercial activity, only to be stopped by the outbreak of World War I. Wages remained very low and a considerable part of the workforce abandoned the sugar plantations when construction work on the Panama Canal became available. Many of the remaining Jewish merchants emigrated to Panama to take advantage of the new economic opportunities there. The wartime threat of possible hostilities involving Denmark made both sides again realize that only a permanent solution of American sovereignty would provide stability.

Final Round

American impetus for a new round of negotiations was spurred by the request in 1915 of the Hamburg-America Line to expand their dock facilities at the major island port of Charlotte Amalie. The U.S. this time was fortunate to have the services of a well educated ambassador to Denmark, Maurice Francis Egan, who worked carefully with Denmark's prime minister, Erik Scavenius, a politician with long experience in foreign affairs and regarded as pro-German, and anxious to make it appear that it was an American initiative rather than a Danish one to resume negotiations.

Of all the ironies in the protracted sales of the Danish West Indies, the final one was the sales price. The Americans were now so desperate to acquire the islands that a bid of $50 million was to be offered as a last bid. Scavenius started off with a more modest $30 million proposal in mind but was bargained down to $25. A Danish referendum (in Denmark only and not among the islands' population) was required to appease public opinion. A private poll taken on the islands themselves showed an overwhelming majority in favor. The referendum was the first nationwide vote in which Danish women participated. The majority of 286,670 to 158,157 was considerable but it was achieved by the added incentive that the Americans would also promise to fully back Danish claims to sovereignty over all of Greenland, an area that had been in dispute with Norway, and was considered a major stumbling block to good relations with that sister Scandinavian country.

What is interesting is an examination of where the no vote was strongest — in pockets of Jutland and in the Faroe islands, an apparent demonstration of the people in those peripheral areas against the central authorities and political parties based in Copenhagen that they not be given such a free hand to sell Danish sovereignty to the highest bidder. This sentiment was graphically demonstrated in a cartoon that appeared in a popular magazine Klods Hans, ("Clumsy Hans"— see illustration) dated January 5, 1917, showing President Wilson in Uncle Sam costume leading the three little black children (the islands) away from their adoptive parents — Mr. and Mrs. Denmark. The father is already hurrying into the house with a sack of gold while his wife is hypocritically shedding tears over the lost little children.

Front cover of Danish satirical magazine *Klods-Hans*, January 5, 1917. The text reads: The rich Mr. Wilson (who has adopted the children for a fine sum of money once and for all) — "Come on boys, let's get going and I will buy you a fine suit and a gold watch with a chain!"

This time, the U.S. made sure not to let money and other considerations stand in the way and did everything necessary to prevent the islands from falling into the wrong hands. The Stars and Stripes replaced the Dannebrog on March 31, 1917, thus ending more than 260 years of Danish colonial rule in the Caribbean and ending the 50-year-long tug of war over their purchase.

Chapter 7

The Gågader:
Denmark's Pedestrian Streets

By the early 1960s, it had become apparent to Danes that duplicating the American level of private automobile ownership, road space and support services was a matter of physical impossibility, even for the most affluent European nations, and were health and environmental considerations to be ignored. Danish planners began to search for ways to cope with the automobile's increasing demands for space and resources.

Today, Denmark is the country in which the "walking street" has achieved the widest public acceptance and has come to be recognized as a standard element of town planning. Since 1962, virtually every Danish town with a population over 20,000, and many smaller ones as well, have converted centrally located shopping streets into pedestrian *gågader*, where vehicular traffic is limited to deliveries and pickups during the early morning hours. These *gågader* have successfully relieved traffic congestion, stabilized retail sales in the inner city and encouraged pedestrian activity among women, children and the elderly. The introduction of walking streets has also increased public awareness of the historic urban environment and heightened interest in maintaining a vital inner city to counteract the consequences of suburban migration.

Any first-time American visitor to the Scandinavian countries inevitably expresses delight at being able to stroll through the city centers at a leisurely pace. The roots of the modern "walking streets" of Europe are not to be found in any single cultural tradition, but rather in the continental response to the common problem of coping with the automobile's impact upon the fragile urban environment. Something had to be done to mitigate the hazardous effects of vehicular traffic upon the historic and aesthetic value of city centers. The solution was to ban cars in the centrally located shopping avenues and turn them into pedestrian thoroughfares.

How did Danes manage to so warmly embrace the concept of pedestrian

42

city streets in the center of their towns? Two specifically Danish factors have been instrumental in winning public support for the *gågader* and in promoting the pedestrian concept beyond the initial planning purposes of traffic control and commercial promotion. First, due to Danish neutrality in World War I and a relatively mild occupation in World War II, Danish towns did not suffer the immense material damage that occurred in most of Europe. As a result, a large number of historically valuable buildings and street networks have been preserved relatively intact. Second, a preference for the small scale is deeply ingrained in the Danish psyche. Danish literature and folk songs sing the praises of the country's small size, its modestly scaled farms and its many small industrial establishments. A lack of affectation is stressed as a national characteristic.

The capacity to make do with limited resources, a virtue in an agrarian society, has been retained in the "human scale" of Danish townscapes. Planning regulations limit the height of most new buildings to three-and-one-half stories, although such tight restrictions have had to be waived for modern office buildings and hotels in Copenhagen and for some housing projects. Nonetheless, the first thing an American notices is that Denmark's capital city, "Wonderful, wonderful Copenhagen," is a city without skyscrapers.

Ironically, the first planned Danish *gågade* was modeled after an American project! City planners in Aalborg, Denmark's third largest city, had read about the architect Victor Gruen and his idea for a pedestrian mall district in Fort Worth, Texas, and proposed a similar plan in 1956. The Aalborg city council shelved the idea for six years before going ahead with the much more modest and temporary experiment of closing off the city's main shopping street to traffic on December 1, 1962. A few days afterwards Copenhagen put into effect a similar trial pedestrianization of *Strøget*, the main shopping street, which stretches from *Rådhuset* (the town hall) to Kongens Nytorv. The *gågade* experience presents an interesting case of a borrowed innovation that rapidly diffused from secondary centers in Denmark after making little headway in the capital.

Strøget, or "the Stretch," is a term dating from the 17th century when it was first applied to Copenhagen's most prestigious showplace for the well-to-do; a Sunday promenade along its length was an expectation of "polite society." The same stretch had long housed the city's finest specialty shops, and many Danish provincial towns imitated the capital's manners by referring to their own most prominent local shopping street as a *Strøget.*'There is a clear identification of the modern pedestrianized *gågader* with an indigenous feature of Danish urban society dating back to the pre-industrial era. Many tourists imagine that the present *gågader* are simply a direct continuation of the pre-automobile *Strøget* tradition (like the famous island promenade, "Las Ramblas" in Barcelona), but in fact nothing could be further from the truth!

Revitalizing the Inner City

In the mid–1970s, European researchers found that the inner city population of Copenhagen had declined from 770,000 to approximately 700,000 persons from 1945 to 1962, while the pedestrian traffic along Strøget fell from 45,000 to 30,000 people daily. The decline in the inner city was more than matched by an increase in the suburban population. Although the city experienced an increase in the number of jobs, out-migration to the suburbs was selective and left behind a population characterized by a low socio-economic profile, living in a ring of decaying slum tenements in the "bridge districts" of Nørrebro and Vesterbro.

The decision of the Copenhagen city council in late 1962 to temporarily close *Strøget* to vehicular traffic met with opposition from local merchants, with suspicion by traffic experts and the police, and with outright hostility from the tabloid press. The large-circulation daily newspaper, *Ekstra Bladet*, predicted that the experiments in Copenhagen and Aalborg were doomed to failure because they were "non–Nordic" imitations of the outdoor orientation of southern European urban life; as such they were clearly unsuited to the Danish climate, mentality and preference for indoor "coziness" (*hygge;* see chapter 12). In the newspaper's editorial opinion, the tradition of the outdoor café, the leisurely promenade and the arcaded public square (*piazza*) could not be made appealing to Danes, who were already firmly committed to the convenience of the automobile.

Despite the newspaper's opposition, the city councils of both Copenhagen and Aalborg went ahead with their plans on a temporary, experimental basis. Immediate public participation, coupled with a 30 percent increase in the volume of holiday sales in both cities, convinced local merchants that their initial fears and suspicions were ill founded.

Traffic experts also responded positively when studies proved that the reduction in the number of motor vehicles using adjacent streets, the loss of parking space, and the conversion of many streets to one-way traffic did not increase travel time through the center of Copenhagen. Statistics collected immediately before and after pedestrianization recorded a 24 percent reduction in the number of motor vehicles during non-peak hours and 34 percent during rush-hour traffic. Police and environmentalists were pleased to note a significant drop in the number of traffic accidents and the amount of air pollution.

The media, including the tabloid press that had originally ridiculed the proposal, then publicized the successful results: a decrease in traffic congestion, an increase in sales along the walking street, and the overwhelmingly positive response of consumers, who had rediscovered a "walking culture" from the pre-automobile age.

By 1977, 58 *gågader* had been established by municipalities in 39 Danish cities. In approximately one-half of the cases, municipalities bore the costs, in two cases local merchants' associations handled the bill, and in the remaining situations the municipality and local merchants' associations shared the costs (as reported by *Detail-handelinstitutet*). In almost all cases, initial gains in sales turnover duplicated the successes of Copenhagen and Alborg. Prior to 1962, Rotterdam and Stockholm had created modern pedestrian shopping streets as part of completely new planned central city district, but in Denmark, the *gågade* idea became integrally linked to a desire to preserve the existing urban environment.

Copenhagen developed the most extensive *gågader* network by integrating Strøget, the university district and a historic square, church, and flower market into one of the longest pedestrian systems in Europe (after Venice and Amsterdam). In Helsingør, on Zealand's northeast coast, the city council rejected the use of flagstones and invested considerable funds in renovating all of the houses along the town's *strøget* to ensure the uniformity of style and historic appearance of the urban core. This action won the praise of architects and urban planners throughout Europe. Although no other Danish city has duplicated the architectural preservation efforts of Helsingør, municipal authorities are so anxious to avoid clashes of architectural styles that modification of

Street entertainment on Copenhagen's main pedestrian thoroughfare (photograph by Ruben Berdichevsky).

facades must win official approval before permission is granted to make any changes.

Two large provincial towns with no objective need to relieve traffic congestion in the urban core also decided to have walking streets; the industrial city of Herning in North Jutland and the port city of Esbjerg on Jutland's west coast. They were both established in the late 19th century. Although neither had the medieval section of narrow, winding streets that typifies most Danish towns, the walking-street concept had become so much of an "architectural and planning imperative" that voters in both towns approved costly projects to pedestrianize their major shopping streets. They felt deprived without a showcase *gågade* of their own.

As in other West European countries, there is a very vocal constituency in Denmark, variously labeled socialist, youth culture or environmentalist, that preaches a counterculture philosophy to the modern, energy-demanding, consumer-oriented society. Before the Arab oil boycott of 1973 that led to a brief period of "car-free Sundays," these groups criticized the suburban trend and called for measures designed to make the inner city a more vital and attractive place in which to live.

Most Danes accepted that the near universal level of car ownership that exists in the United States could never be realized in most of Europe and especially not in crowded Denmark with its tradition of historical preservation and much medieval urban architecture. The level of car ownership in Denmark is below that of many other West European states and about a third less than in neighboring and much larger Norway and Sweden.

Ratio of Passenger Cars in Use to People:
Information Please Almanac, 1999

USA	1: 1.8	Sweden	1: 2.5
Italy	1: 2.0	Norway	1: 2.6
Germany	1: 2.0	Netherlands	1: 2.7
France	1: 2.4	UK	1: 2.9
Austria	1: 2.4	Denmark	1: 3.3
Belgium	1: 2.4	Greece	1: 3.7

Streets and Transport for the People

In Copenhagen and the large university towns of Aarhus, Odense and Aalborg, the population that remained behind in central city areas with decaying housing was made up predominantly of elderly pensioners, childless young couples and students. These are the groups that have a low rate of car ownership and depend upon public transportation. They initially welcomed the *gågade* concept, which was used as a wedge to argue for a "streets for the peo-ple" policy of adapting the urban environment to a more human scale. Street entertainers, musicians and other artists regularly make use of the pedestrian streets as their stage.

Safe and aesthetically pleasing streets and public places offer a refuge for the pedestrian. They are a *sina qua non* for urban thinkers such as Jane Jacobs, Lewis Mumford and Colin Buchanan. Streets comprise more than one-third of the total area in cities and must be viewed, and used, by city residents and commuters alike. The "energy crunch" and disenchantment with suburban living have reinforced these elementary facts, both in the United States and in Europe.

The commercial *gågader* were a product of the prosperity of the 1960s, when expansive growth was taken for granted and retail sales increased sharply in accord with the upward trend of real wages. Walking corridors originated as traffic control measures, but their popular appeal generated unforeseen con-sequences. Likewise, they revealed to the Danish public the mental-hygienic advantages and historic-architectural values of pre-automobile urban life, and encouraged debate on urban planning policies. This debate took on a critical aspect following the energy crisis of 1973 and the realization that the idea of universal car ownership was an illusion and a practical impossibility. Den-mark's level of car ownership is below the average for most West European countries and about a third less than neighboring Norway and Sweden. It is only one-third the level of American car ownership.

The *gågader* also provided a model for the incorporation of a pedestrian-friendly street as part of an overall policy of urban renewal, designed to main-tain the vitality of the inner city and further strengthen public transportation. These policies won approval and popularity in a variety of Asian and South American cities including Tokyo, Israeli West Jerusalem, Tel Aviv, Guadalajara and Buenos Aires.

In the homeland of the automobile, the United States, pedestrian shop-ping streets have enjoyed less success, due to the much higher level of car ownership and the convenience of suburban shopping malls, located on the outskirts of major cities but easily accessible by main highways. Many Amer-ican cities have, in fact, come full circle. Pedestrian shopping districts, intro-duced in the 1970s in the centers of many cities such as Oak Park, Illinois; Poughkeepsie, New York; Eugene, Oregon; Santa Monica, California; Vicks-burg, Mississippi; Memphis, Tennessee; Sioux Falls, South Dakota; and Miami Beach, Florida, were all initially judged to be "moderately successful." All of these cities have since reinstituted traffic along many of the streets that were originally pedestrianized.

American shoppers have preferred their use of the car if provided with adequate and free parking facilities. Few American cities laid out in the checkerboard grid pattern have any historic housing or quaint, picturesque, winding streets that can compete with the Old World's for mystery and romantic allure. In Denmark, by contrast, not a single "walking street" has reverted back to its original status as a trafficked road, according to the Ministry of Housing.

The practical difficulties involved in further restricting the use of private automobiles is a central bone of contention in Denmark's public policy debates, however. A lobby, *Trafik* Forum, has exerted considerable public pressure on successive Danish governments to continue their commitment to building a subway (metro) in Copenhagen. The initial stage of the metro has been completed and now provides more underground or multi-story parking sites, as well as a tunnel connecting Amager (site of Copenhagen's airport on an island) and Østerbro (in the city center). Travelers arriving from abroad can now get the metro at Kastrup airport and journey into the very center of Copenhagen. The new integrated system makes better bus and overground S-train (the present elevated railway system in Copenhagen) connections. It also preserves cycle lanes and enforces more stringent emission controls.

The Forum has a balanced approach to satisfying both car owners and users of public transport. There is general recognition that it would be unfair to impose higher taxes on car owners. Whereas motor traffic has increased everywhere else in Denmark, it has essentially stagnated in Copenhagen since the introduction of the pedestrian streets. The many bumper stickers, first introduced in 1975, carrying the slogan, "Without the automobile, Denmark stands still," continue to be a popular sign that motorists are not willing to surrender more ground to pedestrians.

Chapter 8

Jewish Provincial Cemeteries: A Cultural Landmark to Tolerance

On a recent family trip to Denmark, I came face to face with two realities — one from the past when tiny Jewish communities throughout much of provincial Denmark coexisted in friendship and good will with a society that was "uni-cultural," and the other, from today's much vaunted and extolled "multiculturalism," in which a relatively large community of Muslims, recent immigrants or their children, egged on by imams and agents of extremism, has taken the law into its own hands to create a parallel society.

From the latter part of the 18th century until the beginning of the twentieth, there were approximately a dozen Danish towns in which Jews lived and maintained their religious traditions and obligations and preserved a separate social identity for several generations. All of them eventually withered away due to Danish tolerance. Visible evidence of this can be seen in the provincial Jewish cemeteries and a few buildings that previously functioned as synagogues. Any visitor can observe the beautiful condition of Denmark's ten Jewish cemeteries located outside of Copenhagen. The expense involved in their care is covered by a considerable budgetary allocation provided by the Jewish community in Copenhagen. The local authorities in the ten towns do, however, regard the cemeteries as an important part of their cultural-historical heritage and several of them, like Faaborg, make prominent mention of them in their tourist literature.

How ironic indeed when Denmark suddenly was catapulted into world headlines by the publication of a few cartoons in the newspaper *Jyllands-Posten*. Gentle and ironic satire which many Americans no doubt recognized in the wit of Victor Borge (chapter 15) has long been a Danish art form dating back at least to the many short stories (fairy tales) by Hans Christian Andersen (chapter 17) and used with great success against the Nazis when armed resistance seemed suicidal and hopeless. The object of those satirical cartoons was

49

the political misuse of Islam by extremists and suicide bombers who have carried their fanaticism into the heart of Europe, a claim that has been verified hundreds of times in dozens of locations over the past decade.

Nevertheless, reaction to worldwide 2006 attacks on Denmark, Danes and Danish products by many of the Western media was ambivalent and reminded many Danes how little the outside world cared in 1864 or 1940 when Denmark became the victim of brutal aggression. This time, however, the usual words of sympathy were mixed with condemnation by those, like the appeasers to Hitler in the 1930s, who hoped that if others could be fed to the crocodile, it would grow satiated or they would be eaten last.

Ignorance of Denmark's history and traditions extend to elementary geography. The cartoons in *Jyllands-Posten* were published in Aarhus, (Denmark's second largest city) not Copenhagen, as wrongfully reported dozens of times by much of the American press and even in Christopher Hitchens' recent best-selling book *God Is Not Great* (p. 281). It came as a shock that instead of unequivocal support for an ally and highly respected member of the international community, many voices questioned the wisdom of "purposely antagonizing" Muslim fanaticism.

At times, the Danish delight in irony and a fondness for keeping a low profile have avoided or postponed taking a critical decision. Like the British, "muddling through" has often been the preferred form of dealing with a challenge or confrontation. In 1946–49, the Danish government had the chance to regain the territory of South Schleswig from Germany and could have acted to demand a referendum or simply annex the territory that had been Danish for centuries but was lost in the disastrous war of German and Austrian aggression in 1864 (chapter 26). Although local elections in 1947 indicated that a majority of the local South Schleswig population preferred a referendum of self-determination, the typical Danish choice of avoiding confrontations led to wiser and cooler heads rejecting the opportunity. The Danish government refused the chance to regain part or all of the territory and risk a future confrontation with Germany that might one day give rise to another border dispute (chapter 27).

How much more remarkable it is, then, that in the face of antagonistic Muslim extremism today, before which the "vaunted" ("cowardly" would be the better more accurate term) *New York Times* abjectly surrendered and refused to reproduce any of the Muhammad cartoons, the entire Danish press reprinted all of them in February 2008 to protest the planned assassination of Kurt Westergaard, one of the cartoonists!

Although a few researchers have examined the question of how Jews disappeared from the Danish provincial towns, the evidence does not provide a clear explanation. There was clearly no discriminatory legislation after Jews were granted full civil equality by a special ordinance issued on March 29, 1814,

although some craft guilds prohibited non–Christians from becoming appren-
tices to learn the particular skill. Jews were a tolerated minority, about as numerous as Catholics. They enjoyed a special degree of autonomy for their own
affairs and were responsible for notifying the authorities of any foreign Jew
attempting to permanently settle in their community. There are only a handful
of recorded conversions of Jews to Christianity in the state-supported Lutheran
churches of the country. Later, when civil marriage became an alternative, it
was no longer necessary for one partner to "convert" to another religion.

From the gravestone inscriptions of the two major Jewish cemeteries in
Copenhagen (the earlier one dates from the end of the seventeenth century and
the more modern one from 1876), it is clear that some Jews left the provincial
cities towards the end of the 19th century to settle in Copenhagen where they
died. It may well be that others emigrated to the Danish West Indies (today's
U.S. Virgin Islands, chapter 6) to pursue their business interests or back to their
places of origin in Schleswig-Holstein or intermarried and just opted out.

It should be remembered that, until 1864, the North German territories
of Schleswig-Holstein were affiliated to the Danish kingdom and that Jewish
merchants from these two duchies may already have been familiar with Danish
law and the Danish language before they left the area of Schleswig-Holstein
and adjacent parts of Germany to seek their fortune in the kingdom proper.
The growth of the railroad, expansion of Copenhagen, the loss of Norway in
1815 and the annexation of the two duchies by Prussia and their incorporation
into a united Germany in 1871 also meant reduced commercial opportunities
for Jewish merchants in Denmark.

It is remarkable that each one the cemeteries still tells a unique and fascinating story of the Jewish residents of these small towns — Aalborg, Aarhus,
Randers, Horsens and Fredericia on the peninsula of Jutland; Odense, Faaborg
and Assens on the island of Funen; Slagelse on the western edge of the island
of Zealand (Copenhagen is located on the far eastern edge of this island); and
Maribo and Nakskov on the minor island of Lolland. Fredericia was the
longest lasting Jewish community in Jutland. It was established as a model
community of tolerance by the Danish King Frederick III in 1650 for both
Huguenot refugees and Jews.

What we know from the written record — in the newspapers and municipal archives of the cities where Jews resided — was that they were generally
held in high regard. In no town were they ever more numerous than 3 percent — probably in Randers about 1870 and Faaborg around 1840. There were
no ghettos in any of these towns. All were geographically circumscribed and
Jews residing anywhere could easily walk to a centrally located synagogue
without having to travel by coach or horseback.

The provincial Jewish communities that endured the longest were in Jut-

land at the greatest distance from Copenhagen. The last Jewish services in a
local synagogue in Jutland took place in Randers in the early 1920s. There
was no longer a *minyan* (10 adult Jewish men) to conduct services and the
synagogue was torn down in 1936. In Faaborg, a synagogue was inaugurated
in 1860 but closed after only one generation in 1901. In 1914, it was sold to
the freemasons who have used it ever since and it may still be seen on Kloster-
gade. The earliest Jewish residents were predominantly Sephardim (of Span-
ish-Portuguese ancestry), but almost all of those to arrive after 1800 were from
areas in Germany, Austria and what is today Poland.

   The local authorities today in Faaborg and elsewhere have provided access
to the Jewish cemeteries in these small towns to visitors who must ask permission for the key to enter a locked gate. They are thus protected from the
ugly possibility of vandalism. The serenity and simple beauty of each cemetery
is enhanced by the pathos and beautiful poetic language in Hebrew of the
inscriptions on many stones which are clearly legible — here are just two typical
examples of those I observed and photographed.

   *Radaf tov vihesed ad milayat yamav, Haya tamim bidarko vesa'ad neeman libanav,
   Mimarom yilmadoo aylav zichut viya'amod litchiya likaytz hayamim. (Courtesy of
   the Faaborg Tourist Bureau for permission to visit the cemetery.)*

The Faaborg city gate (photograph by the author).

[He pursued the good and mercy all the days of his life. He was innocent in his ways and a faithful provider for his children. From above they have vouched for him and he will stand amidst eternal life to the end of days.]

Ben arbaim shana. Nasa' lieretz hachaym. Yado haya ptoocha lievyonim, mish'an umavteach leawniyim. Nishmato alta ma'alah vihayta shaluv min-uchato.

[He was 40 years old. He has gone to the land of life. His hand was open to the paupers and a faithful shield and protector of the poor. His soul has ascended to the heavens and he is at rest.]

Tombstone in Faaborg's Jewish cemetery (photograph by the author).

The earliest stones have Hebrew inscriptions only. The ones cited above bear a shorter inscription in Danish underneath the Hebrew text:

Herunder hviler støvet ... (Beneath, rests the dust of...) or

Herunder hviler de jordiske levninger (Beneath, rests the earthly remains of....)

What strikes any modern observer with these inscriptions and those found from the same period on many Christian gravestones is the value placed on modesty, the chastity and faithfulness of women, charity and concern for the poor, the tribulations of this life and faith in some everlasting final reward or resting place. While realists and cynics may argue that these inscriptions can hardly be taken as an accurate account of the character of those whose remains are buried beneath the stones, they do highlight the goals of a generation who could not expect to live into what we would call middle age today. The many children's graves and the headstones indicating that the age of death for many adults was in the early 40s bear this out.

A few of the stones relate the occupation of those buried, such as watchmaker, saddlemaker, shopkeeper, ritual slaughterer, practicing physician, merchant, journalist and even "industrialist" (factory owner). Several provincial Jews were active in shipping while others were among the pioneers in establishing factories for the manufacture of potash, dyeing, tanneries, leather goods, sugar refining, cigars and chocolate. Henri Nathansen, one of Denmark's most famous authors, was the son of Michael from Randers who, as a soldier during the Three Years' War (1848–51) against the Schleswig-Holstein rebels, won Denmark's highest award, *Dannebrogskorset,* and was fatally wounded at the decisive final battle of the war on Isted heath.

Whatever their position in society, they took solace from their hope in a life to come and believed that they and their children would be treated as equals. Whatever their rabbis might have to say about matters of personal affairs in religious observance, marriage, divorce, and adoption, the most ultra–Orthodox religious Jews as well as growing reform-minded and secular elements were thoroughly committed to the principle expressed by all rabbis dating from the third century A.D. in the Diaspora demanding from all Jews recognition that *Dina demalkuta dina*—"The law of the government is the law." No Jew in Denmark could ever attempt to use an argument from Jewish religious law to escape the requirements of the Danish civil and criminal law.

Hans Christian Andersen was sent by his mother to the small Jewish school (their neighborhood where the Jews lived was the poorest section of town) when he had become the victim of bullying by classmates who ridiculed his effeminate nature and fondness for storytelling. Many years later, when a famous author, he wrote a letter expressing his gratitude to the school's headmaster. Andersen was later shocked to find that instead of the very poor folks he had known among his Jewish neighbors as a boy in Odense, Copenhagen's Jewish community included very wealthy families, several of whom would become his patrons in later life.

Multicultural Denmark Today

A few days after my visit to Faaborg, I was strolling through contemporary Copenhagen in the bustling Nørrebro neighborhood. I could see how a major traffic thoroughfare reserved for bus traffic only and where parking for motorists was strictly forbidden had been expropriated as a No-Go area for "ordinary citizens" (i.e., the non–Muslim majority). The lane along a stretch of the neighborhood's major thoroughfare, Nørrebrogade, has been taken over by parked cars that are utilized by shop owners (all Muslim) to store their wares (predominantly fruit and vegetables) or simply expropriated by passersby who have illegally parked, knowing full well that the Danish police and parking officials will not uphold the law against Muslims. This is nothing less than the existence of a separate law for those who now constitute a parallel culture under protection of their own Sharia law that are off limits to all others.

A few years ago, such a development would have been unimaginable. Even taxis are forbidden to use the special bus lane reserved for collective traffic and drivers violating the edict are subject to stiff fines. Actually parking in the lane would have been an inconceivable affront to public order. Many American tourists still marvel at how most Danes are so law abiding that they wait an extra minute or two at crossroads where the light has not yet turned green even though there is no traffic visible on the horizon. Many motorists park in legal zones in the center of Copenhagen and pay up to 26 kroner (more than $5) an hour for the privilege. Today, any vehicles on police or fire-fighting duty in several immigrant areas are accompanied by extra protection if called on to provide emergency service.

Danes returning to Copenhagen from nearby Malmø where Muslims constitute a significant proportion of the population can tell their neighbors that the Swedish police no longer use wheel locks on illegally parked vehicles for fear of provoking a major incident among Muslim residents. Apparently Denmark is still somewhat behind Sweden with regard to acknowledging a "parallel Muslim society." The conclusion is, however, inescapable. The Muslim minority of immigrants and their children/grandchildren feel increasingly emboldened to act beyond the law. For the rest of the world, this presents a different picture than the "Wonderful, Wonderful Copenhagen" from Danny Kay's lighthearted portrayal on film of the life of Hans Christian Andersen.

Upon my return, I read with great satisfaction that a Danish appeals court rejected a suit filed by seven Muslim organizations against newspaper editors who published the controversial cartoons of the Prophet Muhammad. The judges ruled that the caricatures, which have since sparked angry and, in some cases, deadly protests across the Muslim world, did not aim to insult followers of Islam, as the plaintiffs had charged. Appeals court president Peter Lilholt stressed that the Danish judiciary, in accordance with the European Convention on Human Rights, could not "restrict freedom of expression" unless it clearly affected national or public security. The court also emphasized "that terrorist acts have been committed in the name of Islam, and it is not illegal for these acts to be made the object of satirical representation."

From the latter part of the 18th century until the beginning of the twentieth, there were approximately a dozen Danish towns in which Jews lived and maintained their religious traditions and obligations and preserved a separate social identity for several generations. All of them eventually withered away due to Danish tolerance.

Commemorative stamp to celebrate the 300th anniversary of the founding of the organized Jewish community in Denmark.

Denmark of the mid-nineteenth century set a marvelous example in human relations and brotherhood based on mutual respect. It was possible because a small minority had seen how it was incumbent upon them to win the respect of their neighbors. In today's topsy-turvy world, Denmark and other nations are struggling to maintain their noble traditions and culture in the face of provocation from a militant minority of Muslim immigrants that seeks to impose its will and culture/religion on the majority.

Chapter 9

Jutland vs. Copenhagen

Like the archetypal New Yorker who has been everywhere in Europe and traveled to the exotic corners of the earth but has never been west of the Mississippi (a stereotypical few never cross the Hudson into New Jersey), there were, until the modern bridge era, stereotypical images of the "Københavner," who was a super cosmopolitan but had never been across the Great Belt (see chapter 1), and the typical country-bumpkin Jutlander.

Traditionally, Jutland was overwhelmingly agricultural and devoid of any major city. Grazing cattle and sheep and then driving them to market in Germany as well as fishing were also important activities. Strong religious sentiment and ties to the state Lutheran church prevailed in much of Jutland when it had long been on the decline elsewhere and in headlong retreat in Copenhagen. The landscape of Jutland was traditionally quite different than the rest of the country. Until the middle of the 19th century before major reclamation and drainage projects, much of Jutland was uncultivated and had few trees.

Perhaps only Uruguay with its metropolitan capital of Montevideo rivals Denmark for a nation with a capital city that is also the center for all the major political, economic, intellectual, and cultural institutions in the country. Ask any American (except one who is of Danish descent) to name another city in Denmark besides Copenhagen, and the odds are astronomical that he/she won't be able to. This dominance of a single great metropolitan center is even much stronger than with such major national capital cities as London and Paris. Probably nowhere else is a major region within a country the object of so strong a country-bumpkin stereotype as Jutland (Jylland), the peninsula that shares a land border with Germany.

The pace of life everywhere varies between country and city but the contrasts are extreme between Jutland and Copenhagen. It is not just the differences in regional dialects but the speed of ordinary conversation that is immediately apparent even to foreigners who understand no Danish at all. Like capital cities everywhere, Copenhagen has historically been a magnet

The Copenhagen skyline (photograph by the author).

attracting migrants from other parts of the country but in the Danish case, migrants from Jutland can still be identified by the manner and speed of their speech even when there are no other visible differences in appearance or dress. This state of affairs has persisted for centuries and created a sense of mutually suspicious and sometimes hostile stereotypes as well as the source of much good-natured humor which has won a place in Danish literature, theater, film, folklore, linguistics, religion, politics, fashion and social mores. In modern Danish the term "Provinsen," a collective noun denoting "the provinces," simply refers to everywhere but Copenhagen.

Jutland was covered with purple heather and in some northern coastal areas had sand dunes reminiscent of the Sahara whereas the Danish islands were a verdant green of lush, manicured fields and forests. The stereotypes of the Jutlanders and Scots as stingy, uneducated, even primitive and morose still abound and for many observers; the people's character matched their harsh and unforgiving environment. In both areas, fishing was a dangerous occupation and most coastal villages had a score of widows whose husbands had been lost at sea.

Countless folk tales played up the contrasting images of the country bumpkin vs. city slicker and dozens of Danish films and cheap novels followed the same plot of the naïve country-bred girl from Jutland exploited and the victim of sexual predators in Copenhagen. Geographically and psychologically, the central island of Funen (Fyn) was regarded as a kind of a place to pause and think before going on in either direction.

When Hans Christian Andersen visited Scotland, he remarked on the similarities between the Scots and Jutes. This applied to the lingering residue of Nordic/Danish influence in the Scots tongue (*bairn* for child, *hexe* for witch, *dal* for field or valley, etc.), but even more so to the more stoic, reserved, cautious and sincere, direct nature of both peoples in contrast to their more "sophisticated" but often superficial and frequently snobbish characteristics of the English and people of Copenhagen. Jyder often speak of a "højrøvede ["backside up in the air"] københavnersnude" as synonymous with egotistical, snobbish, irritating, and aggressive even if they have never met the person. "Snude" is slang for nose or "snout" and immediately suggests that it deserves a good punch.

For writer Mette Winge, the most obvious difference is that Copenhagen is always looking to boast, exaggerate and search for the latest style to be "in" and "with it" and to impress others, whereas the Jutes make every effort not to be impressed or excited or enthusiastic about anything, They are always the acknowledged masters of the art of understatement.

Several Danish writers of note were "Jyder" such as Johannes V. Jensen, Henrik Pontoppidan, Jeppe Aakjær, and Steen Steensen Blicher, who devoted much of their work to the communities in Jutland where they were born and grew up even though they moved to Copenhagen and resided there for most of their productive lives.

The noun "Jyde" and adjectives "Jysk" and "Jute" for Jutlander provide more than a simple geographic identity marker in Danish. In the past and perhaps even more so today as a result of clever marketing techniques, they have come to mean authentic or high quality, even natural, with regard to both agricultural products and people. A "Jysk kylling" (Jutland hen) and its eggs or "Jysk skinke" (ham from Jutland) are often bought by Copenhagen consumers who are convinced they must be the best "most natural" products without any chemical additives. This is true regardless where the products actually originated and the consumer should be aware that there is an exploitation of the Jutland image in marketing.

With regards to taste and fashion as with politics, Jutland retains a more conservative life style. Not as much expensive French wine is consumed per capita in Jutland as in Copenhagen nor are there anywhere near the number of foreign restaurants offering exotic food as in the capital. Homosexuality and alternative lifestyles are openly celebrated in the capital but often are still regarded with scorn and contempt in Jutland. The socialist and various left-wing political parties have considerably more support in greater Copenhagen than in most of Jutland.

What irks Jutlanders most is that historically, the considerable gaps in education and therefore social access and economic mobility were ignored by the monarchy and its Copenhagen-centered social world that elevated the capital and favored it, and identified the very essence of being Danish with itself. Even such states with a primate city and a stiff centralist form of government as France could not erase or permanently retard the strong sense of regional pride in Flanders, Alsace-Lorraine, Gascony, Normandy, Brittany, and Provence.

Even compared to its small, quite similar neighbor, the Netherlands, where each Dutch province bears its own distinctive regional flag, Denmark's administrative geographic divisions known as *amter* have never displayed such a marker of regional identity. Although there are regional symbols that appear on road markers to distinguish these administrative boundaries, they fall far short of the local patriotism stirred by regional flags. Expressing one's pride in being from Himmerland, Limfjorden, Lolland-Falster, South Jutland, or Fünen was relegated to folk costumes, dialects and folk songs only.

The attempt to reform the absolute monarchy in Denmark and introduce democratic reforms in the 1830s presented a major break with the past by providing for several consultative regional assemblies, one of which, located in Viborg, would represent Jutland. The proposal was voted down and the debates were characterized by an outright rejection of any special representation for Jutland. Representatives from Copenhagen quite rightly pointed out that all the realm's institutions were located in the capital, that everyone with a university education had all been educated there and that a regional assembly of "country bumpkins" would serve no purpose!

At this time, it was the case that almost everybody who had a university education in Denmark had studied at the University of Copenhagen. Jutlanders who were highly educated tended to remain in the capital city after completing their studies. The accepted wisdom of the day was expressed by Orla Lehmann, a leading liberal politician who supported only one consultative assembly in Copenhagen. He proclaimed in 1838 at a public meeting in Copenhagen that "there are no such things as provinces in Denmark" and provoked sarcastic laughter by referring to Jutland's only unique characteristic as its "continentality," i.e., not being an island.

The one major dissenting voice celebrating Jutland's unique character was Johannes V. Jensen, a Nobel Prize winner in literature who criticized the neglect of Jutland by Copenhagen's "distant" rulers and dared claim that the Jutes had long been deprived of their proper role in Danish history. He even asserted that the personality of the Jutes had been better preserved through migration to England and America.

Although the present Danish electoral system is a mixture of proportional and geographic representation and every Dane is technically represented in the Folketing by a member representing his/her area, the geographic part is largely symbolic and there is nothing resembling the high degree of responsibility an American Congressman or Senator owes his/her constituents.

Being from Jutland and defining oneself as such is still considered an advantage if one is seeking to define oneself as trustworthy, dependable, responsible and decent. Countless ads in the local Copenhagen press of individuals seeking to rent apartments use language such as "young, tranquil, responsible Jute nurse from Viborg seeks apartment."

The readers would laugh at someone from Copenhagen using similar language to describe those personal attributes that match his place of origin. It would be just as reasonable for readers to see an ad like "cool, tattooed, bisexual, rock musician Københavner seeks...." This stereotype has even been authenticated several times by individuals who advertised in the local Copenhagen press seeking an apartment and succeeded in getting an interview with the only difference being the presence of the adjective "Jysk" after having tried for months without the "correct" geographic reference.

Times, of course, have changed. Although quite late, Århus, the largest city in Jutland, finally got its own university in 1936. To smooth old feelings of deprivation, Queen Margrethe II was sent to study there rather than the medieval University of Copenhagen — a stone's throw from Amalienborg Palace. A number of other new institutions such as the School of Physiotherapy and Architecture have been placed in both Jutland and Funen to demonstrate that Denmark is no longer synonymous with Copenhagen.

The Sunday issue of Denmark's second largest circulation newspaper, *Politiken*, devoted a special edition to Copenhagen-Jutland stereotypes on September 29, 1997. The newspaper interviewed a dozen journalists, writers, lecturers, media personalities and ordinary Danes from different walks of life. Many of them confirmed the continued reality of regional differences that stereotypes exaggerate.

What makes the issue more complex has been the tendency today of many people to move from their original home to where they find a more congenial lifestyle. This includes Jutes who have found professional advancement in Copenhagen and their opposite number from the capital who have

Folk dancers' costumes in Jutland (photograph by the author).

sought a more "milieu-friendly" (and much less expensive) environment in Jutland!

Typical of migrants from Jutland to Copenhagen who have followed their career desires is Gitte Lokkegaard, who came to Copenhagen to work for the Danish TV3 program *Tak for kaffe* (*Thanks for Coffee*) and has been editing documentary films. She was apprehensive and believed that with her Jysk dialect she wouldn't get the job. She admits that much of her attitude was based on the assumptions of old prejudices. She recalls that as a teenager, she first encountered boys her age from Copenhagen who came to her native Bording, a village between Herning and Silkeborg in Jutland, to take part in a handball tournament. They were much more outward going, fresh, and smartly dressed than the local boys.

Gitte always sensed that her environment was too limiting and she suffered from melancholy at the thought of living the rest of her life in a small town in Jutland. She yearned to see and experience the excitement of Copenhagen. She is happy about her chosen profession and is quite at home now in Copenhagen and loves its pulse and excitement, but she takes great pride in her Jysk origins and resents the jokes that make Jyder their target. For a while, in the 1960s–1970s, a popular form of humor was telling *Århus-historier* (jokes about people from Århus). They were the equivalent of the ethnic humor of racist "Polish jokes" in America and made fun of people from Jutland in general. It is perhaps a sign of the times that the old stereotypes have lost some of their power and such jokes are no longer commonly heard.

Some of the national statistics bear out the continuing (although declining) differences. Whereas 92.9 percent of Jysk couples live in traditional husband-wife marriages and 89.9 percent have their children baptized in the state Lutheran church, the comparable figures for Copenhagen are 78.4 and 75.2 percent. Copenhagen couples and families spend a much higher percentage of their disposable income on eating out and visiting museums and the cinema. Likewise, those from Copenhagen have much larger debts and mortgages than their Jysk counterparts. This is reflected in the fact that between 4 to 5 percent of those in Copenhagen owe taxes based on their last year's income compared to only 1 to 2 percent in Jutland.

The old differences in speech are not only revealed in dialects or accents but in the use of characteristic vernacular expressions. Some of these have traditionally been exploited by politicians seeking to curry favor with the sources of their political support in the various regions, most notably Jutland and Copenhagen. For lecturer Hanne Tanvig from Sydjysk University, the Jutes to a considerably greater degree live in what she calls "an original and reasonable lifestyle," whereas for writer Per Højholt, the Jutes traditionally have suffered from "Jute paranoia"—"think they are the ones who carry the entire country on their shoulders but consider themselves neglected, unrecognized, unloved, ignored, and mistreated."

Chapter 10

The Danish Language

Danish (Dansk) is spoken by just under 6 million people (less than those who speak Hebrew today), mostly in Denmark and Greenland and in the northern parts of Schleswig-Holstein in Germany. It is also still taught as the first foreign language in the Faroe Islands and Iceland.

Many Americans and Brits with scant knowledge of foreign languages find the sounds and rhythms of tongues markedly different from English — Danish and Dutch among them — quite foreign to their ears. The languages seem so different from the listeners' norms that they can even sound somewhat comical, and this is in spite of the fact that Danish and Dutch are languages very closely related to English.

The frequent imitations by English-speaking tourists of Dutch and Danish are a popular amusement, precisely because there is a faint recognition that many of the words sound somewhat like English, particularly when you see them on the written page. Few but the most adventurous and uninhibited short-term foreigners visiting in Denmark or the Netherlands make an attempt to penetrate the veil of the language barrier. This is unfortunate, in that Danish is, perhaps, one of the least difficult languages for native English speakers to acquire.

I have often spoken or lectured about Denmark and have been frequently asked how can a language that sounds so different be so closely related to English. I have developed a ready answer by first reading a text that usually produces the reaction of "I didn't understand a word." I then immediately produce a published version of the text with the explanation that every important word is related to English, and that each related word shares a common origin. Within a minute or two explaining how these cognates are readily apparent in the two languages, a growing realization often dawns on the listener turned reader that indeed, with a determination to put aside prejudice, rapid progress can be made in grasping the essential structure and similarity in vocabulary and syntax of Danish.

Take the test but first ask a Danish speaker to read the text aloud without you seeing it. Then have a go at working out the meaning (the English translation is found at the end of the chapter). If you have difficulty at first, then start by assuming that the closest similarities between the two languages are in the words for parts of the body, family members, the seasons of the year, colors, numbers, and many active verbs (especially the irregular ones):

> Min far kom hjem på skib. Han og hans søster dansede hele aften. Vi sad og drak en kop kaffe. Min bror har blond hår og brune øjne. Vi går til skolen hver dag og lærer mange ting. Rundt om huset står mange træer. Jeg faldt fra et højt trae og brækkede min arm. Vort hus har fire vinduer og to døre. Jeg stak min kniv på brødet. Om natten står månen midt på stjernene højt over huset. Vi ridder hver dag på hest og hjælper hinanden når vi kommer hjem. Min mor sælger røde blomster og min onkel saelger fisk. De koster to og fyrre kroner. Om aften, studerer jeg mine lektier. Sommetider hvis det ikke regner eller sneer, tage vi ud til København i nærheden af mange søer. Kongen har folkets tro. Hans knæer og tæer er godt i orden nu. Skriv alt det jeg siger nu!

If you are encouraged by doing well on this mini-quiz, then hold on. There are a few peculiarities that most English speakers find almost insurmountable — at least when starting out. The monotone pronunciation and glottal stop, also found in so called Cockney speech (where the word *water* is pronounced "wa'a" so that instead of hearing a consonant between two vowels, what you hear is one vowel suddenly choke off followed by an explosive sounding of the next vowel; or when it comes at the end of a word, you sense the sudden choke), takes a bit of practice. This feature of the language is not evident everywhere in Denmark, thus leading to many humorous wordplays. *Gør* (without the glottal stop) means *does*; with the glottal stop, it means *barks*. *Skat* without it, can mean *tax*, *treasure*, or *beloved one*; with it, it is a card game played in southern Jutland. *Mor* without it is *mother*; *mord* (with a silent D and a glottal stop) is *murder*, so that one Dane speaking to another can be misunderstood to have said, "My murder is coming," instead of "My mom is coming." You might make a note that Danes will normally understand a foreigner even if he doesn't know the gender or how to use the glottal stop. In some parts of Denmark, people don't use it at all.

It is the many long compound words that make Danish look frightening such as *Trykkefrihedsselskabet* (in English this would appear as six separate words — "The Freedom of the Press Society"). Many such compound words with six or seven syllables initially baffle English speakers.

Peculiarities of Danish

Probably the biggest headaches for foreigners learning Danish is the existence of two genders (masculine and feminine in other languages but called common and neuter in Danish.) They seem simply designed to trick the foreigner. In other languages, one can often guess which nouns sound or seem masculine or feminine but in Danish, it is a mystery.

The word for *house* in Dansk is *hus*. Simple enough, but a *hus* is a neuter noun so *a house* is *et hus*, *the house* is *huset*, and *the houses* are *husene*, so that the equivalent of our simple and universal definite article *the* requires attaching a final *T* to the end the noun in the singular if the noun belongs to the neuter group. Got it? It's no problem for Romanian speakers who have the same grammatical rule but the rest of us have to struggle! *A big house* is *et stort hus*, but when the same noun is modified by the definite article with an adjective, the adjective also changes to indicate it is modifying a noun — ipso facto we have the form for *the big house* = *det store hus*. *The big houses* are *de store huse*.

With common gender, as in, for example, the word for *book* (*bog*), you get *en bog* (*a book*), *bogen* (*the book*), and *bøgerne* (*the books*—yes there is a vowel change here); English, of course, has some irregular plural nouns like *geese* and *mice*) but Danish has considerably more. We then get *en stor bog* (*a big book*) and *den store bog* (*the big book*) but *de store bøger* (*the big books*).

Here, try one yourself in the common gender (with no vowels). *Ko* is Danish for *cow* (no kidding!). So *a cow* is *en ko*; *køer* is the plural *cows*. *The cow*? *Koen*! *The cows*, *køerne*. *The big cow*? *Den store ko*. *The big cows*, *de store køer*.

The rule of thumb that is supposed to guide you through this maze is that inanimate objects are represented by the neuter gender (ending in t) but there are numerous exceptions.

More familiar to English speakers are the many irregular verbs in the simple past tense; as with English, regular verbs just add–*de* (or–*te*) rather than the English–*ed*, — for example, *arbejder* (*works*) and *arbejdede* (*worked*) — but the many irregular verbs have odd vowel changes or different consonants such as *skriver* (*writes*) and *skrev* (*wrote*).

A remaining oddity of Danish are the numerals from 50 to 90 which, unlike most other European languages (with the exception of French), are based on the so-called *vigesimal* system of units of twenty (a score), formerly also used in Norwegian and Swedish. The tens and ones of numbers above 20 are reversed when spoken or written, so that 21 is rendered *enogtyve*, i.e., one and twenty. This is similar to German, Dutch and Afrikaans as well as archaic and dialect English (compare the line "four and twenty blackbirds" in the old nursery rhyme.)

The numeral *halvanden* means 1.5 (literally "half second"). The numerals *halvtredje* (2.5) and *halvfjerde* (3.5), likewise constructed in this way, are now obsolete, but still implicitly used in the vigesimal (a score of 20) system. Similarly, the time by the clock is *halv tre*, literally "half three," i.e., half past two.

This means that *Tres* (short for *tre-sinds-tyve,* i.e., three times twenty*)* is 60. Similarly, *halvtreds* (short for *halvtredje-sinds-tyve*) means 2.5 times 20, or 50. *Firs* is 80 and *halv-fems* is 90! This remnant of an archaic system from Celtic times is so time consuming/confusing that it has been abandoned for writing checks where a traditional ten-based system is used (as in modern Norwegian and Swedish), i.e., *fir(e)ti* (4 times 10 or 40), *seksti-to* (6 times 10 plus 2 or 62), and *niti-syv* (9 times 10 plus 7 or 97) instead of the formal *syv-og-halvfems.* The simpler system is also used on banknotes (see p. 162).

Danish and English (Anglo-Saxon) at the Dawn of the Viking Age

A few hundred years before the Viking Age, English and Old Norse (the ancestral form of Danish) were undoubtedly very similar. The Old English (Anglo-Saxon) spoken in England before the time of the Vikings was like the Scandinavian and German languages descended from an original Germanic ancestral speech. But as a result of the Viking penetration and settlement in England and the creation of the Danelaw (chapter 25), new dialects developed that enabled both Danes and native Englishmen to better understand each other, especially in the areas of work, home, trade, and agriculture. In Viking times, the common name for all the dialects that later developed into Danish, Swedish, Norwegian, Icelandic and Faroese was "the Danish Tongue" (*dansk tunga*) — a lingua franca used from the shores of Greenland to the coasts of the Baltic and for a short while in Normandy.

Old Norse and Old English were mutually comprehensible to a small degree. If an Old Norse speaker wished to discuss the sale of a horse with an Old English speaker, both of them would know what was involved due to a close similarity in the words for *horse* and *sell* but, due to different rules of grammar, there would be doubt as to whether the sale involved one or several animals.

Such problems in important details required a further approximation of the languages to eliminate confusion. Linguists today believe that something like 600 loan words entered English from Old Norse/Danish and have survived in the modern standard form. These include *knife, knee, knight, knave, gnarl,* and *gnaw* (hence the reason for the spelling of these Danish words which have preserved the initial *k* and *g* sounds that eventually became silent in English), and many everyday terms especially of one syllable: *window, egg, die, sky, take, give, landing, score, fellow, steersman, scream, gear, guest, get, they, blink, loan, ill, low, lift, husband, root* and *law.*

The great majority of loan words did not appear in documents until the early twelfth century; these included many modern words which used *sk*–sounds, such as *skirt, sky,* and *skin.* Among other words appearing in written sources at that time included *again, cake, dregs, fog, freckles, gasp, moss, høns* (hens), *neck, ransack, scowl, seat, sly, smile, want,* and *weak.* At the time of Chaucer, the word for *and* in common use in parts of England was *oc,* closely resembling the Danish *og* (pronounced with a silent *G*).

In the Danelaw, however, the influence was much greater and in effect new Anglo-Danish dialects were created that shaped the eventual English dialects spoken today in Yorkshire, Lancashire, East Anglia and the Lake District. Until the Danish invasions, Old English was a highly inflected language but appears to have lost many of its grammatical endings and verb conjugations as a result of the interaction with Danish. In this way, a more analytic style of language developed that was further changed by the influence of Norman French after the Conquest 1066.

Danish Influence on English

The lasting linguistic effect of the Viking settlements and the Danelaw in England was

1. Many hundreds of words that eventually became part of Standard English,
2. A more simplified grammar in the conjugation of verbs (one form instead of many for each subject in the present tense),
3. Numerous places in the east and northeast of England with Danish names, and
4. Many English personal names are of Scandinavian origin.

There are more than 1,500 Scandinavian place names in England, mainly in Yorkshire and Lincolnshire (within the former boundaries of the Danelaw); over 600 end in–*by,* the Scandinavian word for *village* or *town*— for example, *Grimsby, Naseby,* and *Whitby*; many others end in–*thorpe (farm),–thwaite (clearing),–toft (homestead)* and–*kirk (church).*

The distribution of family names showing Scandinavian influence is still, as an analysis of names ending in–*son* reveals, concentrated in the north and east, corresponding to areas of former Viking settlement. Early medieval records indicate that over 60 percent of personal names in Yorkshire and North Lincolnshire showed Scandinavian influence.

Standard Danish (*Rigsdansk,* i.e., "The Language of the Realm") is the language based on dialects spoken in and around the capital, Copenhagen. More than 25 percent of all Danish speakers live in the metropolitan area of the capital and most government agencies, institutions and major businesses are located in Copenhagen.

This is the form of Danish considered the most "proper," although it has always rankled Danes living outside the capital and in peripheral regional areas where the spoken regional dialects diverge considerably. Standard Danish is thus based on a form of Copenhagen dialect. It emerged as a compromise between the dialect of Zealand and Skåne (Southern Sweden, formerly part of Denmark). The first layers of it can be seen in east Danish provincial law texts such as *Skånske Lov* (*Law of Skåne*). A different Western dialect was recognizable in the west Danish laws from the same ages in Jyske Lov (Law of Jutland).

Genuine regional dialects were formerly spoken by a vast majority of the population, but have declined much since the 1950s. They still exist in rural communities but many younger speakers in these areas generally speak a regionalized form of Standard Danish and sometimes switch back and forth between them. This is known as code switching or using different registers, somewhat like a figure such as President Obama whose rise to the presidency had to be based on his appeal to white voters and use of non-dialectal correct English; while speaking to black audiences, he frequently employs the rap talk of the ghetto and the dialect developed by African-Americans who moved from the deep South to the great industrial centers of the North in the 20th century.

There are three major dialectical divisions:

- *Bornholmic* (*bornholmsk*, sometimes called *østdansk — East Danish*), the dialect of the eastern island of Bornholm — the square insert surrounding the island on the map. This form of Danish has the more familiar singsong melody of Swedish.
- *Island Danish* (*ømål* or *ødansk*), including dialects of Zealand (where Copenhagen is located), Fünen (site of Odense), Lolland, Falster, and Møn.
- *Jutlandic* (*jysk*), further divided in North, East, West and South Jutlandic.

Historically, Eastern Danish included what today are considered southern Swedish dialects. This is the end result of the loss of the originally Danish provinces Blekinge and Halland (Skåne) to Sweden in 1658. The island Bornholm in the Baltic also belongs to this group, but remained Danish. A few generations ago, the dialects spoken in the southern Swedish provinces sounded much more like Eastern Danish than Swedish, being similar to the dialect of Bornholm. However, modern means of communication have fostered the speech forms of Standard Swedish.

The Danish Spelling Reform of 1948

In 1948, a spelling reform was carried out to distance the appearance of Danish from German. Prior to that time, nouns had been capitalized. The double Aa/aa was replaced by the "balled å" as in Swedish (Å/å). The double aa is, however, still in old town names (Aarhus and Aalborg) and in personal names (Aage). Doing away with the capitalized nouns actually enables the reader to read a text more quickly.

Danish Abroad

Iceland

Historically, the colonial territories such as the Faroes, Iceland and Greenland were directly ruled from Copenhagen and all higher education took place in Denmark so that the local languages were either neglected or used only at home. Iceland declared its independence in 1944 and immediately set up its own educational system with Icelandic as the language of instruction. Danish has long remained the preferred first foreign language learned at school but in 1994, a committee appointed by the Ministry of Education proposed that English should eventually replace Danish as the first foreign language taught in both primary and secondary school. This recommendation was the subject of considerable debate.

It may be said that while many young Icelanders today prefer learning English (and American English at that rather than the old very formal British language taught under Danish rule), the authorities, university and cultural institutions of Iceland recognize that this would entail a serious loss of cultural continuity and the close relationship not only with Denmark but the rest of Scandinavia. As of today, Danish is still the preferred first foreign language closely followed by English.

Greenland

Greenland (chapter 5) currently enjoys a special autonomous position within the Danish kingdom and is represented by a special mandate in the Folketing (unicameral legislative body). Both Danish and Inuit (Greenlandic) are official languages. In 1953, Denmark passed a new constitution making Greenland a Danish county and ending its colonial status. Nevertheless, Danes serving in the local administration remained at their posts and Greenlanders have only very slowly replaced them. Greenlandic was previously entirely a spoken language and is only distantly related to kindred native languages spoken by the aboriginal population in Canada. Greenlanders must master Danish if they hope to have any career, job or educational opportunities outside of Greenland.

Danish in South Slesvig (Schleswig) in Northern Germany

Danish is spoken in varying degrees among a population of approximately 40,000 people south of the German-Danish border and within the state of Schleswig-Holstein as far as the administrative border between Schleswig and Holstein along the Eider River. This amounts to about 10 percent of the total population in the territory. The degree of knowledge ranges from full fluency to a restricted secondary, largely conversational understanding on a simple level or primarily for literary purposes. For a detailed analysis of the language conflict along the German and Swedish borders, see chapters 26, 27, and 30.

Dano-Norwegian and the Language Struggle in Norway

Denmark ruled over Norway for more than 450 years and the Danish language became the spoken and established standard literary language of the country, notably in the larger towns and in the official administration, education, the law, and the church and used by all of Norway's great writers. Some Norwegians alive today can tell anecdotal stories of how their great-grandparents had grown up with the notion that Danish was God's holy language because this was the language of the Bible (i.e., the Bible at home that they had read and used in church when they were children). In the small villages amidst the fjords, people spoke rural dialects that differed considerably from the Danish spoken in town.

Norway had been an independent kingdom in the Middle Ages but lost its independence as a result of the catastrophic Black Plague that ravaged the country in 1349–1350, resulting in the death of approximately one-third of the population, including a large part of the educated class. Under these circumstances there was no hope of continuing a separate administration and Denmark assumed control. By 1400, written Danish was introduced and took precedence over the rival rural dialects. No separate university existed and all higher education took place in Copenhagen, putting further emphasis on the need to learn and use Danish as preparation for any career. The Norwegians pronounced Danish in the manner they had been accustomed to in their own native speech but the Danish dialect created was essentially no more distant from the language of the realm that became standard Danish than the dialects of Jutland, Bornholm, or Skåne (southern Sweden).

With growing demands for an independent Norway following Sweden's assumption of rule following the Napoleonic Wars, many Norwegians began to speculate and debate the issue of whether it would be desirable to "recover" their ancient language or simply continue speaking the Danish (now referred to as Dano-Norwegian) they were accustomed to for centuries. The prospect of an independent nation intensified the debate.

Ivar Aasen (1813–1896), a playwright, poet, lexicographer, anthropologist and folklore enthusiast became the proponent of a major reform of the many spoken Norwegian dialects into an amalgamated standard — something he imagined would have become the eventual national literary standard Norwegian of the country had it been allowed to continue its independence in the 15th century. It was actually no one's spoken language but the idea attracted support particularly in the rural areas where many Norwegians felt that townspeople with a formal education and their cultivated Danish had dominated society. Aasen termed the new variety of Norwegian "Nynorsk" ("New Norwegian") and worked zealously to establish the standards of grammar and spelling.

The first newspaper in Nynorsk appeared in 1858 and by 1885, the Norwegian *Storting* (parliament) recognized Nynorsk as a national language on an equal footing with Dano-Norwegian. In 1905, the Norwegians established their independence from Sweden after a referendum that won a 99 percent majority. The language issue remained divisive. Changes in name (referred to variously as *Bokmaal*— "the language of the book" and then *Riksmaal*— "the language of the realm") and spelling to make the Danish used in Norway more distinctive were considered window dressing that failed to convince proponents of Nynorsk that it was the worthy national language of their renewed nationhood. An ideological battle has continued since then.

Nynorsk has also chosen another name (*Landsmaal*— "the language of the country") although some people are not happy with this either because it gives the sense of speakers who live only in the countryside. Further spelling reforms and attempts to find some middle ground with a compromise form of Norwegian between the two existing varieties have led to more confusion. A mathematical key is used to prescribe how many documents from postage stamps to currency to university studies must use one or another variety (or both). The *Riksmaal* variety is still close enough to Danish in its spoken form that there is considerable mutual intelligibility between its speakers and those of Danish. For Danes, the spelling of the dominant form of Norwegian (i.e., Dano-Norwegian) resembles how they imagine young children would naturally and mistakenly spell Danish words.

Influence of English on Danish

In the medieval Danelaw, it was Danish that was the dominant language and profoundly influenced the Anglo-Saxon speech that evolved into English.

For the past 70 years, it has been the other way around. Prior to this, German and Dutch originally exercised a major influence on Danish through the agency of migrants, merchants, court functionaries, royal marriage and trade. This was followed by the influence of French from about 1650 to 1900 and lastly by English, especially the American variety since the end of World War II. English has been making inroads on both spoken and written Danish through Hollywood films, popular music and American preeminence in many scientific and technological fields. Unlike France that adopted a special law, *Loi Tourbon*, in 1994 to protect the French language (demanding the use of French words and expressions to replace borrowings from English) from undue English influence and the other Nordic counties, notably Iceland and Norway, Denmark has essentially maintained a hands-off policy. There is a *Dansk Sprognævn* (Danish Language Advisory Board) but its recommendations do not have the force of law.

Countless idiomatic American/English expressions have been adopted wholesale without any attempt to make them appear less foreign. For example, "brain drain" is good Danish today but the comparable term in Norwegian is *Hjerneflugt* (literally "brain-flight"). One can daily come across many advertisements in Danish newspapers where the main heading is entirely in English, such as a clothing ad showing a well dressed young man with the title in large print reading, "Fooling Around and Having a Good Time." The assumption is made (correctly) that it is not necessary to waste time and space to translate the main message into Danish.

Most Danes under the age of 50 with a high school education can enjoy a British or American film on television without the necessity of reading the Danish subtitles, although occasionally, as I have observed, American pronunciation frequently causes some translators who majored in English (when the British variety was the only one considered to be correct) to make errors, such as translating Newark (New Jersey) as New York.

I found Danish to be a beautiful language but that is after initial curiosity and doubt whether I could speak it well. It is certainly an indispensable tool for an appreciation of Danish literature, history and the many contributions of a remarkable people. Like Hebrew, with only 6 million current speakers, its creativity, range and pathos make it a language of much greater value than numbers alone can predict. As with the speakers of other minor languages, there is a strong sentiment among Danes that they have been overlooked and that instead of having only three previous Noble Prize winners, a dozen more deserving authors would have won the prize had they written in English rather than Danish.

The Language and Danish Predilection for Understatement and Irony

No matter how well one learns a language from books and videos, its everyday use in conversation cannot be mastered fully until one appreciates how native speakers use it to reflect aspects of national traits and social relations that have developed over many centuries. With Danish, this means an appreciation of the many untranslatable words, especially unstressed adverbs such as *vel, jo, da, mon, dog, nu, and nok,* that lend a special shade to the meaning of the whole sentence. These can be translated in English only by much longer expressions such as *indeed, I shouldn't wonder, really, well, but, certainly, more or less, however* and *probably.*

> FRUEN: *De kan vel også lave ganke almindelig hverdagsmad?*
> KOKKEPIGE: *Ja, frue, men jeg bryder mig ikke om at spise den.*

> LADY OF THE HOUSE: *You can certainly also make just plain, ordinary, everyday food, can't you?*
> COOK (a young girl): *Yes, madam, but I don't care to eat it.*

Well, are you ready for your Danish translation test?

Translation of Danish Text on Page 65

My father came home by ship. He and his sister danced the whole evening. We sat and drank a cup of coffee. My brother has blond hair and brown eyes. We go to school every day and learn many things. Around the house stand many trees. I fell from a tall tree and broke my arm. Our house has four windows and two doors. I stuck my knife into the bread. At night the moon stands in the middle of the stars high over the house. We ride every day on a horse and help each other when we come home. My mother sells red flowers and my uncle sells fish. They cost forty-two crowns. In the evening, I study my lessons. Sometimes, if it doesn't rain or snow, we take a trip (take) to Copenhagen in the neighborhood of many lakes. The king has the trust of the people; his knees and toes are in order (okay) now. Write all that I say now!

A Postscript on My Experience as a Translator between Danish and Hebrew

I regarded it as a great honor that during my residence in Israel I was called upon to undertake a translation from Danish to Hebrew of the electoral laws to the Folketing as part of an effort by the Israeli Knesset to compare and possibly borrow elements of other parliamentary electoral systems to replace Israel's unwieldy proportional representation. Unfortunately, my translation is still gathering dust in the Knesset archives.

As one of a handful of individuals with professional experience working with the two languages and the economic, political and social realities of Denmark and Israel, I was particularly delighted with the remarks of the well-known Danish Jewish journalist Herbert Pundik, for many years the executive editor of the Copenhagen daily newspaper *Politiken*, who, upon receiving the Modersmål (Mother Language) Award for his proficient use of Danish, spoke of his experiences as a correspondent for many years in Israel. I share with Pundik many years' residence and involvement in the two nations and languages and so fully understand and appreciate him when he remarked:

> Danish is good for your nerves.... Danish lends itself only poorly to rhetoric. Pathos lies quite distant from the tones of the language. Many other languages are so dramatic that they exert a beguiling effect on the listeners. It is not impossible but very difficult to mislead listeners when one speaks Danish, for it is a language that uncovers falsehood.... In the 15 years my wife and I lived in Israel, often under extremely stressful conditions without a regular physical contact with Denmark, it was a balm for the soul to be able to flee from the unstoppable assault of intensive seriousness to the Danish language's more restrained tones and understatement. Danish had a calming effect on our surroundings.

Chapter 11

The Rebild Celebration, Danish Americans and U.S.-Denmark Relations

What do Walt Disney, Danny Kay, Richard Nixon, Hubert Humphrey, Ralph Bunche, Walter Cronkite, Pat Boone, Raymond Burr, George Romney and Victor Borge have in common?

They have been awarded a special honor to be the keynote speaker at an annual public festival, the only one of its kind outside the United States that has celebrated American Independence Day since 1912 and underscores the cordial and fraternal ties that generally have linked the two countries as well as the recognition of the contributions made by Danish Americans. The great majority of keynote speakers (there are two every year, one from Denmark and one from the U.S.) are distinguished business executives, senators, congressmen and governors, members of the Folketing (Danish parliament), Danish prime ministers, ambassadors, government ministers, scientists, film stars, entertainers, journalists, academics, authors and, on several occasions, their majesties, King Frederick IX, Queen Margrethe II, her sister Princess Benedikte, and the two princes, Joachim and Frederick.

Nevertheless, the event, all cynicism aside, is a rare example of honest sentiments of appreciation, gratitude and fraternal ties linking two countries that, in spite of many differences, have much to be proud of and share in celebration. The only prominent one of Danish birth among speakers from the American side was, of course, Victor Borge (more correctly, from both sides since he was a dual citizen and left instructions in his will for his ashes to be buried in both places).

He arrived as a penniless immigrant in 1940 (chapter 15) and achieved the American dream without having intended to. Victor Borge left behind a mass audience with an enormous appreciation of his talent who became a

76

generous benefactor providing aid to Jewish refugees who, like himself, had to flee their homelands.

Danny Kaye's Danish connection consisted in his starring role in the Hollywood musical portraying the life story of Hans Christian Andersen (*Wonderful, Wonderful Copenhagen*). Hubert Humphrey was of Norwegian descent but that was good enough for the organizers of the Rebild festivities.

It is quite remarkable that the man responsible of the original idea of celebrating American Independence Day in his former homeland in order to pay tribute to the opportunities he had received as an immigrant was Max Henius, who, like Borge, was a Danish Jew (his father Isidor had walked from Poland to Denmark in 1857), the founder of the Dansk Spiritfabrik in Aalborg, producer of the world famous Akvavit (chapter 13). As Jews, both had prospered and felt a deep affection for Denmark but Henius could not resist the even greater appeal for individual opportunity offered by America and Borge was forced to flee by the impending German invasion and knowledge that his anti–Nazi repertoire in the world of Danish entertainment and cinema had made him a prominent target for German reprisals.

The "Denmark and America love each other" story is not entirely idyllic and was marred by two brief periods of discord during 1918–22 following the adoption of aggressive anti-immigrant sentiment and legislation against the use of foreign languages in civic, educational and church organizations in the wake of World War I and the period 1966–73 when American involvement in the Vietnam conflict cast a shadow over relations, particularly among the younger generation, in Denmark.

The Story Behind the Festival in the Rebild Hills

The idea to make use of an area of rugged Danish moorland as a gathering place for Danish Americans to meet each year with family, friends, and acquaintances in their birthplace originated with Max Henius. These emigrant rallies, as they were referred to, later came to be known as the Rebild Celebrations. He and other organizers among Danish immigrants in Chicago helped raise funds for the purchase of the 190 acres of land, enabling them to present a national park to the Danish government in 1912. The park was to be open to the public year round with special celebrations enacted for the benefit of Danish Americans and their guests on July 4 and other American days of remembrance.

Due to the sudden death of King Frederick VIII on May 14, 1912, the first Rebild Celebration was delayed until August 5. Almost 15,000 people joined together in the Hills where they cheered the new King Christian X, whom the Rebild Committee had presented with the deed to the property known as the Danish American National Park.

The website of the Rebild Society states it is a non-political organization with the goal to further friendship between Denmark and the U.S., confirm the fundamental belief that friendship is the foundation of coexistence despite the violence so prevalent in our times, prove that a little and big nation can work together on an even footing both culturally and historically, and help members actively participate in the celebration of the American Independence Day. The event is held in the Rebild Hills outside of Skørping, Denmark.

Danish Americans: A Proud Yet Modest Community (No Contradiction)

Unlike most Americans of Swedish, Norwegian and Finnish descent, Danish Americans were less likely to establish cohesive ethnic communities of their own. While the other Scandinavian immigrants tended to congregate with their own countrymen, the Danes spread out nationwide and comparatively quickly disappeared into the "melting pot." A large preponderance of Danish immigrants were single men who searched for brides among women of other national origins and subsequently they were more likely to use English and teach English to their children, avoiding the appearance of mono-ethnic or "ghetto" communities.

The one Danish name that left an imprint on the map of colonial America is ironically my own birthplace! Jonas Bronck after whom the Bronx is named, was probably a Dane, either originally from the Faroe Islands or Jutland's west coast, who sailed for the Dutch. In 1638, Bronck and his new bride arrived on the *Brandt van Troijen* from Hoorn, Holland. He had contracted with the Dutch East India Company to purchase a tract of land on the mainland portion of the New Netherland colony, well beyond the area of Dutch settlement in Manhattan protected by a stockade. Bronck, to his credit, also signed a deal with the local tribal chief, recognizing local custom and insuring (as much as possible) his survival. On some early maps, the Bronx is referred to as "Brouncksland." (Some Swedes believe he was really one of them, though it appears that another branch of the family, prominent in Sweden, is the root of that claim.)

Why They Left Denmark

Immigration from Denmark on more than the scale of a few isolated families only began in 1840, when the first Mormon Danes arrived. Denmark's laws were comparatively benign toward dissident sects and the Mormon missionaries found their most fertile ground for new converts in Denmark and Iceland. A considerable number of Danish Americans belong to the Mormon Church. Between 1849 and 1904, some 17,000 Danish Mormons and their children made the journey to the "Mormon Zion" in Utah, making Danes second only to the British in number of foreigners recruited by the church to the state. In total, the Mormon migration accounts for about 10 percent of all Danish immigrants to the U.S.

The large-scale immigration of Danes to America was the result of both a push and pull factor. The push was a rapid population growth and urbanizing society hemmed into a small country following the loss of South Jutland after the disastrous Danish defeat in 1864. Official Danish statistics for the period 1801–1925 reveal that about 10 percent of the population growth (excess of births over deaths) emigrated, whereas for Norway and Sweden it was considerably greater, on the order of 25 percent. For the period 1861–1910, the rates for all three Scandinavian countries rose to about 30 percent.

It is remarkable that Denmark experienced the second highest rate of population growth in Europe during the 19th century, an amazing 164 percent, second only to Russia's 189 percent. The considerable excess of births over deaths was due to a sharp fall in mortality, improvements in health care, a great rise in agricultural production and better nutrition than elsewhere. The small confines of the country made it difficult for the younger generation to maintain the size of farm properties, resulting in the choice of migration to the cities or emigration abroad. Several of Hans Christian Andersen's fairy tales, most notably "The Little Match-girl," relate the poverty and grim conditions of a city that could hardly have been referred to at that time as "Wonderful, Wonderful Copenhagen."

It should be remembered that in the case of Denmark, statistics for the period after 1864 do not include the substantial number of ethnic Danes in Schleswig under German rule, many of whom had the additional "push factor" of being forced to do compulsory military service in the armed forces of a country that had been responsible for aggression against Denmark.

Official Danish sources document that approximately 165,000 citizens left Denmark with the intention of permanently settling abroad, more than 90 percent choosing the United States as their new homeland. The desire of many families who had come under German rule was to find both personal and political freedom and economic opportunity on a much larger scale than Denmark could offer. The pull was the availability of cheap land and a much more flexible society in which the individual could to begin a new life.

Annual July 4th celebration in the Rebild Hills (photograph by the author).

The Number of Danes Living in the United States

Danes are defined as people who marked their ethnic origin as "Danish" on the census surveys in 1990 and/or 2000.

	1990	*2000*
Total number	1,635,000	1,431,250
Percent of total U.S. population	0.7	0.5

Change 1990–2000: -203,750
Percent change (1990–2000): -12.5 percent

According to the U.S. Census of 2000, the states with the largest populations of Danish Americans are as follows:

- California:— 207,030
- Utah:—144,713
- Minnesota:— 88,924
- Wisconsin:— 72,160
- Washington:— 72,090

Danish Americans who continue the usage of the Danish language number about 30,000. According to the U.S. Census Bureau, in 2000, 33,400 people spoke Danish at home; the figure was down to 29,467 five years later (2005 American Community Survey); the decrease rate was about 12 percent. The Library of Congress has noted that Danish Americans, more so than other Scandinavian Americans, "spread nationwide and comparatively quickly disappeared into the 'melting pot'.... The Danes were the least cohesive group and the first to lose consciousness of their origins." Historians have pointed to the higher rate of English use among Danes, their willingness to marry non–Danes, and their eagerness to become naturalized citizens as factors that contributed to their rapid assimilation, as well as their interactions with the already more assimilated German American community.

Among names of prominent Danish Americans (born in the U.S. of full or partial Danish ancestry, including those born in Denmark who became U.S. citizens) are Gutzon Borglum (sculptor who designed and carved the monumental heads of four American presidents on Mt. Rushmore), Victor Borge, Lloyd Bentsen (unsuccessful candidate for vice-president, 1988), Buddy Ebsen (actor), Lauritz Melchior (opera singer), Viggo Mortensen (actor), Veronica Lake (actress), Lady Bird Johnson, Jacob Riis (photographer) and Ted Sorenson (speechwriter and co-author with President J. F. Kennedy of *Profiles in Courage*).

One common factor prevailed in the search for a new life, whether on the prairie or in Chicago and New York. It can be found in the memoirs and diaries of many immigrants, like Peter Martins, world-famous ballet dancer, who wrote in *Fjernt fra Danmark* (*Far from Denmark*, 1983) that America stood as a test for their sense of self-worth, free from all the limitations, regulations, considerations, rules and barriers they felt were the price of living in a Danish society that measured a man or woman by one's background, formal education, titles, diplomas, wealth, pedigree, church or labor union membership, and connections with influential privileged individuals.

Danish Americans Confront Imposed Americanization

Although too small to form any special "ethnic vote," Danish Americans have been active and prominent citizens in many communities, yet they found themselves in the middle of an unwanted and unexpected brief storm that threatened their idealized portrait of themselves as loyal American citizens. Danish communities wholeheartedly supported American entry into World War I and many found President Wilson's peace program and promise of self-determination the solution to regain the long-lost province of Slesvig, home to many Danish immigrants or their parents who retained their sense of Danish nationality under German rule before leaving to settle in the United States (see chapters 26–27).

The Danish church in America and Dana College, an accredited baccalaureate college of the Evangelical Lutheran Church in America, located in Blair, Nebraska, promoted greater use of English in the churches and schools of Danish American communities than prior to 1917, aware of the provocative statements of former President Theodore Roosevelt in 1912, warning against the continued presence of "hyphenated Americans." President Wilson voiced similar sentiments following America's entry into the war but it was William Lloyd Harding, Republican governor of Iowa who, in a moment of pique, lashed out at the nearest examples of "ethnics," the Danes in his vicinity who were an easy target because many of them had hoped for American entry into the war to help secure the liberation of Slesvig but whose original homeland, Denmark, remained stubbornly neutral even after the U.S. declared war on Germany.

On May 23, 1918, the governor issued an order prohibiting the use of foreign languages at public meetings, including church services. Anybody who found this offensive should just stay home. At the July 4 celebration of Independence Day in the city of Sac, Harding delivered an address and sarcastically described the Danish residents of nearby Elk Horn and Kimbalton as ungrateful: "Imagine a man who has been pulled out of the muck and crap found in Denmark, brought over to an American farm that he can probably buy for $3 an acre. By God Almighty, can he ever pay back what Iowa has done for him?"

Danes throughout America and among the most distinguished members of the Rebild Committee, who had shown their American patriotism at every occasion as volunteers for the armed forces and through buying war bonds, were shocked. The Des Moines *Register* was appalled and compared Governor Harding to the German Kaiser, praising the Danish community throughout Iowa as model of patriotism and extolling their virtues. Harding was defeated in the next election and left office in disgrace over a pardons scandal.

Danish American Relations: Americans in Denmark and the Janteloven

This episode, the only stain on Danish American relations, was quickly forgotten but the next period of soured relations over American participation in the Vietnam War, although not on any official level, helped polarize a substantial portion of Danish youth, already politically active on the socialist and extreme left of Danish politics, into activist and sometimes violent anti–American demonstrations occasionally overshadowing the Rebild festivities.

Paradoxically, Denmark has frequently been elevated by the American political left into the image and model of a modern "liberal" welfare state with cradle-to-the-grave security, anti-militarism, concern for the environment, conservationist "green" policies, an open society welcoming immigrants and those seeking asylum, and a nation of physically fit nature enthusiasts. Americans with such views and hopes have, however, after a period of extended residence in Denmark, come to realize that in spite of their initial enthusiasm, they often feel that much of what they had imagined as the noblest of causes and the social solidarity they so envied leaves them with a feeling that "something is rotten in Denmark."

The Danish weekly newspaper *Information* ran a series of articles in January 1981 on *Americans in Denmark—Who Are They and Why Have They Come?* Those who had found a permanent job, were well integrated, and had even mastered Danish were critical of the lack of initiative, high taxes and, as one individual named Steve put it,

"I was brought up to do things and get ahead. When I started work here, my colleagues told me immediately to set the pace slower. I learned that the system is arranged to benefit the slowest. Individualism and diligence aren't tolerated."

This attitude, called "janteloven," negatively portrays and criticizes success and achievement as unworthy and inappropriate. The term stems from a small, mythical Danish town, Jante, created by the Norwegian/Danish author Aksel Sandemose in his novel *A Fugitive Crosses His Tracks* (*En flyktning krysser sitt spor*, 1933; English translation published in the USA in 1936). Sandemose's novel portrays the town (modeled after his native Nykøbing, Mors) at the beginning of the 20th century as one where nobody is anonymous and reflects a strong sense of envy and a behavior that refuses to accept "excessive individuality." It refers to a snide, jealous and narrow small-town mentality that places all emphasis on the collective, while punishing those who stand out as achievers.

There are ten different rules in the law as defined by Sandemose. They can be summed up with *"Don't think you're anyone special or that you're better than us."* The ten rules state:

1. Don't think that *you* are special.
2. Don't think that *you* are of the same standing as *us*.
3. Don't think that *you* are smarter than *us*.
4. Don't fancy *yourself* as being better than *us*.
5. Don't think that *you* know more than *us*.
6. Don't think that *you* are more important than *us*.
7. Don't think that *you* are good at anything.
8. Don't laugh at *us*.
9. Don't think that any one of *us* cares about *you*.
10. Don't think that *you* can teach *us* anything.

A further rule recognized in the novel is:

11. Don't think that there is anything *we* don't know about *you*.

A considerable proportion of Americans in Denmark during the last forty years had come in order to reject much of American society rather than for any specific attraction or connection with Denmark. Some had been strong critics of the war in Vietnam but the majority expressed the major factor as disappointment with the extreme materialism, rat-race mentality of competition, and ever-present danger of violent crime. Quite a few were active on the far left.

Recent elections have reversed the long-term trend of left-wing governments seeking greater and greater collectivist solutions, higher taxes, and so-called liberal policies for Denmark's problems. Many of the Americans residing in the country have also come to realize that these desirable high ideals of social solidarity come with what many perceive to be a stifling social conformity.

Chapter 12

Hygge and Happiness

More than fifty years ago, Denmark was the most homogeneous society in Europe with only Jews and Greenlanders as minorities in some distinctive way, although both groups were native-born Danish citizens and fluent in Danish. The only family names that betrayed a foreign origin were German, French Huguenot and Dutch groups that had entered the country centuries ago and had long been assimilated. The Huguenots had arrived as refugees from persecution and been welcomed into Protestant Denmark, and the Dutch had been invited by King Christian IV to settle and drain the marshland east of Copenhagen on the island of Amager (today the site of Copenhagen airport) and along Jutland's west coast.

Today's foreign-born immigrant population stands above 5 percent and is rising. They came starting in the 1960s to fill workplaces in the booming economy and then stayed on. I arrived in 1966 to visit my girlfriend and got a job the next day. In a few days, I had become a skilled rubber worker at the Dansk Gummi Fabrik in Gladsaxe! I inserted huge rubber mats into a grinding machine and with my stopwatch-like measuring instrument made sure they were precisely ground to the correct thickness.

Although considerably smaller than the immigrant populations of diverse Asian and African origin in Germany, France or Great Britain, the new immigrants in Denmark have had children and grandchildren and the country finds itself for the first time with a population quite distinct from the native majority and unsure as to what the task should be — integration, assimilation or a multi-ethnic society. There is still a debate and an uncertainty as to who is responsible for what, even though ethnic/religious/racial ghettos have emerged in urban areas such as in Nørrebro and Vesterbro in Copenhagen and elsewhere alongside city centers in almost all the major Danish cities.

Had the Danish electorate in 1947–48 been aware that Denmark would not remain a totally homogeneous society in the future, would citizens then have been less afraid to meet the challenges of absorbing the people of South

Schleswig including a new German minority when they were offered the possibility to sponsor a plebiscite and agree to possible annexation of the territory? (See chapter 27) We will never know what might have been but my guess is yes. The potential "new Danes" of 1947–48 were closely related to Danish culture and history, unlike those of today.

Denmark currently faces a more difficult problem. It has become a victim of its own self-image. A proud nation with a thousand years of history, with the oldest monarchy and flag in Europe, has frequently demonstrated a reluctance to lose its identity. It maintains the krone as a currency and refuses to accept the euro. It only narrowly approved membership into the European Union after several referendums, yet many Danes, particularly among the younger generation, want to demonstrate to the world and to themselves (to their subconscious image of being tolerant) that they are ready, willing and able to become a multi-ethnic society.

Elsewhere, it seems more and more people have rejected being lumped together with others and even agitated to separate from their neighbors such as the Slovaks and Croats but in Denmark, the prevailing talk is of tolerance and multi-culturalism. Today's supporters of immigrant rights in Denmark are, however, often unsure whether this entails any commitment to Danish culture, language, history, society and government. Immigrants may acquire citizenship and learn a new language but still feel they are essentially different and wish to preserve vital aspects of their own traditions and culture.

Two distinguishing features of Danish social life, often commented on by foreigners, are *hygge (pronounced hoo-geh)* and the Danish cuisine. Both are acquired tastes (if at all). *Hygge* is a term most foreigners spending time in Denmark come to know and regard as very much in harmony with the Danish national character, but not necessarily their own. It has been translated as a cozy, warm, snug, comfortable, stress-free feeling, sometimes compared to the German word *Gemütlichkeit,* but less formal. It is a personal concept but one shared by all Danes wherever they live and from whatever social and economic niche of society they stem from. It is the antidote to glumness, a danger that creeps up on one with the dreary winter climate.

Hygge probably wasn't to be found in medieval Denmark. It has become such an important element in Danish social relations as a result of overabundance. According to newspaper columnist Anne Brockenhuus-Schack, "You can't *hygge* yourself very much if you're cold and hungry." The Danish winter is certainly long and dark, but summer days are long and the nights can be remarkably bright and balmy. Anthropologist Henny Harald Hansen relates *hygge* directly to climate: "It's a term that has grown out of our cold and darkness, when we come together around a source of heat. Our ancestors surely didn't decide to settle here in December!" Certainly, Danish life has traditionally been much more centered around home and hearth than in warm, Mediterranean lands with their marble floors!

A common ingredient in all definitions is good food, good company, comfortable furniture, soft music, easy lighting (candles in particular), and a fine cigar to follow for the gentlemen (and appreciated by a few ladies as well). Of course, this was before anti-smoking became the height of political correctness. Nevertheless, there are still traditional circles where *hygge* trumps even the prohibitions against smoking.

The *Time Out Guide to Copenhagen* writes that *hygge* is anti-confrontational, anti-boisterous, friendly, easygoing and jovial. *Hygge* is a part of open fires, a little alcohol, good conversation and homespun fun. You can have a *hygge*-evening, a *hygge*-chair, or even sit in your favorite *hygge*-corner.

It can be used as a noun, verb or adjective:

Hyggen er vigtig hvis der skal vaere en god stemning. [*Hygge* is important if there is going to be a good atmosphere.]

Kom, lad os hygge os! [Come on and let's *have a relaxing time.*]

Et lille, hyggeligt hus med græs på taget. [A *snug little adorable* house with grass on the roof.]

The italics portion of the translations gives an indication of how many different expressions are covered by the one Danish word. There are also special types of *hygge* to match the season and occasion such as jule*hygge* (Christmas *hygge* that almost all Danes prepare for days in advance); for example, *Kom og besøg vores butik med masser af julehygge!* (Come and visit our shop with its load of Christmas *hygge*.) It is frequently used in connection with food, snacks and candy.

As a verb, it can mean to create a particularly pleasant and enjoyable atmosphere. As a reflexive verb (*hygge* sig) it means to ensure conditions are right for you to have a cozy and stress-free time even if you are alone. It doesn't have to take place while at home. You can be at work or anywhere. As a causative verb (*hygge* om nogen) it relates to doing what it takes to make someone else feel confident, protected, safe and comfortable.

Danes often turn the expression on its head to be ironic and sarcastic by applying it to situations that are really painful or to boring tasks that have to be endured: *Jeg vil gå hjem og hygge mig med at male min lejlighed* (I'm going home to have a cozy time painting my apartment), or in typically very UN-Danish situations and circumstances such as *Stalin hyggede sig med at slå alle sine politiske fjender ihjel* (Stalin found it so cozy to kill all of his political enemies). It is also used an adverb as in *Hvor bor I dog hyggeligt!* (Oh, how cozily you live!).

The youth rebellion/uproar and "counter-culture" that characterized the

1960s and '70s in much of the world was loud and aggressive in Denmark. Politically active Danish youth among those committed to the New Left sought to demonstrate to the rest of the world and themselves that their country and its reputation as a decent, law-abiding and peaceful place made them feel uncomfortable and that the older generation, as everywhere else, were smug, self-satisfied, stodgy, and guilty of many of the same prejudices as elsewhere. To be sure, such prejudices existed and still exist as they do in one degree or another everywhere. I experienced them myself but I knew that they were not representative of the great majority of Danes who accepted and warmly welcomed me.

Many on the political left came to regard Denmark as too provincial, akin to the same narrow, homogeneous "duck pond" that drove ambitious artists and writers in the past like Hans Christian Andersen to seek their fortune abroad. They turned inward and strove to create their own vision of a new, hospitable Denmark which in the words of one of their favorite songs would welcome anybody and everybody no matter who or from where. This was quite unlike their ambitious relatives who, in previous generations, left the duck pond of little Denmark and gave up the much greater security of an advanced welfare state to realize their ambitions in the United States or Canada.

A dozen or more pop groups, writers, singers and poets lashed out at what they considered the old-fashioned image of Denmark as a homogeneous country out of touch with the new cosmopolitan, ultra-liberal, "the world is one" philosophy. Kim Larsen, Shubi-Dua, Trille, Benny Andersen, Gnags, Elisabeth G. Nielsen, Niels Hausgaard, Benny Holst, Erik Clausen and others were part of a new beat generation who all yearned for a greener and more culturally diverse Denmark. Their songs of protest were unilaterally in favor of what they considered to be the oppressed, no matter how much their isolation may have been self-imposed and due to strict prohibitions to socially consort with Danes or absorb any part of the prevailing culture.

The group *Røde Mor* (Red Mother) produced a recording in 1976 with a song called "*Hjemlig hygge*" (home *hygge*) in which *hygge* is lampooned and Denmark is represented as the epitomy of a corrupt land sacrificed on the altar of international capital and modern technology. It became fashionable to speak of uhygge! The prefix *u-*, meaning "not," is used in the same way as the corresponding prefixes *un-*, *non-*, *il-*, and *im-*, in English. I guess this was what Hegel meant by dialectics. *Hygge* has led to uhygge. Will there be a synthesis? Like oil and water?

Most Danes don't want to lose *hygge* and probably most resident foreigners are not likely to feel any attachment to it, if their cultures (Turkish, Arab, Nigerian, Haitian, Mexican, Greek, Italian, and even American) promote totally different kinds of behavior, social relations, demonstrations of affection, cuisine, boisterous and festive celebrations and the admiration of extrovert personalities.

But Are They Happy?

With all this *hygge* and the many cradle-to-the-grave entitlements of social welfare, national health insurance, and unemployment benefits, including maternity and paternity leave, is it any wonder that Danes are so happy? Or is there something lurking beneath the surface that even Shakespeare was aware of when he had Marcellus comment that "There is something rotten in the state of Denmark" (*Hamlet*, Act 1, scene 4, 87–91)?

In a study compiled in 2006 by the British University of Leicester covering data from 178 countries to "map happiness across the world," Denmark ended up in first place, a statistical achievement, but one that left many observers wondering, although the international and especially the American media were quick to explain the result by granting their seal of approval on the Danes' good access to healthcare and education. The nations that followed Denmark were Switzerland, Austria and Iceland, the Bahamas, Finland, Sweden, Bhutan, Brunei and Canada.

The report's author, Adrian White, said the results showed that people in Europe should be aware of how privileged they were. Most of Africa and the former Soviet republics scored worst. Burundi, Zimbabwe and the Democratic Republic of Congo were the world's least happy places. The report did, however, contain some surprises. The tiny Himalayan nation of Bhutan, ruled by an autocratic monarch, came in eighth, whereas nations such as France and Japan ranked 62nd and 90th (both of which offer their citizens comprehensive welfare and health entitlements). The United States came in 23rd and Britain, 41st.

Benjamin Holst, a Danish journalist, questioned the results and mentioned poignantly that Denmark's high suicide rate — among the highest in Europe and approximately equal to the suicide rate in the United States — should make people question the study and avoid any smugness by Danes over their ideal society. "I'm not sure about these studies and I really wonder about the suicide rates in Denmark," he said. "I mean, is it that we're so happy we kill ourselves? I really wonder about that."

Researchers at the University of Michigan commented that Denmark's prosperity, stability and democratic government placed the country at the top of White's "happiness" rankings, which he used to produce a "World Map of Happiness." Critics, including many Danes, suggest that the studies, which measure indices of social and economic welfare, confuse contentment with happiness. *Hygge* at its core means contentment but not necessarily happiness and certainly not ecstasy.

When President Obama visited Copenhagen in late 2009 to try to win approval of Chicago's selection as the site for the 2012 Olympic Games, the American TV talk show personality Oprah joined him and spent a few days in Copenhagen. She portrayed Denmark as a veritable paradise in terms that were embarrassing for many Danes, including instant, on-the-spot judgments about which she had done no research whatsoever, claiming that Danes customarily leave their bicycles unlocked everywhere.

That was last true about fifty years ago. No mention was made of any requirements for any benefit for entitlements such as the stipulation of having been continuously employed full time for the previous three years before qualifying for generous unemployment benefits, being a member of a state-recognized unemployment insurance fund for at least a year (towards which you pay dues), actively seeking work and being ready to accept gainful employment even if not exactly in your profession. No mention of the fact is made that due to a very well managed economy, unemployment in Denmark, at just over 3 percent, is one-third that of the American rate (where benefits now continue for "only" two years). Denmark as the "happiest country in the world" was also discussed and debated on Bill O'Reilly's *The Factor* TV show and exaggerations about "most Danes paying taxes amounting to 75 percent of their income" were also picked out of thin air to entertain viewers.

These programs highlight the tendency to use Denmark as a lightning rod for critics of traditional American society and values on the left as well as for those on the right who warn against the inevitable decline of a society weighed down by excessive entitlements. Responses to the O'Reilly and Oprah comments on the internet by many Danes and foreigners married to Danes reject the idea of the Danes being so happy. One reader, Alan Robinson, wrote in more realistic terms in January 2010 to the British daily newspaper, *The Independent,* that had published a story on the most happy country study, commenting. "My wife is Danish and I've lived in Denmark myself longer than I've lived at home in the UK. And guess what? Sit 10 Danes round a table with a pot of coffee and give them a piece of sticky cake each, and they'll sit there for an hour uttering banalities to each other and having a great time. That's how Danes see happiness. Anything that is "hyggelig" is happiness. However, someone needs to explain the high Danish suicide rate, and the expression on people's faces as they walk around town. Happy Danes? I'd say content, but not particularly happy."

Many Americans who come to Denmark ecstatic over what they felt was a more humane and rational civilization eventually become disillusioned by the prevailing *jantelov* mentality (see Chapter 11 on the Rebild festival). What I found is that many more Danes than Americans and other foreigners live a healthy and active lifestyle and are involved in an array of cultural, social, athletic, physical and intellectual activities in countless associations and clubs that promote a sense of well being. This is a wholly admirable trait which is often neglected in much of the commentary by pundits and two-day visitors like O'Reilly and Oprah when discussing Denmark.

Chapter 13

Food and Drink

Nothing beats a prolonged stay in Denmark to become acquainted with all the mouth-watering dishes that are found in Danish cuisine. It may be the easiest way, because the retail outlets in the United States marketing authentic Danish products are few and far between. Danes have a reputation for being *madglade* (crazy about food), but they don't drown it in sauces or steam it to death or spice it to hell. There are three traditions that must be observed with care that are usually involved in dining while in Denmark so that you can *hygge* (see chapter 12) yourselves while enjoying a good meal or snack. The *hygge* tradition is very strongly a part of most cordial dining experiences with good friends. Remember the three S's that go together—*spisning* (eating), *snak* (conversation) and *skål* (the toast to accompany drinks in honor of those present or past memories or good times to come).

Now that you know a lot more about the Danish language (chapter 10) and can recognize many cognates, *skål* (skoal) should immediately be recognized as closely related to the English word "skull" or shell. If you believe the first purported origin of the toasting tradition (Viking victory fest drinking out of the skulls of their slaughtered enemies), you may find the whole affair a bit repulsive and cannibalistic. The second theory presents the custom in a much more pleasant light as simply a useful implement to help in presenting a fond farewell to a dear departed one or offering good wishes and luck and health.

The *skål* tradition ranges from individual toasts in succession and a collective *skål* shouted out by all those present and drinking or by diners. As one might imagine, in a series of individual *skåls* in which everyone salutes each person individually, one tends to become rather intoxicated by the end. At some cordial get-togethers, people will frequently improvise their own extended speech or toast, especially when celebrating a marriage, anniversary, birth of a child or another major life event. It is the equivalent of cheers, *le'chaim*, salud, sláinte, prost or bottoms up.

Let me introduce this chapter with the warning that my tastes focus on a few traditional, hardy staples of the Danish diet and that I never dined at an expensive gourmet restaurant during the seven years I lived in Denmark. My plebeian tastes are simply presented as a starting point for a first-time visitor who, no doubt, will receive many words of good advice from tourist guidebooks, hotel managers, and gourmet-loving friends or relations who know the country well.

First, as with any gustatory adventure, one must approach an introduction to Denmark's cuisine with the proper mindset. Danish food is a delight because it whets, tickles and tantalizes and fulfills the appetite. However, it is not the food items themselves but the whole food culture, the *hygge* atmosphere and intimate and cozy milieu in which the diners socialize with each other, that distinguishes the Danish dining culture, the object of which is to ENJOY.

Danish cuisine features the products most suited to its cool and moist northern climate: barley, potatoes, rye, beetroot, greens, berries, and mushrooms. Dairy products are a world-class specialty. The products of modern Danish agriculture and the fishing industry supply the country and provide for a large surplus of food exports that made Denmark an especially desirable target in the rivalry between Great Britain and Germany in two world wars.

Don't Confuse the Swedish Smörgåsbord with the Danish Smørrebrød!

The Swedish culinary term *smörgåsbord* should not be confused with the Danish *smørrebrød* tradition. The former is the world-celebrated Scandinavian buffet meal with multiple dishes of various foods on a table usually prepared in connection with a celebration during which the guests may freely pick and choose a variety of both cold and hot dishes. The equivalent Danish feats is called the large cold table (*det store koldbord*).

The Danish *smørrebrød* (originally *smør og brød*, for "butter and bread"), commonly translated as "open sandwiches," usually consists of a piece of buttered rye bread (rugbrød), a dense, dark brown sourdough rye bread, and *pålæg* (literally "on-lay"), the topping. This topping can be simple or elaborate, decorated homemade cold cuts, pieces of meat or fish, cheese and spreads. A slice or two of *pålæg* or several shrimp/herrings are placed on the buttered bread, and then *pyntet* (decorated) with the right toppings to create a tasty and visually appealing item. A lunchbox with three or four (or more) of these tasty tidbits was traditional working-class fare but the more elaborate and pricey ones are now featured at exclusive dining spots or for tourist consumption.

Danish bread is a very important part of the Scandinavian table and the polar opposite of sliced American white bread. It forms the basis of *smørrebrød*. The simplest and most common *ret* (serving) is *leverpostej* (liver paste). Many Danish kids grow up on this and become addicted.

The simplest *koldebord* offers bread, butter, cheese, herring and several types of liqueurs, but smoked salmon, sausages and cold cuts are also served. This was originally considered an appetizer for a gathering of people and eaten while standing before dinner. Eventually, restaurants stopped serving them as appetizers and presented them as a main course. They are still a popular feature of sea cruises and were part of the tradition of the old ferries between different parts of Denmark.

Traditional Scandinavian delicacies of meat and fish favored smoking, pickling and other food preservation techniques that prolong the storage life of products. The island geography of Denmark meant that before industrialization and advances in refrigeration and transportation, it was difficult, time consuming, and costly to travel great distances or to ship products. These factors have thus helped mold the traditional eating habits of the Danish people.

Where Did "Danish" Pastry Originate? (Not Denmark!)

Although Americans are fond of their "Danish," they are amused to find out that such pastries in Denmark are called *Wiener-brød* meaning bread from Wien, i.e., Vienna. In the last half of the 1800s, unemployed young bakers from Vienna were offered jobs in the Copenhagen area, because there was a need for bakers at the time. They brought with them their formula for a special sweet bread, where the dough is folded a number of times with extra butter, using a very time-consuming technique. After the Viennese bakers left again, the new "sweet bread" had become so popular among Danes that the Copenhagen bakers continued to develop the new dough process, eventually turning it into the delicious Danish pastry known today all over the world.

The Traditional Danish Herring — Historical Staple

Due to its control of the Sound and Kattegat, separating the Danish island of Zealand (where Copenhagen is situated) and the Swedish coast (for centuries this southernmost area of Sweden, known as Skåne, was part of the Danish kingdom), at one time, Denmark had a monopoly on the entrance and exit to the Baltic from the North Sea and was master of the enormous herring catch throughout these waters.

The long familiarity with the excellent varieties of herring found in this area and skilful preparation made this delicacy a staple product on the table of Danes for centuries. As a first course or visit to the buffet table, the consumer will enjoy varieties of *marinerede sild* (pickled herring). The most common herring is marinated either in a clear, sweet, peppery vinegar sauce (white herring) or in a seasoned red vinegar (red herring). It may also come in a variety of sour cream-based sauces, including curry or mustard sauce.

The preferred base and toppings are buttered, black rye bread, topped with white onion rings and curry salad (a sour cream-based sauce, flavored with curry and chopped pickles), and served with hard boiled eggs and tomato slices. Fried herring in vinegar *(stegte sild i eddike)* offers additional variety. For extra festive occasions, a prepared *silderet* (herring dish) features the herring pieces in a serving dish along with sliced potato, apple pieces, onions and capers topped with a dill sour cream or mayonnaise sauce.

Specialty Retail Food Stores: The Oste- and Fiskeforretninger

One charming and quaint (at least for most American visitors) aspect of the Danish urban picture is the continued presence of many food retail specialty shops that sell just cheese (or fish, or pastry and bread products). Supermarkets have spread far and wide and the number of such specialty shops has decreased, but they will undoubtedly persist in spite of the competition and lower prices offered by the big supermarket chains.

The cheese (*osteforretninger*) and fish specialty stores are my favorite. Yes, you can smell them from the distance. Danes love cheese, almost all of which has a much stronger taste than the cheeses that are popular in the United States. Go into one of these *osteforretninger* and you will be offered a few samples that are sure to convince you to take something home.

Most of us recognize Danish Blue (the cheese) as a specialty dessert to be enjoyed with liquor or coffee. This is a light blue, veined cheese that is semi-soft, in drum or block shape, and with a white to yellowish, slightly moist, edible rind. It is made from cow's milk and has a high fat content (25–30 percent). It takes eight to twelve weeks to age. Rods are used before aging to pierce holes and distribute the mold. It was invented by Marius Noel, a Danish cheesemaker who wished to imitate a Roquefort-style cheese. It has a milder flavor characterized by a sharp, salty taste. Danish Blue is often served crumbled on salads or as a dessert cheese with fruit, but the Danish way of eating it is on bread or biscuits.

The other Danish specialty cheese many foreigners know and love is havarti, a washed curd cheese that doesn't have a rind, and is smooth with a cream to yellow color. It has small and irregular openings and a buttery aroma. It can be somewhat sharp in the stronger varieties but still has a sweet taste and is slightly acidic. It is typically aged about three months and when left at room temperature the cheese tends to soften quickly. Flavored variants of havarti that are more and more popular include garlic, caraway, dill, jalapeño (a great example of multi-culturalism), basil and coconut. It is popular with chardonnay, sauvignon blanc and pinot noir wine, accompanied with figs, smoked turkey, raisins, walnuts, pears and apples. Other Danish cheeses you are not likely to find in American supermarkets and should try frequently reveal their geographic origins with names like Fynbo, Maribo, Molbo, Tybo and Samsø. Some of these varieties when aged into old cheese (*gammel ost*) are really powerful and would require special permission from U.S. customs authorities (just joking, but better check before you put one in your suitcase).

Beer

The perfect accompaniment is a few rounds of ice cold snapps and/or cold Danish beer. According to Danish tradition, the ice-cold snapps helps the fish swim down to the stomach. Also, the high alcohol content helps dissolve the fat left in the oral cavity after eating the fish, allowing the diner to more readily taste the different dishes.

Two Danish giants, Carlsberg and Tuborg, are renowned throughout the world and have given Denmark its reputation as a master brewer. The Carlsberg group was founded in 1847 by J.C. Jacobsen after the name of his son Carl. The company's main brand is Carlsberg, but it also brews Tuborg as well as several local beers. After a merger with a Norwegian brewery in 2004, Carlsberg became the fourth largest brewery group in the world and currently employs around 45,000 people. Many Danes swear by their preference for the one or the other, while others claim that the rivalry is much like Pepsi and Coca-Cola and, when blindfolded, only a few drinkers can tell them apart.

An experience you must try, especially around Easter and Christmas–New Year, if you like beer, is the strongest one in Denmark (or anywhere perhaps), aptly named Elephant. Outside the Carlsberg Brewery (take the tour and sample their selection) in Copenhagen is one of the most famous sculptures in the country. It is a tower resting on four elephants carved in granite from the Danish island of Bornholm (see chapter 3). The four elephants each bear the initial of one of Carl Jacobsen's four children: Theodora, Paula, Helge and Vagn.

This landmark, known as the Elephant Gate, has been the entrance to the brewery since 1901. To the west of the gate, Carl Jacobsen's motto is inscribed: *Laboremus pro Patria* (let us work for our country). After an experimental trial in West Africa, where they like strong beer, the Elephant brew was launched in Denmark on November 9, 1959. Just one 8 oz. glass will certainly put you over the limit.

Akvavit

Akvavit (sometimes spelled *aquavit*) is literally (in Latin) "the water of life" and the preferred strong alcoholic drink (40 percent alcohol, 70 proof) that goes with typical meat, fish and cheese dishes, especially the selection from *det store koldebord*. Like vodka, it is distilled from either grain or potatoes. The flavor is provided by herbs, spices, and fruit oils such as caraway seeds (the dominant flavor), cardamom, cumin, anise, lemon or orange peel, and fennel. The Danish distillery Aalborg makes an aquavit distilled with amber.

Akvavit complements beer well, and its consumption is very often preceded (or followed) by a swig of beer. Some connoisseurs disagree with this practice, claiming beer ruins the flavor and leaves an aftertaste.

The earliest known reference to aquavit is found in a 1531 letter from the Danish Lord of Bergenshus castle, Eske Bille, to the last archbishop of Norway in which the archbishop is offered "some water which is called Aqua Vite and is a help for all sort of illness which a man can have both internally and externally." It remains a popular belief that akvavit will ease the digestion of rich foods. In Denmark it is traditionally associated with Christmas lunch.

Gammel Dansk (Old Danish) & Cherry Heering

Now this alcoholic drink is indeed a matter of taste. It was favored by hunters and fishermen going off early in the morning to hunt for their prey during long hours in the cold. It is preferred today by many Danes for breakfast (after a hangover), at wedding anniversaries and birthday celebrations. It is brewed with a large number of herbs and spices, making it similar to other *stomach bitters*, such as *Campari* or *Jägermeister*. These herbs and spices include laurel, ginger, star aniseed, nutmeg, cinnamon, Seville orange, gentian and rowanberry. It is certainly worth trying once and several ice hockey and football stars claim that a quick drink at halftime has brought them good luck.

Another popular Danish dessert liqueur (40 proof) is Cherry Heering, a Danish cherry liqueur that has nothing to do with herring, invented in the late 1700s or the early 1800s by Peter Heering. It is dark red and has a flavor of black cherries that is not too sweet. It has frequently been misunderstood as Cherry Herring and Cheery Heering.

The Danish Hotdog and Hotdog Stand (Pølsevogn)

The original fast food outlet in Denmark is the hotdog stand on wheels (see photo), the old reliable outlet for a snack that REALLY satisfies. It offers Denmark's famous thin, red, and very long (12-inch) sausages, *røde pølser* (red hotdogs), served on a small, rectangular paper plate along with a side order of bread. When the sausage is served in a traditional bun, it is called a hot dog. It is commonly served with remoulade, which has a mild, sweet-sour taste, and a medium yellow spread made of a mayonnaise base served with pickled cucumber and fair amounts of sugar. The more exotic kind contains hints of mustard, cayenne, coriander, and onion, with starch, gelatin and milk as thickeners. The consumer has a wide choice of condiments, including ketchup, mustard, onion (either raw or toasted, i.e., *ristede*) and thin-sliced pickles placed on top.

Another variety is the French hotdog (*Fransk hotdog*) which is a sausage stuffed into a special long roll. The roll has a hole in the end, into which the hot dog is slipped into, after the requested condiment has been squirted in (ketchup, mustard, different kinds of dressing). Americans who like a more beefy or kosher style frankfurter avoid the red ones.

The rolling hotdog wagons are typically made of metal with an open window to the street, and a counter where one can stand and eat the sausage. A few more specialized wagons include limited seating, usually both inside and outside. The number of sausage wagons has continually declined as competition from convenience stores and gas stations has increased.

In regards to meat eating, the Danes primarily eat pork rather than beef. Pork roasts, pork cutlets, tenderloin and chops are all popular. Ground pork is used in many traditional recipes requiring ground meat. While still in first place, pork has lost ground to turkey, beef and veal in recent years. Beef has become more and more popular in recent decades as the standard of living and availability has increased. Denmark has a century-old tradition for dairy products, so cattle bred for meat were rare and much more expensive.

Potato recipes are almost ubiquitous in Danish cooking. It has captured this important position in spite of its relatively short career in the Danish kitchen. The potato was first introduced into Denmark by the French Protestant Huguenot immigrants who arrived in the town of Fredericia in 1720.

Danish hot dog stand (*pølsevogn*) in the city center of Kolding.

King Frederick V encouraged widespread cultivation on the moor and grass-lands on the Jutland peninsula, by enticing German and Dutch immigrants to move to Denmark and cultivate potatoes. They became so much a staple of the diet that a number of colloquial expressions evolved such as *Jeg er en heldig kartoffel!* (I am a lucky potato!), expressing the luck of the common man.

Most tourists who have been to Norway, where potato consumption still ranks at the top of the list on a per capita basis, will feel relief at arriving in Denmark with its much more varied menu.

Getting hungry? Thirsty? God rejse (bon voyage) and god appetit!

Chapter 14

Piet Hein:
Renaissance Man

Shakespeare characterized a famous Danish prince, Hamlet, and indeed all of us as the victims of the "slings and arrows of outrageous fortune." The same might be said to apply to the entire Danish nation. Its endurance and many achievements in the arts, sciences and democratic institutions were in the last century and a half twice jeopardized by invasion and occupation (1864 and 1940–45) by an aggressive Germany. Many foreign observers and even Danes such as Hans Christian Andersen questioned whether a nation that had so long placed its trust in good will and mutual respect rather than armed resistance to aggression could long endure.

How ironic indeed when Denmark suddenly was catapulted into world headlines by the publication of a few satirical cartoons by the newspaper *Jyllands-Posten* aimed at the campaign of terror by Islamic extremists and the political misuse of Islam. Gentle and ironic satire has long been a Danish art form dating back at least to the many short stories (fairy tales) by Andersen and used with great success against the Nazis when armed force to resist seemed suicidal and hopeless.

How much more remarkable is it, then, that in the face of antagonistic Muslim extremism today, before which the "vaunted" ("cowardly" would be the better more accurate term) *New York Times* abjectly surrendered and refused to reproduce any of the infamous Muhammad cartoons, the entire Danish press reprinted all of them in February 2008 to protest the planned assassination of Kurt Westergaard, one of the cartoonists! Since then, an actual attempt on his life was made at his home in Aarhus in February 2010.

From 1940 to 1945, four prominent Danes — physics professor and 1922 Nobel Prize winner Niels Bohr, entertainer Victor Borge, engineer and poet Piet Hein, and architect and interior designer Arne Jacobsen — all took a stand against the Nazis and the occupation of their country. The last three were wholly unknown outside the borders of their small homeland while Bohr was a distinguished world figure and Noble prize winner in physics. Each went into exile but they did so not to abandon the fight but to help promote the cause of their homeland and the plight of their fellow citizens trapped at home and refute the great Nazi lie that Denmark had wisely sought "German protection."

The German occupation of Denmark was initially in the form of a special lenient administration allowing life to go on normally without any interference except "necessary security measures," until the fall of 1943 when an attempt to deprive Jewish citizens of their rights and deport them provoked mass resentment. The four men who left before then not only helped give reliable information about their country under occupation, but gained publicity that furthered their own illustrious careers and made them world famous. We can take heart from their example at a time when the lack of will to openly confront militant Islam characterizes much of Western Europe and elsewhere.

Recently, one of the leading publishers in the United States, Random House pulled a book, *The Jewel of Medina* by first-time author Sherry Jones just prior to the publication date. The reason was clear — a "politically correct" American academic believed it was inflammatory against Muslims. The publishers say they had received "cautionary advice" not only that the publication of this book might be offensive to some in the Muslim community, but also that it "could incite acts of violence by a small, radical segment." How stark the contrast between such publishing giants (and cowards) as the *New York Times* and Random House, long considered to be among the leaders in the world of letters and freedom of expression, with the heroic stand of the Danish press.

Each the four Danes had a Jewish connection — either a Jewish wife (Piet Hein), one Jewish parent (Niels Bohr; chapter 22) or being wholly of Jewish origin (Victor Borge, born Børge Rosenbaum, chapter 15, and Arne Jacobsen, chapter 20). Each was an innovative and respected person in Danish public life at the time of the German invasion and occupation of their country in April 1940. For practical reasons, they were all advised by colleagues not to provoke Denmark's strict policy of neutrality and to refrain from making anti–Nazi statements. To their credit and the credit of all Danes, they refused to be cowed and when no other practical alternative was possible, chose exile.

Like other Danes with Dutch names, Piet Hein was a descendent of Dutch colonists invited to Denmark by King Christian IV in the 17th century for their skills in constructing dikes and drainage works as well as shipbuilding. He was named for an illustrious ancestor, a 17th-century Dutch naval hero (or pirate) who preyed upon Spanish fleets in the Caribbean and is considered to be Holland's equivalent of Sir Francis Drake. His decision to study both physics and philosophy at the University of Copenhagen was considered eccentric. After all, people told him, it had never been done before.

Piet Hein was born in Copenhagen and was an only child. His father was a civil engineer and it must have been a remarkable example of being a chip off the old block, a sure sign of things to come, that his father designed the roller coaster at Tivoli Gardens (a perfect blend of science and art). His mother, Estrid Hein, was a noted eye doctor and active in *Dansk Kvindessamfund* (Danish Women's Society), the feminist organization that helped secure the right to vote for Danish women. She was the daughter of Octavius Hansen, a leading jurist and politician whose home was the scene of frequent social gatherings attended by the leading figures of art, science and politics throughout Scandinavia.

It was his mother's influence and his interest in her work that led Piet Hein to design several innovative optical devices that earned him his first source of income from successful patents. These included lampshades that reduced glare and spread light much more evenly than was possible earlier and were at the same time strikingly attractive.

As a doctor, his mother was involved in much of the humanitarian and social work of the League of Nations in Geneva. It was due in great measure to her influence that Piet Hein felt so international. There was also a bit of the pixie about her. She designed what people called an "individual national costume" that incorporated elements from diverse regions of Denmark.

An ardent Danish patriot yet a passionate advocate of world brotherhood, Piet Hein combined the attributes of a true Renaissance Man–inventive scientific genius and artistic sensitivity. Piet Hein harmonized a vision of one humanity and one world with an immense love of his Danish homeland and language. If this seems like an impossible task, it is no more so than the equivalent ideal compromise he found by merging the rectangle and the circle into the super-ellipse, a brilliant design element in urban, furniture and tableware design as well as in dozens of other applications. He was a genius in such diverse fields as mathematics, physics, engineering, poetry, painting, furniture design and philosophy.

His elf-like persona made him an ideal "pixie" but he was an intellectual giant and a friend, collaborator and correspondent with Nobel Prize–winning physi-

Engineer-architect-pixie poet Piet Hein

cists Niels Bohr (whose ideas on nuclear physics he popularized for ordinary Danes) and Albert Einstein as well as with film legend Charlie Chaplin (a fellow pixie). He was often referred to as the Hans Christian Andersen of modern Denmark and compared to Plato and Goethe as a philosopher or the Book of Ecclesiastes in the Bible. He never tired of admonishing the world to free itself from conventional wisdom, insisting that the "trick is not to let yourself be hypnotized by traditional solutions."

Piet Hein studied art at the Swedish Academy in 1925–26 and then physics in the 1930s. While at the University of Copenhagen, he attended lectures by the German physicist Werner Heisenberg (see chapter 22), famous for his Uncertainty Principle. Piet Hein immortalized his life and knowledge in short, aphoristic poetry, accompanied by simple drawings, thereby creating more than 7,000 of what he called *grooks*. If any more proof of his versatility is called for, he was able to draw the illustrations to the *grooks* with his left hand while writing the text with his right!

A few sample *grooks* among the many hundreds that he himself translated into English will give the reader an immediate idea of their poignancy, humor and relevance. The drawings are equally important and the potentially interested reader can acquire several volumes published in the United States during the 1950s and '60s.

Prayer
Sun that givest all things birth, shine on everything on earth!
If that's too much to demand, shine at least on this, our land.
If even that's too much for thee, shine at least on me.

A Toast
The soul may be a mere pretense,
The mind makes very little sense.
So let us value the appeal
Of that which we can taste and feel.

He began what appeared to be a whimsical hobby under the pen name of Kumble in 1940 following the German invasion of Denmark. At the time, he was president of the anti–Nazi Union and had to go underground. The first *grooks* reflected his views but managed to be circulated freely for a time because their imaginative and subtle use of irony was often lost on the Germans. In spite of his deeply felt love for Denmark, he could poke fun at himself and fellow Danes who he felt tended to overdramatize their conception of their own country. In an introduction to a film he collaborated on for the Danish Ministry of Foreign Affairs and the Industrial Council, he designed a globe on which Denmark filled up one hemisphere and the rest of the world had to be content with the other half. This globe became a popular novelty item for many Danes who shared his ironic sense of humor.

Piet Hein had another motive for his Denmark globe. He wanted to show how a small country, "poor in natural resources," could still make a major impact on the world due to its human resources. Piet Hein (he is always referred to by both names) was a master of the art of coining aphorisms that speak to us from the heart, the mind and the gut all at once. They often contain a subtle irony that makes us reflect on the few lines long after we have read them. He was able to achieve this in the languages he spoke fluently — English, German, French, Italian and Swedish as well as his native Danish.

Without a doubt, his most remembered and honored achievement was the mathematical formula that enabled him to design what he called the super-ellipse, the perfect compromise between the rectangle and the circle. The problem was originally presented by Swedish designers' difficulty in planning a traffic loop in the roughly rectangular city center of Stockholm.

The spatial advantages of using his mathematical formula in buildings as well as tables, chairs, lampshades, placemats and tableware has been estimated at 15 percent. The super-ellipse was the basic form used in the design of Mexico City's Olympic Stadium, Stockholm's Sergel Torg (at the city center) and many other similar projects throughout the world. The technical brilliance of Piet Hein's super-ellipse solution and its applications as an important element of what became known as "Danish design" or "Scandinavian Modern," coupled with his flamboyant personal life and attractive whimsy, made him the choice for *Life* magazine's cover story (the first Dane to be so honored) in October 1966, with his portrait encased in a super-ellipse and the captions "Piet Hein, Denmark's pixie poet with his slide rule," and "Piet Hein peers from his super-ellipse."

In his university days in Copenhagen in the 1920s, the young Piet Hein hit on the idea for the Soma Cube. This is a 3 × 3 × 3 cube (i.e., made of 27 unit cubes) that can be built out of seven different pieces, each composed of three or four small cubes; it became the ultimate three-dimensional puzzle. Psychologists have also used the cube to test spatial skills. An article on the Soma Cube in *Scientific American* stimulated thousands of readers to make their own models and build imaginative shapes. Parker Brothers brought out a game based on the cube in 1969. If you know a child who is a budding engineer, there is no better gift than the Soma Cube. It carries a label warning against "addiction."

All of Piet Hein's achievements stem from the fusion of art and science. His super-ellipse was the most beautiful blend of the two. Many of his *grooks* also make the same point. He believed we must avoid narrow specialization and instead strive to build bridges between the "hard" technical and natural sciences and the "soft" humanistic ones. His artistic talents go beyond his poetry. He was an accomplished painter, defining art as a way of thinking about all subjects. He asserted in the *grooks* and in serious essays that the great cultural divide was not between the haves and the have-nots, but between the knows and the know-nots. He said: "After all, what is art? Art is the creative process and it goes through all fields. Einstein's theory of relativity, now that is a work of art. Einstein was more of an artist in physics than on his violin. Art is this: art is the solution of a problem which cannot be expressed explicitly until it is solved."

When he was 10 years old, Piet Hein was sent to Metropolitan Skolen, a traditional school for well-to-do boys, where he had difficulties because of his iconoclastic views on everything, including patriotism. His suggestion that one should leave the room when the national anthem was played did not receive approval from his teachers or fellow pupils.

This is all the more ironic in hindsight, for it was Piet Hein who wrote what is certainly one of the most beautiful expressions of love for Denmark, "*Når den lyse lærker synger over Danmark,*" written in 1947 just after the World War II. It is among the most beautiful tributes to his homeland in song and devoid of any arrogance. The poem has been set to music and tells of skylarks flying over waving fields of wheat and the crashing of waves on the shore. The stanzas reveal that the mature Piet Hein was anything but the young cynic of his school days.

Piet Hein was an admirer of women and was married four times and had five sons. One of his wives was a Jewish woman from Argentina and Piet Hein spent several of the war years there and attracted the attention of the anti-Nazi cause. He had quite definite ideas about women and even wrote on the subject, as we would expect from a true Renaissance Man. He believed that a woman's "soul," or what we might call personality, was the more dynamic factor in attractiveness than physical appearance, and that "lady" was often the term applied to a woman who for propriety's sake refused to have a sense of humor, an essential ingredient in any human relationship.

He maintained an apartment in the center of Copenhagen but was emotionally tied to two estates, Damsbo and Egeskov, on the Danish island of Fünen. His son Hugo continues to direct production of the many Piet Hein art objects and devices that have earned international acclaim. The cities of Rungsted and Næstved recently inaugurated Piet Hein streets and Piet Hein was recently included in a popular write-in vote as one of the 100 most famous Danes. He was indeed a Renaissance man of multiple talents, typifying the best in Western civilization uniting the arts and science and a Great Dane.

Chapter 15

Victor Borge:
The Clown Prince

No other Dane became as well known in the United States and Canada and beloved as the Danish American pianist Victor Borge, who enchanted and delighted world audiences for three generations, from the time of his arrival in the United States as a refugee fleeing German occupied Denmark in 1940 until his death in 2000. Known as the Clown Prince of Denmark, he drew upon the tradition of gentle and ironic satire used by another Great Dane, Hans Christian Andersen. No one else has used a love and respect for classical music in such a genuinely affectionate, gently mocking and humorous way. His humor was remarkable. It was the antithesis of slapstick and relied on clever ploys, outrageous juxtapositions, word gags, logical absurdities and the totally unexpected. He never cheapened a performance with base sexual innuendo. Perhaps his philosophy was best described in his own words that "the shortest distance between two points is a smile."

His many honors include knighthood by the five Scandinavian countries, a special Medal of Honor awarded by the Liberty Centennial Committee at a gala ceremony at Ellis Island and awards by the United States Congress, the United Nations, the International Humor Treasure Award and a special honor by the Kennedy Center in 2000. Victor Borge left behind a mass audience with an enormous appreciation of his talent. More than this, he was a self-made man who became a generous benefactor providing aid to Jewish refugees who like himself, had to flee their homelands. Together with New York attorney Richard Netter, he created the Thanks to Scandinavia Scholarship Fund that has brought more than a thousand Scandinavian students and scientists to study in the United States.

His name is enshrined in Victor Borge Hall, located in Scandinavia House in New York City and at Victor Borge Plads, a major Copenhagen square. On his grave in Greenwich, Connecticut, stands a statue of the Little

Mermaid. It is no exaggeration to say that more than any other individual he helped personify the best bonds of good friendship and mutual respect between the United States and Denmark.

He was not just simply a comedian or a musician. Like the other "Great Danes," his vocal opposition to the Nazis even before their war of aggression against his homeland put him in the forefront of those who risked everything to speak out and be heard when so many others of his countrymen and most Europeans preferred the convenience and safety of being silent. Due to his comic revues satirizing Hitler and the Nazi regime, Victor Borge was physically attacked by Danish Nazi sympathizers.

Born Børge Rosenbaum, he was a child prodigy. His parents Bernhard and Frederikke were both distinguished musicians and from a Jewish family that had long been resident in Denmark. He gave his first recital at the age of eight and in 1918 was awarded a full scholarship at the Royal Danish Academy of Music and starred in a major concert in 1926. Although considered a success as a classical pianist, Victor Borge launched a career that stemmed from his irrepressible humor. He had hit upon an unusual formula that he made his own and explained that "for those people who take music seriously, I'm a musician and to people who don't take anything seriously, I'm a clown."

Victor Borge grew up in the middle-class neighborhood of Østerbro in Copenhagen and absorbed the culture of a family of professional musicians and parents who honored Jewish tradition but were committed to integration within Danish society. His father had played the violin in the Royal Danish Philharmonic Orchestra for 35 years. Victor began to learn to play the piano from his mother when he was three years old. His penchant for wry humor and party tricks were apparent at gatherings in his parents' home when he would volunteer to play compositions of his own in the style of Beethoven or another famous composer, convincing the guests that these were the works of the great masters.

As a musical comedian, he launched a dual career as an actor in Denmark's moving picture industry and as a musical revue entertainer in the 1930s. In the period 1935–1940, he appeared in numerous comedies, theatrical and musical revues throughout Denmark and in several major Danish films as a character actor. They were *De tre, måske fire* (*The Three, Maybe Four*), *Alarm, Frk. Møllers jubilaeum* (*Miss Møllers' Anniversary*), and *Der var en gang en vicevaert* (*There Was Once a Superintendant*).

One of his comedy routines brought him into the political spotlight when he lampooned the Nazis by asking what the difference is between a dog and a Nazi. "A Nazi lifts its arm." These remarks made him a marked man and his name was among those who were to be immediately arrested following the German army's invasion of Denmark on April 9, 1940. Already in 1939 on a visit to Stockholm to appear in a review he had confided in several friends that he knew "which way the wind is blowing" and expected a German invasion of the Scandinavian countries.

Borge managed to secure passage on the last American passenger ship, the S.S. *American Legion*, leaving northern Europe in 1940. "As he later said, 'Churchill and I were the only ones who saw what was happening; he saved Europe and I saved myself....'"

Arriving practically penniless and with no knowledge of English, Victor Borge nevertheless quickly drew attention to himself and by 1941 had become a member of Bing Crosby's radio program, appearing on that show for 56 weeks. In 1942, he was accorded the honor of being named "the best new radio performer of the year" by the American press. To celebrate American democracy, Victor appeared together with Frank Sinatra in the film *Higher and Higher* and *Meet the People* in 1944. While the war was still on, he managed to arrange to secretly return to occupied Denmark disguised as a seaman when he was made aware that his mother was on her deathbed. In 1948, Victor Borge became an American citizen.

Television brought him additional fame and instant recognition through appearances on the *Ed Sullivan Show* in 1949 and his own one-man show, *Comedy in Music*. After opening in Seattle in February 1953, the show ran for an extended stay on Broadway at the Golden Theatre for 849 performances, a total that set an all-time record for a running solo appearance. The show was transformed into a televised episode of *Omnibus*, a 90-minute, commercial-free program funded by the Ford Foundation. His 90-minute video *The Best of Victor Borge* has sold more than 3 million copies. In his career throughout the 1950s to the end of his life, he performed on the average of 100 or more nights a year.

The brand new Danish Jewish Museum in Copenhagen was in part made possible by a generous donation of $250,000 by Victor Borge. The site for the museum was chosen, to a large degree, for its significance to Danish Jewish history. The original building was constructed by Christian IV, the first Danish king to invite Jews to settle in Denmark in 1622. When the Germans occupied Denmark during World War II, the royal collection of Hebraica and Judaica was hidden there to protect it from Nazi depredation. The Judaica collection held by the library is still one of the best such collections in Europe. The museum was designed by award-winning architect Daniel Libeskind, who designed Berlin's Jewish Museum, and whose design was originally selected by a special commission to rebuild the Twin Towers in New York.

Americans of my age (68) remember his two most famous routines — "Inflationary Language" and "Phonetic Pronunciation" — with special affection. Few of his fans know that the "Phonetic Pronunciation" routine was used as a diagnostic tool by medical doctors to determine if the hearing loss suffered by some soldiers was due to a psychosomatic cause and curable or the result of physical injuries and therefore likely incurable.

The "Inflationary Language" skit was created to "keep up with inflation" and was a triumph of zany humor which uniquely required the participation of the audience mentally trying to keep pace with telling of the story and struggling to unwind the distorted words. In case you've never hear it, here is a brief sample (not as funny on the written page because you don't have to guess so much):

> Twice upon a time, there lived in Sunny Califivenia a young man named Bob. He was a third leiuetelevenant [*sic*] in the U.S. Air Fiveces. Bob had been fond of Anna, his one-and-a-half sister, ever since she saw the light of day for the second time. And all three of them were proud of the fact that two of his fivefathers had been among the creninetors of the U.S. Constithreetion. They were dining on the terrace. "Anna," he said as he took a bite of a marinineded herring, "You look twoderful threenight. You never looked that lovely befive." The table was tastefully decorninded with Anna's favorite flowers: threelips.

The beauty of this insane exercise in manipulating language is that the "real word" dawns on the listener just in time to get mentally ready for the next inflationary word — you've got to think but the effort is worth the humor. Even if you have hear the main "Inflationary" routine several times, you still have to wrack your brain to grasp. "I nined the elevenderloin with my fivek."

Other fans prefer any one of a dozen zany piano duet routines where Borge and a partner/rival played through each other's arms to reach the far end of the keyboard or raced from one end of the bench to the other to finish playing in unison.

Victor Borge, the inimitable Danish-American humorist and pianist.

When taking a holiday from his comedy routines, Victor Borge performed as a talented soloist concert pianist and conductor. In an interview with an Associated Press reporter, Borge explained that he never had to "psyche himself up" for a performance. He said, "Luck, good fortune and stamina always keep me performing.... The moment I walk on the stage, no matter what my mood, if I have any regrets, feel sick or in pain, all that disappears. That is when the climax of my day occurs."

Just thirteen days before his death at age 91, Victor Borge gave an interview most of his fans in America may find revealing. It appeared in the Danish newspaper *Berlingske Avis* on Sunday, December 10, 2000, and in addition to fond recollections and expressions of love for his deceased wife, he revealed a somber side very much in contrast to his public face of eternal good humor. Only his fans able to read the original Danish (since, as far as I know, it has not appeared in print in English) could appreciate how he had faced the cruel realities of the renewed specter of anti–Semitism.

The interview was conducted by Jakob Kvist, and in the piece Borge began by discussion his personality: "I am naturally in good humor. That's my nature. Therefore I am also in very bad humor when I am not in good humor.... Either I am at the very bottom or I'm at the very top rather than somewhere in between."

When asked if he used humor as a "shield," Borge replied, "Yes — in very large degree — it has protected me. In reality, I am very shy.... I always stood a bit in the background. I didn't like being celebrated and still don't. Naturally, I do like it in a way but not as the center of things." Borge went on to say that humor was a natural part of his personality, something that came to him "unconsciously." He also noted that it had its drawbacks — he didn't want people to think he was "clowning around and trying to be funny all the time." This could be a challenge, though, because, as Borge realized, "I am funny and I can't help that. It's just like people who stutter. They can't stop."

Borge attributed the shaping of his persona in part to "fate," but also cited his experiences growing up as a Jew in Europe during the Nazi era. "With Nazism, it was persecution. You could never be sure.... It made me modest, made me reluctant to push myself forward and be aggressive. For that reason too I have always stood in the background."

Borge also described humor as a form of self-protection when faced with anti–Semitic audience members, and seemed clearly to have been strongly affected — though not afflicted — by his experience:

> I can remember when I stood on stage and could see people even if I couldn't hear them, I could make out one or another was muttering, "Jew." I could see it in their expression ... and that has in a way tormented me my whole life. But there are always people like that. You just have to clench your fists. And it always amazed me why I should be punished for something I didn't do.

When asked whether humor and tragedy were natural companions, Borge was unequivocal: "Yes. Why does one laugh a few years later about things that go wrong? At the moment they happen, yeah, they are terrible but when you think back about them and speak about them then you can die of laughter."

He also reiterated that he was not a clownish figure, and did not want to be viewed as one. "A clown is not himself.... He puts a mask on and so becomes someone else. But I am myself when I stand on the stage. I am authentic in that sense. It is not fabricated in any way." He went on to comment on the importance of spontaneity in his career, saying that "I count on it and if I hold a speech, I never prepare myself. I wait until all the other speakers are finished, and so I use something that comes automatically. My best speeches are completely spontaneous." When asked about acting "funny" when he wasn't in a good mood, Borge's experience and professionalism were readily apparent: "I can't help myself. I am funny.... I know that the things I do are funny because they are surprising and there aren't others who work like that.... I have knowledge and training behind me [and] I use my knowledge and ability ... and it always works."

When asked about an interview in which he said he didn't understand where the time had gone, Borge replied, "I can't understand that it has taken so long to go so fast." When Kvist inquired of Borge how he felt about his advanced age, Borge countered, "I am not old. My body is old but I haven't changed.... Yes, my physique is weakened a bit ... but my spirit hasn't changed." Borge was also asked if he ever regretted that life's events had forced him to leave Denmark to pursue a career, to which he replied "No," though he did add, "but the USA is a strange country in many ways."

In the interview, Borge went on to discuss his status as a man with a foot in two countries, as well as his plans to mingle his ashes with his beloved wife's creamated remains upon his death. They would be buried together in the U.S., but a portion of their remains would also be sent to Denmark for burial in his native land. The ashes are interred at Copenhagen's Western Jewish Cemetery. As a nod to his Danish heritage, Borge also obtained permission to have a copy of Denmark's famed "Little Mermaid" statue placed at his grave in his adopted homeland.

Upon his death his daughter, Frederikke Borge, wrote in his obituary,

> He died peacefully, no pain. He died of terminal life. ... I think he meant the world to me, as every father does to every daughter, but he meant a lot to a lot of other people, which made me proud to be his daughter, and he was a very decent and generous man, which also made me proud. I think he brought laughter to the world, and I think he was a very gifted musician, and I'll miss him terribly.

So will we all.

Victor Borge left a foundation for several important causes dear to his heart, among them the Danish Jewish Museum in Copenhagen, one of the city's keenest attractions for many tourists. The museum, with its Daniel Libeskind–designed interiors, officially opened in 2004.

Like his contemporary, Piet Hein (see Chapter 14), Victor Borge was fond of aphorisms. Those for which he is most remembered include the following:

- Humor is something that thrives between man's aspirations and his limitations.
- There is more logic in humor than in anything else. Because, you see, humor is truth.
- I wish to thank my parents for making it all possible ... and I wish to thank my children for making it necessary.
- If I have caused just one person to wipe away a tear of laughter, that's my reward.

And finally, his saying, the first part of which was chosen by Borge and co-author Niels-Jørgen Kaiser as the title of Borge's 2001 autobiography (in Danish), *Smilet er den korteste afstand*: "A smile is the shortest distance between people."

Chapter 16

N.F.S. Grundtvig: Spiritual Father of the Nation

N.F.S. (Nicolai Frederik Severin) Grundtvig (1783–1872), clergyman, historian, poet, religious and political reformer, theologian, writer, philosopher, philologist and researcher of Norse mythology and folklore, may sound like a comical name for many English speakers, few if any of whom have heard the name before, but it resonates through Danish society, church life, politics, folklore, education and concepts of freedom, and participation in civic affairs, social responsibility and politics.

Almost one hundred and forty years after his death, he still casts a long shadow and is regarded as the unequivocal holder of the title of "spiritual father of the nation." For several decades, he and the philosopher Søren Kierkegaard occupied opposite ends of the religious and political spectrum and engaged in a debate that still continues.

A recent poll taken by the Danish daily newspaper *Kristeligt Dagblad* among members of Denmark's parliament (Folketing) posed six questions about Grundtvig and the "folk high school movement" for the system of adult education he inspired. About one-fourth of the respondents (44 of the total 179 members of parliament) were asked if they had attended such an adult high school and what significance Grundtvig has had on their political work and views.

A clear majority answered positively and many gave concrete examples. Forty percent answered that they had frequently attended folk high school courses (compared to about 10 percent of the general adult population). What is noteworthy is that not only is there continued enthusiasm for Grundtvig's ideas and the folk high schools from the two traditional, centrist liberal parties (Venstre and Radikal Venstre) but also from both the far left (SF — Socialistiske Folkeparti) and the far right (Dansk Folkeparti).

Among what has traditionally been the strongest political party, the Social

Democrats, special mention was made of the folk high schools run by the Labor Movement. The respondents were keen to give Grundtvig full credit for their practical work and regard him as no less a figure of veneration among the Danish working class than Marx. Where else in the West can this be said of a man who was a pastor and the author of hundreds of psalms and who retains such a strong hold on a party that is by definition both socialist and largely secular?

The most fundamental aspect of his view of Christianity was its role among the world's nations and peoples, each through their distinct culture. Both Hans Christian Andersen and N.F.S. Grundtvig envisioned a society characterized by economic and social solidarity where "few have too much and even fewer have too little."

Even among those who did not point to a direct connection between their political work and Grundtvig's philosophy, there was a readiness to accord his views great importance for modern-day Denmark. In his sketch of the folk high school, *Skolen for livet og akademiet i Søro* (*The School for Life and Academy at Søro*, 1838), Grundtvig explained that it took him thirty years to "get Rome and Latin out of my system," and in a poetic vein wrote that "all letters are dead even if written by fingers of angels and ribs of stars, all book knowledge is dead that is not unified with a corresponding life in the reader."

By 1940, there were approximately fifty folk high schools for adult education in Denmark, short of the high watermark of the Golden Age following the rapid expansion of these schools after the Schleswig-Holstein war of 1864. The 1980s saw a remarkable resurgence of the folk high school movement, even if its clientele, including urban unemployed and refugees, changed considerably.

N.F.S. Grundtvig (1783–1872) was, at the time of his death, already an almost mystical figure. For him, a people's history is part of universal history and can be best understood through an examination of how hundreds of generations have blended "spirit and dust" to create a mosaic of diverse cultures.

His ideas for the folk high schools stressed they would provide "a school throughout life" and make available the fine tool of literacy that had previously been reserved for a privileged class, hence the importance of language, the most important instrument and essential ingredient for learning, self-awareness, creativity and social participation. For Grundtvig, it was essential for Danes to use their native language to sing and relate their love for Mother Denmark through the generations.

An outstanding example of Grundtvig's abiding legacy is that he authored 271 of the 754 hymns contained in the Danish Hymnal. Many of Grundtvig's prolific writings, however, remain unpublished and only a very few of the published ones have been translated into English

In 1791 at the age of eight, he was sent to live at the home of a pastor in Jutland, and went on to study at the Cathedral School of Aarhus (Aarhus Katedralskole) until he graduated in 1798. He left for Copenhagen two years later to study theology and was accepted at the University of Copenhagen in 1801. In 1805, Grundtvig took a position as tutor in a house on the remote island of Langeland and for the next few years studied Shakespeare and the great German writers. He achieved some recognition upon publication of *Northern Mythology*, a minor drama, *The Fall of the Heroic Life in the North*, and shortly thereafter, at age 27, he achieved national notoriety by boldly denouncing the clergy of Copenhagen who demanded that he be punished.

Upon his father's death in 1813, Grundtvig applied to be his successor in the parish but was rejected. From 1813 to 1815, he attempted to form a movement to support the Norwegians in their struggle for independence and proclaimed that their separation from Denmark was God's punishment for the weakness and failings of the Danish church.

Grundtvig developed the view and argued that Christianity was not a "theory" to be derived from the Bible and elaborated by scholars. He questioned the right of theologians to elaborate on the Bible by interpreting the scriptures, translated from ancient languages. The result was that Grundtvig was publicly prosecuted for libel and fined. The state Lutheran church forbade him to preach for seven years. During this time he published a collection of theological works and studied Anglo-Saxon to pursue his interests in Nordic mythology. Finally, through royal protection, he obtained permission to preach again and received the position of pastor of the workhouse church of Vartov hospital.

Laws for compulsory school education were only passed in 1814. When Denmark took the first steps towards democracy in the 1830s with the establishment of advisory assemblies, Grundtvig played a major role in drawing attention to the necessity of an appropriate modern education for the masses instead of the old academic routine and Latin-based formal education of academies that had not changed in the curriculum since the Middle Ages. He undertook three trips to England during the period 1829–31 that had an immense impact on his thought. In the 1830s, he published several pamphlets on education, stressing the critical importance of the living, uncensored spoken word rather than reliance on books in the mother tongue of the people. He echoed the sentiments of Hans Christian Andersen who had to attend a traditional "scholarly academy" where Latin was the most important subject and heavily influenced an academic-style Danish remote from the language of the people.

He turned out to be the very opposite of his father, a conservative clergyman in a country village, who was content with a theology that can best be described as pietistic. Because of his radical ideas, abrasive behavior and polemical writings, Grundtvig was for a considerable part of his life a Lutheran minister, either forbidden to preach or allowed to preach but not administer the sacraments. It was only through the intervention of King Christian VIII on his accession to the Danish throne that Grundtvig, at the age of 55, finally received a permanent (albeit a minor) position as chaplain to Vartov, a Copenhagen church home for elderly women.

He was one of the most influential people in Danish history, as his philosophy gave rise to a new form of nationalism in the last half of the 19th century. He was married three times, the last time in his seventy-sixth year.

Between 1837 and 1841 he published *Sang-Værk til den Danske Kirke* (*Song Work for the Danish Church*), a rich collection of sacred poetry followed by a selection of early Scandinavian verse (1838). From 1844 until after the First Dano-Norwegian War (also known as the Three Year's War, 1848–50), Grundtvig took a prominent part in politics. In 1861, in spite of his earlier non-conformist views, he received the titular rank of bishop but without a see. His preaching attracted large congregations, and a following among a large segment of the Danish people. His hymnbook effected a great change in Danish church services, substituting the hymns of the great national poets. He wrote or translated about 1500 hymns in all.

He started collecting fairy tales, legends, songs, traditions, and beliefs in the 1840s and published *Gamle danske minder i folkemunde* (*Old Danish Legends Alive in Folklore*), 1854–57. Grundtvig was the first in Denmark to systematize a folklore collection, meticulously noting the origins of texts within Denmark and abroad. His foremost achievement was the collection and publication of folk ballads which resulted in the first four volumes of *Danmarks gamle Folkeviser* (*The Old Folk Songs of Denmark*), 1853–83.

His Views as a Pastor, Not a Theologian

Grundtvig's theological development continued throughout his lifetime. He promoted wisdom, compassion, and equality. He opposed all compulsion, including exams, as deadening to the human soul. Instead, he advocated unleashing human creativity according to the universally creative order of life. Only willing hands make light work. His work was steeped in the national literature and supported by deep spirituality.

He always called himself a pastor, not a theologian, and emphasized the distance between his ideas and academic theology. The chief characteristic of his theology was the substitution of the authority of the "living word" for the written scriptures. He desired to see each congregation act practically as an independent community. His views were bitterly attacked by very conservative elements of the Lutheran church and the various pietistic sects with their emphasis on God's written word, most notably "the Inner Mission."

Debate with Kierkegaard

A number of scholars have referred to Grundtvig as the apostle of Christian humanism and responsible for the character of the Lutheran church in Denmark as opposed to that in Germany. These included Hal Koch, a professor of Theology who played a key role in arousing national unity during the occupation and opposed all measures that violated the spirit of the Danish constitution, national consciousness and the Church. Another was the German theologian who taught at the Danish University of Aarhus, Regin Prenter, who called Grundtvig "the quintessential Dane ... for except for Luther himself, there is no one who has so consciously and so successfully made the national expression of the Church of the reformation the very content of his lifework as he did." Grundtvig took seriously the creation idea of man as a divine experiment and remained true to the vision of the Old Testament Hebrew Bible that God was the God of Creation before the God of Redemption as personified by Jesus.

This meant that human beings were first part of God's plan of creation and their life together as social beings in nations: "I believe in God, the Father, the Creator." The Danish philosopher Søren Kierkegaard (see chapter 18), who disputed Grundtvig on key points of Christian faith, had argued that the Christian message summoned by the Gospel was directed entirely towards the individual seeking salvation through grace. Jaroslav Pelikan, a religious historian and contributor to the book *The Rescue of the Danish Jews; Moral Courage Under Stress* (edited by Leo Goldberg, New York University Press, 1987), has argued that "Kierkegaard and Grundtvig were contemporaries who were born to be contrasted. Kierkegaard expressed with unique power the recognition that each person is individually accountable before God, but Grundtvig recognized with a profundity that was born of the Hebrew Bible ... that the imperatives of biblical faith are not individualistic." By this, most Danes understood the Grundtvig legacy that they had a collective social and national responsibility towards their fellow citizens, the Danish Jews.

Patriot and Danish Nationalist

Grundtvig is remembered as a Danish patriot and spokesman for the Danes left behind the border in occupied Slesvig. He was not, however, a narrow-minded nationalist. He argued for the right of self-determination and proclaimed in a poem that "All belong to a people who so regard themselves." This characterization of modern, non-exclusive nationalism has been frequently cited in the current debate over immigration policy and how society should be open to the acceptance of immigrants from other cultures and lifestyles. Those who believe that it is incumbent on new immigrants to actively seek integration and acceptance point out that the following verse calls for the requirement that all should have "an eye for its history and an ear for its language." He inspired Slesvigers with the will to resist and taught that coercion could never triumph over freedom.

During the years that followed the loss of Slesvig, the Danish people turned inwards and found pride and inspiration in Grundtvig's approach to national feeling that included a more lenient church, a fundamental optimism with regard to the capacity of ordinary people, love of the Danish language and a romantic attachment to the past.

His poem below on the diametrically opposed national character of the Danes and Germans in Slesvig inspired the national movement to recover the lost territory:

> *Som paa Fattig-Kirkeegaarden*
> *Strengt er efter Maale-Snoren*
> *Al den tyske Ret og Orden*
> *Danskens Lyst er Rosen-Floren*
> *Med alt Mildt det Lattermilde*
> *Friheds Drik af Glædens Kilde!*

> As in a poor church cemetery,
> Disciplined by a measuring yardstick,
> Are all the German's rules and regulations;
> The Danes' delight is the rose's bloom,
> All lenient and mildly laughing;
> It is Freedom's drink, our source of joy!

Chapter 17

Hans Christian Andersen

The year 2005 marked the 200th anniversary of the birth of Denmark's greatest writer, whose works have been translated into more languages than any author (second only to the Bible). The event was marked not only in Denmark but throughout Europe with many festivities, exhibitions, seminars, exhibits and tours of his hometown of Odense and where he lived in Copenhagen for many years. Most Americans have basic misconceptions about Andersen and his work, based on having seen the romanticized film about his life starring Danny Kaye and use of the term "fairy tales," usually considered appropriate only for children. Almost all of his 156 short stories or "adventures" (a better meaning of the Danish word *eventyr*, usually translated as "fairy tales") can be appreciated on two levels — one for adults and one for children.

The subjects of many of these stories also come as a surprise for those who have always regarded him as a kindly old grandfather telling his fairy tales to adoring grandchildren, the theme of a sculpture in New York's Central Park that portrays Andersen reading to children perched on his knee. The themes of his lesser known short tales include time travel, adultery, murder by decapitation, death, grim poverty and social inequality, child psychology, intense drama, split personality, husband-wife relations, snobbery, social climbing, Jewish identity, and a deep, abiding love for his Danish homeland.

Your children may have enjoyed the colorful characters, wizards and creatures of the Harry Potter series or *The Wizard of Oz*, but what have they learned of any value for later life? Most Andersen short stories have left a moral legacy about life, its struggles, human nature and the beautiful innocence of childhood. It is ironic that his work is much better known and appreciated by tens of millions of children in China or Russia, who continue to love Andersen, than in America or Britain.

When Leningrad was under siege in World War II and the city surrounded and starving, the production of all consumer goods was reduced to the absolute minimum. People were eating sawdust and paper could not be spared to publish literature. The publication of only one book of fiction was allowed in 1942 — *The Tales of Hans Christian Andersen.*

Andersen as Social Critic

It strikes most contemporary Americans as amazing or unbelievable when told that, after the Bible, Andersen's most popular "fairy tales" are the most translated work in all of literature. Close to two-thirds of them have been translated into more than sixty languages (more than Shakespeare's most popular plays). The Andersen Museum in Odense, his birthplace, boasts a display of several Andersen short stories in more than 120 languages, including Esperanto, Basque, Khmer, Estonian, Maltese, Korean, Albanian, Gaelic, Catalan, Icelandic, Yiddish, and Volapük. "The Nightingale," in translation, is a favorite Andersen tale read in Chinese elementary schools today.

Many of Andersen's tales feature talking animals, inanimate objects and fantastic creatures with their distinctive personalities, but they all teach us something about human nature and relations or the innocence of childhood. As a teacher of a course for "senior citizens" on Andersen's "fairy tales" at Central Florida Community College, I was not surprised that the turnout was comprised almost entirely of women (85 percent). They all claimed that men would hardly be interested in "simple children's stories" yet at the end of the last class, in summing up what they got out of the course, attitudes had changed profoundly. Several women spoke with tears in their eyes about how the stories had struck a powerful chord with them and even the

In the garden of "Roligheden" near Copenhagen, Denmark. 1869 photograph.

gentlemen spoke about how they had been totally surprised by the range of Andersen's interests.

Most of his stories have indeed stood the test of time. Andersen, at the time of his death, ranked with Charles Dickens as the world's most popular author and, like Dickens, he stood clearly on the side of those at the bottom of society, the socially weak, dispossessed and persecuted. Many Andersen stories defended children, women ("Story of a Mother"), the disabled ("The Steadfast Tin Soldier") the poor ("She Was No Good," "The Little Match-girl"), the humble ("The Gardener and the Aristocrat"), social outcasts and "climbers" who live by their wits ("Little Claus and Big Claus," "The Ice Maiden," "The Tinderbox"), and the Jews ("The Jewish Girl," "Only a Fiddler"). He delighted in ridiculing the ostentatious, the wealthy, nobility ("The Emperor's New Clothes"), snobs ("There Is a Difference," "Kid's Talk"), bureaucracy and the press ("Clumsy Hans"), and church hierarchy. He also expanded his themes to include time travel ("The Galoshes of Fortune"), psychological relations ("The Shadow"), and even husband-wife relations ("Father's Always Right").

Andersen's homeland was also faced with a dilemma by world events and the growing power and aggressive designs of German nationalism. He had to reconcile his Danish patriotism with his gratitude to wealthy patrons and publishing houses in Germany that had responded favorably to his work when he was still an unknown in Denmark. This was doubly difficult, for he had been ridiculed and harshly criticized by Danes at home in positions of power and influence in the literary world. These critics argued that his humble background and use of the common, ordinary spoken language of the people fell far short of what was expected from a great writer. Like Mark Twain, his characters spoke the language of the street and not of the academy. He had to overcome all this, as well as insulting personal remarks about himself as ugly, ungainly, uneducated, unmanly in appearance and overly sentimental.

His dilemma was heightened by the attack on Denmark launched by Prussia and Austria in 1864 that tore away the provinces of Schleswig and Holstein and then by Prussia's assault on its Austrian ally two years later in 1866 (the Seven Weeks' War), followed by the Franco–Prussian War in 1871. The three examples of Prussian militarism and expansionism were painful for Andersen.

He had achieved his early most notable successes that established his reputation as a great writer in Germany and been wined and dined by the nobility of many of the small principalities and was always welcomed as an honored guest at the home of the prince of Weimar. Andersen returned this love and respect with a deep admiration for high German culture and was shocked by the Prussian path under Bismarck to world-power status and the unification of the small German states into a powerful and militaristic empire.

The Schleswig Wars

In the disastrous war of 1864, Andersen confided to his diary that his heart had been broken by the events and that he would turn his back on those Germans who had launched or supported this aggressive war of conquest against his beloved homeland. In a letter to his close friend, Edvard Collin, Andersen questioned whether the Danish language would still be spoken and his works read in their original language in a hundred years time, so fearful was he at the threat of Denmark's total submergence by a united Germany. Many Danes with snobbish pretensions made an effort at using both German and French loan words in their speech and writing, a habit that Andersen satirized in his story "The Goblin and the Woman."

The Danes had defended their historic territories before in 1848–51 and had been encouraged that either (or both) England and Sweden would not let the country's territorial integrity be violated by a major European power bent on expansion. Neither lifted a finger. Only Schleswig was defended by the Danish armed forces as Denmark had already declared it had no interest in preserving the allegiance of Holstein, an area populated wholly by German speakers who had indicated their desire to become part of a larger German Confederation (Chapters 26).

The Multimedia Special to Celebrate the 200th Anniversary

In collaboration with museum exhibitions; airport, bookstore window and shopping displays; lectures; concerts; and radio and television documentaries, a national celebration was held in 2005 to celebrate the 200th anniversary of Andersen's birth. A major national television series was produced featuring the recollections of twelve prominent Danes who were interviewed by noted Lutheran minister, TV personality, writer and lecturer, Johannes Møllehave. Each guest was asked to recount when he or she first became aware of Andersen's magical name and stories. The programs evoked considerable interest and generated thousands of comments from viewers and readers.

The female mayor of Aarhus, Louise Gade, chose "The Goblin and the Woman." The woman in the story is much more cultured than her gardener/husband who thinks his wife is putting on airs by writing poetry. She has a fond affection for her nephew, the "assistant schoolmaster," Mr. Kisserup, to whom she shows some of her poetry, demonstrating her patriotic attachment to old Danish words in preference for the snobbish use of German.

Nothing better illustrates the universal appeal of Andersen than the memories of Nasser Khader, a Palestinian-born immigrant who mastered Danish after arriving as a young adult and was elected to the Danish parliament. Khader relates how his illiterate grandmother told him stories set in an Arab environment but which in fact were retellings of Andersen stories. His favorite is "The Emperor's Old Clothes," reflecting his rejection and disgust with the many Middle Eastern rulers he recalls who, like the Emperor, surrounded themselves with handpicked yes-men.

The most well known among the twelve guests was the then prime minister, Anders Fogh Rasmussen, the dark-haired, eloquent politician whose conservative coalition supported President George W. Bush during the invasion of Iraq to depose Saddam Hussein. Fogh Rasmussen chose "The Steadfast Tin Soldier" as a favorite that children and adults enjoy on different levels. It is one of Andersen's most beautiful stories with a sad ending. The one-legged tin soldier and his beautiful porcelain ballerina remain steadfast in their love in spite of all the ups and downs and cruelties of fate, a story of faithfulness in the face of adversity.

Holger Bech Nielsen, a professor at the Niels Bohr Institute of Physics in Copenhagen, is a top scientist in the field of high energy physics whose favorite story is "The Water Drop," a look into science fiction, where the microcosm of a single drop of water holds all the struggles of human existence. "The Flea and the Professor," chosen by Andersen's biographer, Jens Andersen, is one of the strangest of all Andersen's stories. It has erotic undertones and may have been an attempt by Andersen to express contempt for the literary elite of Copenhagen who had initially rejected him. A professor and a trained flea have a strange affection for each other until an eight-year-old exotic beautiful princess who had seized power from her parents falls in love with the flea! Is this story deep social commentary or pure slapstick? Try reading it and come up with your own interpretation.

"The Shadow" is a psychological drama preferred by Niels Birger Wamberg, a writer and literary historian. It demonstrates how far ahead of his time Andersen was, for when he wrote most of his stories, Freud's research was hardly begun. It is the story of a good and learned man's subconscious, or "other self," symbolized by his shadow. The shadow takes over the role of an independent person and subjugates the man's consciousness. Wamberg believes the story reflects Andersen's humiliation and desire for revenge against his former patron and close friend, Edvard Collin who wrote to Andersen that he could not bring himself to use the intimate second person form of address, "du" (indicating a close relationship), in conversation and correspondence with Andersen (preferring instead the more formal and polite form "De").

The former bishop of Copenhagen, Erik Norman Svendsen, presented a view of Andersen's religious sentiments in the choice of "The Story of a Mother." A mother goes to the ends of the earth to recall her child from Death. She gives up everything dear to her — her eyes, her bleeding heart and beautiful hair — in order to get to Death's garden before the soul of her child arrives there. When she encounters Death, she is allowed to look into "the well of Death" where she sees two human souls, one of which will have a happy life and be a blessing to the world. The other soul is marked by fear, sorrow, poverty and woe. She knows that one of these two is her son but she cannot make out which his fate is to be. Her choice is either to recall the soul and bring back to life only one or to let them both rest in the peace of death. Andersen could have chosen a happy ending but he preferred to rely on the Christian hope of the Resurrection and life everlasting.

Birthe Schall Holberg, a former Minister of Agriculture and the Interior, brought a story that is just as touching and reveals an aspect of Andersen's deep yearning to express his art. "The Snail and the Rosebush" reflects introvert and extrovert personalities. They are diverse aspects of human nature that dominate in different types of people. Like the rosebush, Andersen had to give the world everything within himself to be fulfilled, no matter what the cost. Holberg recalls her surprise and delight upon learning that the story in translation is a favorite among Chinese schoolchildren.

Asger Aamund, a business executive, chose the humorous portrayal of Cupid in "The Naughty Boy," who has the audacity to go around shooting people through the heart with his arrows, even the unsuspecting and unready, even your parents and grandparents, causing them to fall in love!

Birthe Ronn Hornbech was the Assistant Minister of Police who grew up in the country and enjoyed the many evenings her aunt would come to visit and read Andersen's tales to her. As a country girl, the story "There is a Difference" was her choice. It is an analogy dealing with the social distinctions of both flowers and plants in the garden, on the one hand, and people in society, on the other. Andersen wrote it to castigate the arrogance of those who consider themselves better than others because of their wealth and social position yet he ends without a call for social justice, preferring to take the view that the sun was made to shine on everyone — the evil just as much as the righteous.

Ulrich Beuning, a film consultant, explained his preference for "Clumsy Hans" and believes that had Andersen lived longer, he would have made a first-rate film screenwriter. Clumsy Hans is the rejected, ignorant third son in a family where his two brothers are paragons of virtue, scholarship and polite manners as well as encyclopedic (and useless) knowledge. One knows the Latin dictionary by heart (Latin was Andersen's most hated subject when he tried to make up for his lack of a formal education) and the other is familiar with all the laws. The story is a satire and attack on much of the formal education that was considered essential in early 19th-century Denmark. Both older brothers use cod liver oil to "talk more smoothly" but Clumsy Hans outwits them both and wins the hand of the beautiful princess!

The last guest was Mogens Lykketoft, a former Minster of the Treasury, who chose the well known "The Ugly Duckling," which may readers and critics consider to be autobiographical. For Lykketoft and many others, reading this story was an important act of self-therapy not to be bitter and seek revenge but rather to develop one's natural talents and beauty. Even if these talents and skills are not evident at first, they will inevitably bloom.

Andersen's "The Most Incredible Thing" ("*Det Utroligste*"): A Tale for All Time

Although none of the twelve participants in the television special on the 200th anniversary mentioned this story, it is my favorite. Andersen wrote this tale in 1872. It was his response to a question that would torment other authors and intellectuals in his lifetime and during the 20th century — how to deal with the problem of evil and imminent threats to our civilization. The response has ranged from abject surrender to open confrontation. The first was personified by Stefan Zweig, the great Austrian Jewish author, who committed suicide in Brazil in 1942, after completing his memoirs, so aptly titled *The World of Yesterday*. Zweig believed that the humane cosmopolitan civilization he had known was doomed by the evil bestiality of Nazism and could not defeat it. It is perhaps fitting that he is not remembered today whereas a dozen German, Russian, American, British and Italian authors rose up to the challenge of both fascism and communism and fought them with every fiber of their being — Erich Maria Remarque (*All Quiet on the Western Front*), Thomas Mann ("An Appeal to Reason," *Buddenbrooks, Joseph and His Brothers*), Ignacio Silone (*Bread and Wine*), George Orwell (*1984, Homage to Catalonia*), Aleksandr Solzhenitsyn (*The Gulag Archipelago, One Day in the Life of Ivan Denisovich*), Ernest Hemmingway (*For Whom the Bell Tolls*) and others.

Remarkably, the great Danish "fairy storyteller" from "oh so peaceful and tranquil Denmark" belongs in the latter group. His story "The Most Incredible Thing" turned out to be a prescient warning to future generations. It was taken up by the Danish Resistance Movement that had struggled during the early years of German occupation (1940–42) to rally support for active sabotage and an end to the government's policy of appeasement.

Opposing appeasement, a Danish resistance movement took shape. Among those active was a group of scholars led by professors Paul Rubow and Elias Bredsdorff who encouraged and helped publish new editions of "The Most Incredible Thing" with illustrations that were an open call to resist the occupation and vindicate Andersen's belief that, in the face of pervasive, aggressive, violent evil, only eternal vigilance, armed preparedness and vigorous, unreserved military action, are the only means to ensure the survival of civilization.

The Plot of "The Most Incredible Thing"

The story opens as many other Andersen tales with the search for a husband for the king's daughter, who will be rewarded with half the kingdom. The challenge for the many aspiring suitors is to perform the "most incredible thing" and they outdo one another with grotesque, absurd pranks from spitting on their own backs to eating themselves. A day is set aside for an exhibition of unbelievable things and the immediate winner in this competition is the maker of a great hall clock which has a series of moving figures that symbolize important features of our civilization and duly appear each hour.

These features and their respective times are as follows:

- Moses writing the first commandment to symbolize there is ONE true God at the hour of 1:00.
- Adam and Eve in the Garden of Eden at the stroke of 2:00.
- The Three Wise Men bringing gifts to the manger at the birth of Jesus at the stroke of 3:00.
- The four seasons at the stroke of 4:00.
- The five senses at the stroke of 5:00.
- A gambler symbolizing good fortune rolling dice that come up "double sixes" at the strike of 6:00.
- The seven days of the week at the stroke of 7:00.
- A choir of monks singing the eight o'clock evensong at the stroke of 8:00.
- The nine muses representing the arts at the stroke of 9:00.
- The Ten Commandments at the stroke of 10:00.
- A group of dancing boys and girls who sing a rhyme, "All the way to heaven, the clock struck eleven."
- A night watchman wearing a cap and carrying the "morning star," a truncheon tipped with spikes who, at the stroke of the midnight hour, sings the song "Twas at the Midnight Hour Our Savior He Was Born."

Everyone agrees that this was the most marvelous, charming and incredible thing. It represents all the values, beliefs and aspects of our civilization and life on earth we hold dear. The artist who made it is a sincere and generous young man who is kind and loves his parents. The crowd considers him a worthy candidate to marry the princess.

The day for the wedding arrives and everyone in town is celebrating when suddenly a "tall powerful bony fellow" strides forth and announces that "I am the man to do the most incredible thing" and he swings his powerful axe at the craftsman's clock and leaves it in ruins. He boasts to the crowd, "I did that. My work beat his — I have done the most incredible thing."

The people and the judges of the competition as well as the king are astounded and terrified. In a certain sense, of course, the arrogant, evil lout who has destroyed the most incredible thing ever produced inherits the mantle of "greatness" in a perverse way. This is the raw terror and contempt of civilization that characterized the Nazis of two generations ago and Al-Qaeda and the Islamist fanatics of today.

Their very contempt for what is most important and cherished by us instills a pervasive fear. No one can challenge him. The judges agree that he is entitled to the title of having done the most incredible thing by destroying what was the most incredible thing and the king must observe his own rule about marriage to the princess because "a law is a law." The judges declare that "to destroy such a work of art is the most incredible thing we've ever seen!"

Translated into today's realities, this absurd respect for the "law" because a "law is a law," even if it affords no protection to those who bound themselves by it, is the very same ultra-legalistic attitude of all those who insisted that the U.N. could not endorse the joint American and British action against Saddam Hussein following the unanimous votes of 16 U.N. resolutions. The final of these resolutions before the invasion promised "dire consequences" but then did nothing except urge restraint and the adoption of another resolution because "a law is a law."

The reaction of the lout in the story is exactly that of a Hitler, Pol Pot, Mao Tse-Tung, Kim Il-Sung, Mussolini, Ceausescu, Ahmadinejad and Saddam Hussein. In Andersen's words, "From the way he strutted and swaggered about, you'd think that nothing could ever bowl him over."

When all seems lost and the wedding ceremony is about to begin, the church doors are flung open and behold, all the works of art in the clock that had seemingly been destroyed stride down the aisle and march up to the bride and groom. How have they been reassembled? Because, as Andersen writes, "Dead men cannot walk the earth. That's true, but a work of art does not die. Its shape may be shattered but the spirit of art cannot be broken."

The clock begins to strike the hours again and all the figures reappear at their customary time. At the stroke of twelve, the watchman appears. He confronts the lout and smites him on the forehead with his "morning star" truncheon, killing him on the spot.

The people are amazed and now remark that indeed they have lived to see the most incredible thing. The princess summons the craftsman who had made the clock, proclaiming that he shall be her husband and lord. The assembled crowd is overjoyed and relieved and all bless the hero who has come to the rescue and no one was even envious of him because they knew he had acted while they had been paralyzed by fear.

In the 1942 Danish publication of "The Most Incredible Thing," the final picture portrays the watchman who strikes down the lout as a Jewish rabbi with hat and beard standing above the fallen, semi-naked, Aryan-looking "muscle man" who is pinned to the floor by the twin tables of the Ten Commandments inscribed with Hebrew letters and surrounded by a crowd of ordinary Danes in 1940s dress.

Andersen would undoubtedly have been pleased that his story about resistance to evil and the faith he had in the values of our civilization would inspire his countrymen in World War II at a time when opportunists and those who had favored a policy of appeasement for Denmark preached that resistance was hopeless. The moral of the story is just as true today.

Denmark currently has a small force of soldiers in Iraq and Afghanistan, a long-time reversal of previous left-wing governments' policy not to be identified with the War on Terror (as it was called until recently). The infamous cartoon rage in the Islamic world against Danish interests and random threats to carry out acts of terrorism against both military and civilians only increased initial public support for the forces.

Although support among the general public has waned and been replaced with growing disillusion as the conflict drags on without any prospect of a resolution of some kind, the renewed interest in Andersen and his work prompted by the 200th anniversary of the author's birth have caused a new evaluation of how relevant some of his "minor" stories are for our time. Andersen was indeed a "Great Dane," probably the Dane who has made the greatest impact on the consciousness of more people from more cultures around the world than anyone else.

P.S. Readers are also referred to Ramona Koval's interview of me about the life and work of H.C. Andersen on Australian National Radio in October 2007. It may be found on the internet at www.abc.net.au/rn/bookshow/stories/2007/_2057716.htm.

Chapter 18

Søren Kierkegaard

I agonized for a long time on how to introduce a chapter on the work
of Søren Kierkegaard (as might be expected of anyone daring to write a brief
summary of the monumental treatises, volumes and essays of one of the greatest minds among more than three thousand years of philosophic inquiry).
Who am I as an authority? Nobody! But like most readers who have attempted
to struggle through a course in Philosophy 101, listened to college students
arguing passionately over existentialism, or seen a few Woody Allen movies,
dropping his name is regarded as the "in" thing to do to acquire credentials
as an intellectual or profound thinker. I don't subscribe to any of those ploys.
What makes him worthy of a chapter in this book is not simply his Danish
background as a contemporary of Hans Christian Andersen and Johannes
Grundtvig, but an acknowledged genius whose work has long survived him
and who expressed many of our deepest thoughts and doubts about life and
ourselves.

I begin with what I consider to be the five most profound statements
from his work that speak to all of us:

1. "One sticks one's finger into the soul to tell by the smell what land one is in. I
   stick my finger in existence — it smells of nothing. Where am I ? Who am I?
   How came I here? What is this thing called the world? What does this world
   mean? Who is it that has lured me into the world? Why was I not consulted?
   Why not made acquainted with its manners and customs instead of throwing
   me into its ranks, as if I had been bought by a kidnapper, a dealer in souls?
   How did I obtain an interest in this big enterprise they call reality? And if I
   am compelled to take part in it, where is the director? I should like to make a
   remark to him. Is there no director? Whither shall I turn with my complaint?

Did he leave anything out? I don't think so. By the way, the director is
not God. Before going any further, let me state unequivocally that in spite
of all you may have heard about Kierkegaard as the father of existentialism
or associated with such dictums as "life is absurd" and has no meaning as

interpreted by Sartre, Kafka, Heidegger, Camus, and dozens of others who rejected God and religion in order to justify all and any behavior, this was not Kierkegaard's view. He believed because as an individual he felt there was no other place, person or idea to turn to. Kierkegaard has this to say about God:

2. "To stand on one leg and prove God's existence is a very difficult thing from going on one's knees and thanking Him."

You can argue about God until the cows come home. What you must do eventually is to take a "leap of faith" and recognize his plan of salvation.

3. "Since my earliest childhood, a barb of sorrow has lodged in my heart. As long as it stays, I am ironic — if it is pulled out I shall die" (1847).

Yes, life is tough and there are no shortcuts. My best advice, learn to live with it and make it a source of ironic diversion and humor.

4. "The truth is a trap; you cannot get it without it getting you; you cannot get the truth by capturing it, only by its capturing you" (1854).

So there! Take that, all you readers who have sought/are seeking the truth and/or salvation in some political ideology. It is not there for you to seek, pursue and capture.

And for those of you who are worried about what others think of you, the media, political correctness, etc.:

5. "The truth is always in the minority, and the minority is always stronger than the majority, because as a rule, the minority is made up of those who actually have an opinion, while the strength of the majority is illusory, formed out of the crowd which has no opinion — and which therefore the next moment (when it becomes clear that the minority is the stronger) adopts the latter's opinion, which now is the majority, i.e., becomes rubbish by having the whole retinue and majority on its side. While the truth is again in a new minority" (1850).

Well, you don't have to be a psychiatrist to know that this man was a loner and

Sketch of Søren Kierkegaard by Niels Christian Kierkegaard, ca. 1840. Kierkegaard Manuscripts, Royal Library of Denmark.

that he must have had to cope with a great deal of misfortune on the order of a Job. His Lutheran faith with its emphasis of the dour values of guilt, suffering, sin and piety represent the polar opposite of Grundtvig's inspirational optimism (see chapter 16), his natural contemporary rival. For Kierkegaard, the individual is subject to an enormous burden of responsibility with an eternal choice hanging over his/her head of eternal salvation or damnation. Anxiety is the inevitable outcome, but instead of parallelizing the individual with the choice made on the threshold of eternity, Kierkegaard found that the dreaded burden is also the road to experiencing an exhilarating freedom of realizing one's own identity. This individual self is the life-work which God judges.

There is no *mediation* between the individual self and God by priest or by logical system (as in Catholicism and Hegelianism respectively). There is only the individual's own *repetition* of faith.

Woody Allen turned mocking Kierkegaard into a gag and source of much of his humor in a number of films, most notably in *Love and Death*. His life and "philosophy" may be what many people call existentialism in the sense that life is absurd and has no meaning, but it is a secular existentialism in which the logical choice to be made by the individual is simply to seek pleasure and evade all responsibility. This extends even to the absurd point of denying death; reducing love to lust; ridiculing meditation, contemplation, psychoanalysis; and spoofing "anxiety" and "choice" over trivia.

Dialogue from the film *Love and Death*:

BORIS: And so I walk through the valley of the shadow of death. Actually, make that "I run through the valley of the shadow of death"—in order to get OUT of the valley of the shadow of death more quickly, you see.

* * *

BORIS: Oh, if only God would give me some sign. If He would just speak to me once. Anything. One sentence. Two words. If He would just cough.

SONJA: Of course there's a God! We're made in His image!

BORIS: You think I was made in God's image? Take a look at me. You think He wears glasses?

SONJA: Not with those frames.

* * *

SONJA: Judgment of any system, or a priori relationship or phenomenon exists in an irrational, or metaphysical, or at least epistemological contradiction to an abstract empirical concept such as being, or to be, or to occur in the thing itself, or of the thing itself.

BORIS: Yes, I've said that many times.

* * *

[last lines of the film]

BORIS: The question is, "Have I learned anything about life?" Only that human beings are divided into mind and body. The mind embraces all the nobler aspirations, like poetry and philosophy, but the body has all the fun. The important thing, I think, is not to be bitter.... If it turns out that there IS a God, I don't think that He's evil. I think that the worst you can say about Him is that basically He's an underachiever. After all, there are worse things in life than death. If you've ever spent an evening with an insurance salesman, you know what I'm talking about. The key is to not think of death as an end, but as more of a very effective way to cut down on your expenses. Regarding love, heh, what can you say? It's not the quantity of your sexual relations that counts. It's the quality. On the other hand if the quantity drops below once every eight months, I would definitely look into it. Well, that's about it for me folks. Goodbye.

Woody Allen as the anti–Kierkegaardian "philosopher" has undoubtedly appealed to millions of fans as the arch representative of secular and materialistic hedonism, a lifestyle that became the choice of many in modern Western societies in the 20th century. In doing so, Allen also denied himself and his own roots, changing his family name; ridiculing, mocking and rejecting his parents' Orthodox Jewish background; and attacking the State of Israel to verify his ultra-cosmopolitan and liberal views.

What makes Allen, many Jews, and others on the ultra-liberal and left-wing progressive side of contemporary issues so contemptuous or ignorant of Kierkegaard? Rabbi Milton Steinberg writing in the *Menorah Journal* (1949), expressed the view that "although a thorough Christian — or as he would have put it, infinitely interested in becoming one — Søren Kierkegaard addressed himself neither to Jews or Judaism. But they have overheard him. In part because they could not help it.... Jews are well advised to be on the alert for what they can learn not only about him but about themselves also."

Rabbi Steinberg was shaken by the depths of evil manifested during the Nazi regime and World War II. He took issue with the prevailing ethos of many in his contemporary American Jewish community whose optimism and beliefs in human progress and perfectibility and their concerns about material success had made them woefully shortsighted in confronting life's challenges and the potential destructive power of evil.

Kierkegaard's Life

Judging from his philosophy, the reader will already have guessed that Søren Kierkegaard must have had a stern upbringing and a life full of tragedy. His father Michael was a melancholic, anxious, deeply pious, and fiercely intelligent man. Five of his seven children died before he did and, driven to despair and convinced that he had earned God's wrath, Michael, like Job in the Bible, cursed God. Søren's only surviving sibling, Peter, became Bishop of Aalborg. The religious strain in the family ran deep.

Kierkegaard attended the Copenhagen School of Civic Virtue, where he studied Latin and history, among other subjects. In 1830, he entered the University of Copenhagen and was drawn to literature and philosophy. Perhaps it was Kierkegaard who set the modern style of those young men who are budding philosophers and would-be intellectuals by adopting an outlandish hairstyle. A friend attending his brother's wedding celebration in 1836 wrote: "I found his appearance almost comical. He was then twenty-three years old; he had something quite irregular in his entire form and had a strange coiffure. His hair rose almost six inches above his forehead into a tousled crest that gave him a strange, bewildered look."

Regine Olsen and Graduation (1837–1841)

Kierkegaard met "the love of his life," Regine Olsen, in May 1837. They were instantly attracted to each other. In his journals, Kierkegaard wrote devotedly of Regine as "the sovereign of his heart" and, in September 1840, he formally proposed to her yet he soon felt misgivings and doubts about the prospects of the marriage and the effects it might have on his future career. He broke off the engagement in August 1841, though it is generally believed that the two were deeply in love. Kierkegaard wrote in his journals that his "melancholy" would make him unsuitable for marriage.

His father died at age 82 in 1838, leaving behind the wish that his son should finish his education in theology. Perhaps the father's wish was motivated by the desire to atone for his having cursed God. Kierkegaard wrote in his diary, "I had so very much wished that he might live a few years longer, and I look upon his death as the last sacrifice which he made to his love for me; ... he died for me in order that, if possible, I might still turn into something. Of all that I have inherited from him, the recollection of him, his transfigured portrait ... is dearest to me, and I will be careful to preserve [his memory] safely hidden from the world."

With his family's considerable inheritance, Kierkegaard was able to fund his education, his living, and several publications of his early works.

Early Writings and *The Corsair* Affair (1841–1846)

Kierkegaard's first noteworthy works were his university thesis, *On the Concept of Irony with Continual Reference to Socrates*, 1841, and his masterpiece and arguably greatest work, *Either/Or*, 1843. In the same year *Either/Or* was published, Kierkegaard discovered that Regine Olsen was engaged to be married to a civil servant. This fact affected Kierkegaard and his subsequent writings deeply.

On December 22, 1845, Peder Møller, a young author and student at the University of Copenhagen, published an article indirectly criticizing Kierkegaard's work *Stages on Life's Way*. It complimented Kierkegaard for his wit and writing ability but questioned his ability to marshal his talents so as to write coherent, complete works. Møller also wrote for *The Corsair*, a Copenhagen satirical paper that lampooned almost everyone of notable standing. Kierkegaard responded with a satire of his own, describing Møller's article as an attempt to impress Copenhagen's literary elite. This created a lively controversy with the editor, a talented writer and poet in his own right, Meir Aaron Goldschmidt.

Kierkegaard openly challenged *The Corsair* to satirize him. And Goldschmidt took Kierkegaard up on his offer to "be abused." The periodical unleashed a series of articles ridiculing every aspect of Kierkegaard's appearance, voice, habits and views. This aroused intense public interest and for the next few months Kierkegaard became the victim (or so he imagined) of harassment on the streets of Copenhagen. This only reinforced Kierkegaard's views about the whims of public opinion and the integrity of the individual to stand fast against criticism and even ridicule.

In spite of Kierkegaard's running disputes with both Goldschmidt and Grundtvig, all three were Danish patriots devoted to love of their homeland, the Danish language and Denmark's cause in the dispute with the Schleswig-Holstein separatists. Only readers of Danish can appreciate Kierkegaard's love and enthusiasm for the Danish tongue and the extraordinary contributions he made to its literary form with his finely chiseled and elegant language.

Kierkegaard was a detractor of George Wilhelm Friedrich Hegel, the German philosopher, who was the acknowledged leading thinker in the field during the 1830s and 1840s. Kierkegaard's main point was the belief in personal immortality and he was appalled by Hegel's substitution for God by what the German philosopher called the "Absolute Spirit," the submission of the individual to the will of the state.

What is truly remarkable about Kierkegaard was his determination to remain an isolated non-conformist battling even the established Lutheran church in Denmark, which one might think should have been in ally. He opposed Grundtvig's lenient humanistic approach to religion and attacked church officials and the Danish bourgeoisie for following what he believed was a superficial and hypocritical adherence to church doctrine. Although an ordained minister, Kierkegaard never took a position as pastor.

His Death and Legacy

At his creative peak he published 12 books in 18 months (1843–44), using many pseudonyms, sometimes even satirizing his own books under a different name. Kierkegaard was suddenly stricken with a spinal disease as well as epilepsy and collapsed in the street during one of his daily walks in October 1855. He died a few weeks later, on November 11, 1855.

The Austrian Wittgenstein, the Spaniard Unamuno, the Englishman Robert Poole were all men of letters and philosophers who learned Danish specifically to read Kierkegaard (why else would you unless you had a Danish girlfriend or boyfriend? That's why I did). Kierkegaard has also had a considerable influence on 20th-century literature. Writers deeply influenced by his work include W.H. Auden, Jorge Luis Borges, Herman Hesse, Franz Kafka, Flannery O'Connor, Rainer Maria Rilke and John Updike. Kierkegaard also had a major impact on psychology and therapy, and several prominent psychologists have cited him as an important figure in their research and work including, Erich Fromm, Viktor Frankl, Rollo May and others — oh yes, and quite unintentionally, the American film producer Woody Allen.

Chapter 19

Arne Sørensen and Danish Unity

On the eve of World War II, various so-called Right-Wing authoritarian regimes of the conservative, traditional, national and religious type, namely Ethiopia's Emperor Haile Selassie, Austria's clerical-fascist regime of Engelbert Dollfuss and Kurt Schuschnigg, Poland's president and military leader General Jozef Pilsudski, Yugoslavia's General Simovic and his supporters in the armed forces and Greece's leader Ionnas Metaxas all resolutely opposed the expansionist ambitions of Hitler and Mussolini. Although remote from the background of traditional politicians on Denmark's liberal social democratic stage and the traditional conservative upper middle class, Arne Sørensen, the founder of a far right political party helped initiate the first call for active resistance to the German occupation. His name today is unknown outside of Denmark but his legacy and odd-man-out status deserves to be recalled.

Those on the political left like to bask in the false glow of Hollywood's traditional bias that created dozens of movies dealing with how heroes, often portrayed by macho types such as Humphrey Bogart, Gregory Peck, John Garfeld and Gary Cooper (praised to the sky when he played the hero of *For Whom the Bells Toll* but reviled when he acted as the brilliant architectural genius whose designs are rejected by his colleagues) outwit and outfight the fascists, Nazis and homegrown conservative politicians who are Southern racists, anti–Semites and misogynists, or worst of all, the very symbol of evil, Senator Joseph McCarthy.

The idea that the wartime resistance to the Nazis anywhere could have been initiated by a right-wing or fascist party (as they were labeled by the political Left in Denmark before the war) is supposed to be an oxymoron. In general, a very large proportion of liberals and many Jews accept the thesis that to be right wing is ipso facto to be fascist and anti–Semitic or, the contrary, that to be a Liberal means you necessarily must be anti-anti–Semitic. Neither is necessarily true.

Just before the outbreak of World War II, liberal left social-democratic/

labor-dominated governments in Britain, France, Belgium, the Netherlands, and Denmark were all reluctant to oppose German expansionism and aggressive Nazi designs. Under the German occupation, collaborators were found to offer a façade of home rule under German protection. During the "honeymoon" between Stalin and Hitler from August 1939 to the invasion of the USSR on June 22, 1941, the governments and communist parties in these countries more than just acquiesced in the occupation. They opposed any renewal of the war effort and discouraged attempts at sabotage or resistance of any active kind.

In Denmark, Christian X was a puppet king. He did not choose, as did other monarchs such as The Queen Wilhelmina of Holland and King Haakon of Norway, to flee to England and help in the establishment of a government in exile. During the first three years of the occupation and in full agreement with the Danish government, the king warned his fellow countrymen not to participate in acts of sabotage against the German occupation forces. This was the government line that he adhered to and which also guaranteed Denmark a special relatively mild status, including no discriminatory measures against the Danish Jews until the planned deportation in October 1943.

The first steps calling for active resistance in occupied Denmark were taken by a small ultra-rightist party often denounced by many observers before the war as fascist and known as "Dansk Samling" (Danish Unity) and its charismatic founder, Arne Sørensen (1906–1978). The party was founded in 1936 and contested elections in 1939, 1943, 1945, 1947, 1953 and then once more in 1964. Based on a form of Christian nationalism, it presented itself as a "third way" between socialism and liberalism. Its rejection of Denmark's parliamentary system of multiple political parties, each catering to selected interest groups, led to accusations of fascism, although it clearly rejected anti–Semitism and denounced Nazi doctrines as evil, pagan and a threat to Western civilization.

Sørensen was born in 1906 in the northwestern Himmerland region of Jutland and originally educated in business administration but became a teacher, journalist and author taking part in the debate over Denmark's social, economic and political future. He attracted attention by criticizing the traditional parties of both the right and the left. He expressed support for dynamic leaders who were not bound by catering to divisive and selfish interests, a view that initially was understood as support for a Mussolini or Hitler in Danish politics. What he meant was a leader who could rally a large segment of the people across party, regional, confessional and class lines.

Arne Sørensen came from a humble rural background far from the center of power in Copenhagen. His father was a smallholder eking out an existence and unable to provide support for his ambitious son. In quick succession, the young Sørensen became drawn to the capital, involved with politics, a modern poet, a freelance journalist for the great liberal Copenhagen daily *Politiken* and a teacher. He gradually veered away from the radical-socialist milieu and adopted a vision of a third way in politics between with the traditional standpoints of the labor movement and the conservative free market.

Although Sørensen was dismayed by the parliamentary form of Danish democracy, any brief attraction he may have had for European fascism quickly faded with the growing fanaticism of Hitler's anti–Semitism and its anti–Christian ideology. Added to this repulsion was the growing conviction that a large part of the Danish public had failed to rally around any strong sense of national will, a conviction aided and abetted by the social democratic party in power, which failed to understand the threat of German expansionism. He became strongly involved in the movement to protect Denmark's border with Germany.

In the 1939 election to the parliament when Dansk Samling received only 8,000 votes and no seats, it had appealed unsuccessfully to all the Danish parties to present a common Danish front in South Jutland, the critical border area where an aggressive German minority was increasingly being financed and encouraged to exhibit irredentist demands for a revision of the 1920 border in Germany's favor.

Sørensen had been in touch with both ethnic Danes in the German-occupied South and with refugees who were able to provide realistic and reliable information on the anti–Nazi "confessional church" led by Dietrich Bonhoeffer whose 700 pastors had been imprisoned by the Gestapo. His newly found interest in the border issue brought him into contact with the distinguished historian Vilhelm la Cour in the summer of 1940. La Cour's joining Dansk Samling created a stir and brought the party new prestige. By the autumn of 1941 both Sørensen and la Cour had been arrested by the government for their publication of illegal leaflets calling for a restoration of Danish pride and resistance to the German occupation.

It continues to rankle some historians and pundits that it was the "anti-democratic" Dansk Samling on the far right of the political spectrum under Sørensen's leadership that took the lead as early as the spring of 1941 to call for active resistance against the German occupation. For all those without ideological blinkers, it is not difficult to understand. Dansk Samling's stand was based on Danish nationalism, anti–Nazism and a continued mistrust of the established parties' politicians for appealing to small and divided constituencies primarily about immediate bread and butter issues that ignored larger national questions and the ethical and moral standards derived from Christian principles.

In the spring of 1942, British Special Operations Executive (SOE) began to infiltrate agents into Denmark by parachute to organize armed resistance. The Danish agent in charge of operations, Christian Michael Rottbøll, contacted Danish Unity's leaders as the most promising initial address with a request for assistance. They both arranged for the accommodation, identification documents, and ration coupons for the agents as well as transmission locations for the radio operators. Active members of Danish Unity (a few of them were former volunteers for Finland during the 1940 Winter War) organized the Holger Dansker resistance group that carried out sabotage against the German occupying forces and their installations.

At this juncture, the king and government under duress and the fear of German reprisals still continued to broadcast appeals to the Danish population not to engage or help in sabotage or threaten the relations between the civilian government and the German occupying forces. The Danish communist party had only just begun to recover from the shock of the German invasion of the USSR in June 1941 and begun to seriously mount an effective campaign of resistance, after almost two years of having criticized the Allied war effort as "the preservation of the British and French colonial empires."

Following the German invasion of the Soviet Union, the Danish Communist Party was made illegal and immediately went underground. Throughout 1942, it organized to carry out a resistance against the occupation forces but it was not involved in the first serious acts of sabotage carried out by students and former Danish volunteer veterans who had fought in the 1940 Winter War on the Finnish side. On January 25, 1943, a group of students who had previously been refused membership in the communist resistance group due to the mistrust held by its members toward what Stalinist ideology still regarded as elitism and the bourgeois character of the group set fire to a stock of German listening devices at *Dansk Industrisyndikat* in Hellerup (suburb of Copenhagen).

Only after this action were the students accepted into the group, and this caused a change of name from the original KOPA (*Kommunistiske Partisaner*, Communist Partisans) to BOPA (The "B" for Bourgeois). In the last election of the Danish parliament under German occupation in the summer of 1943, Dansk Samling was still officially regarded as a legal party and able to participate. It won three seats and a popular vote of over 40,000. The vote was also a wakeup call for the majority party, the social democrats, to undertake a major shift in policy and defend Danish rights even if it meant a break with the occupying German forces. The fact that Dansk Samling was still a legal party and allowed to participate in the national election of 1943 as a bone thrown by the German occupation authorities to bolster their claim that they were not interfering with the Danes' right to manage their own affairs gave the Communists added prestige as the major political force of the Resistance. Their pre-war stand as pacifists committed to neutrality was thus largely forgotten and forgiven.

In September 1943, the Danish Freedom Council in London was created as a shadow government in exile. This attempted to unify the many different groups that made up the Danish resistance movement. The council was made up of seven resistance representatives including Arne Sørensen and the Danish Communists and one member of SOE. The resistance movement had grown to over 20,000 by the summer of 1944 and, in the lead-up to D-Day, acts of sabotage markedly increased. Though the D-Day landings were to be in Normandy, SOE believed that the more German soldiers who were tied up elsewhere in Europe, the fewer that could be present in northern France. Therefore, the more acts of sabotage in Denmark, the more German troops would be tied down there.

In 1944, the Danish Freedom Council stepped up its efforts and more than 11 million copies of underground newspapers were published. That June, following a declared state of emergency, the entire city of Copenhagen went on strike. Infuriated, German troops flooded the city, cut off water and electricity, and established a blockade. From this time, all Danes under occupation looked towards London and the Freedom Council as their legitimate government in exile.

By then, Sørensen had reached London, where he was instrumental in trying to formulate a policy that would gain recognition for the Danish minority in the North Schleswig region following the collapse of Nazi Germany. He was encouraged to believe that the British would favor the internationalization of the Kiel Canal and involve Danish troops to occupy a zone North of the Canal.

In the first postwar election in 1945, Dansk Samling won 64,000 votes and increased its representation to four representatives but the Communists emerged as the major force profiting from their wartime resistance (however belated). It proved a major disappointment for Sørensen who saw his fears realized that the old-style politics of division and cultivation of special interests would return as the standard format of Danish politics.

By the liberation of Denmark on May 5, 1945, the communists were widely seen as the most effective underground resistance movement. This was due in part to their greater experience in military training that included several dozen veterans of the Spanish Civil War and the rise in prestige of the party due to the success of spectacular sabotage actions, especially the destruction of several factories in Copenhagen. The Danish communist Party emerged from World War II with the prestige of having been active in the resistance and their status as an illegal underground organization as early as June 1941.

Both la Cour and Sørensen became deeply involved in the postwar effort to support the Movement of the Danish Minority in Germany (SydSlesvig Forening SSF — The South Schleswig Association) that experienced an explosive growth from 1945 to 1947. The Danish government was astounded by the renewal of sentiment for Denmark and a forty-fold growth in membership compared to the 1939 size of the Danish minority. They were, however, careful at making any demands for a new plebiscite and were reluctant to be swept up by emotions.

The failure of most of the traditional Danish political parties and the opposition of the communists to any border change and a general desire to return to normalcy meant that Danish Unity had no further prospects for continued growth. It has since stagnated and declined. The grandiose plans and commitment to win back part of South Schleswig formulated by Sørensen and others among nationalist circles were regarded by the majority of the Danish public as too ambitious and risky.

Dansk Samling still exists today as a political organization but not a party. Many of its former supporters lost faith in its ability to present a realistic alternative to the traditional Danish multi-party system catering to special interests. It opposed Denmark's membership in the European Union and is highly critical of the large-scale immigration from North Africa, the Middle East, and East Asia that has created a substantial foreign population of residents or citizens who do not identify with Danish history, language, values and traditions.

Former supporters of Arne Sørensen believe he made a critical mistake in joining a postwar government after the rejection of his South Schleswig policies and became Kirkeminister (a Danish Minister of Religious Affairs tied to the state-affiliated Danish Lutheran church), a position without any real influence and easy to satirize and even lampoon. Opponents have laughingly referred to the remnants of the party as a form of "Danish Disunity."

Danish Unity continues to be against "all-isms." It unabashedly proclaims that its central point is to embrace and cultivate all that is essentially Danish and the belief that Denmark cannot just be the address of new immigrants but that the home of the Danish people and all that it has created of lasting value, the Danish language, its Christian heritage, tolerance, culture and ideals without any disrespect for other peoples.

The Wikipedia entry on the internet under the title "Danish Resistance" mentions the Holger Danske Group but has nothing to say about Dansk Samling or Arne Sørensen in its list of prominent members of the Freedom Council. The Holocaust Research Project, a Jewish website called HEART (Holocaust Education and Archive Research Team) mentions both BOPA and the Holger Danske group but is likewise silent about Dansk Samling and Arne Sørensen.

These sites and others proudly give full credit to the Danish communist party as the leading element in the Danish resistance. This is the same hard-line Stalinist party that endorsed the Soviet invasion of Finland in December 1939 and called the outbreak of World War II on September 1 as a war between European imperialist powers that meant nothing for the international working class except needless bloodshed.

Arne Sørensen, like other conservative politicians such as Winston Churchill and Charles De Gaulle, stood defiantly and consistently against the Nazis at a time (Sept. 1939–June 1941) when the Communist parties and their fellow travelers on the International Left under the tutelage of Moscow regarded the war as a conflict between rival imperialist powers and not in the interests of the working class. This line was followed even more vigorously when Churchill became prime minister in May 1940, following the defeat and occupation of France and Denmark, and vowed never to surrender. In defeated France, De Gaulle was attacked by the Communist press for trying to rally a "Free French" Resistance and his conservative background was prominently mentioned as a reason why workers should not be duped into following him. In January 1941, the British House of Commons voted 297 to 11 to shut down the *Daily Worker* Communist newspaper because of its subversive anti-war stance. Notwithstanding these facts, much of how World War II has been treated in Hollywood displays collective amnesia and insists on idealizing the "heroic Left" as the only source of the Resistance.

On the same day that Denmark was invaded by the German army (April 9, 1940), Stalin's henchmen were busy murdering thousands of Polish army officers in the Katyn Forest, an unprecedented atrocity of the most gruesome proportions, an event denied by the Soviet and Danish Communist parties from 1943 onwards until admitted by them during the last days of the existence of the USSR.

Arne Sørensen, like the Danish prince Hamlet, suffered "the slings and arrows of outrageous fortune." He left a legacy that should not be forgotten.

Chapter 20

Arne Jacobsen: The Father
of Danish Design

From 1940 to 1945, four prominent Danes — physics professor and 1922 Nobel Prize winner Niels Bohr, entertainer Victor Borge, engineer and poet Piet Hein, and architect and interior designer Arne Jacobsen — all took a stand against the Nazis and the occupation of their country. The last three were wholly unknown outside the borders of their small homeland while Bohr was a distinguished world figure and Nobel prize winner in physics.

Each went into exile but they did so not to abandon the fight but to help promote the cause of their homeland and the plight of their fellow citizens trapped at home and refute the great Nazi lie that Denmark had wisely sought "German protection." Each was Jewish or had a Jewish connection — either a Jewish wife (Piet Hein), one Jewish parent (Niels Bohr) or were wholly of Jewish origin (Victor Borge, born Børge Rosenbaum, and Arne Jacobsen). Each of them for practical reasons were advised by colleagues to flee the country so as not to provoke Denmark's strict policy of neutrality and to refrain from making anti–Nazi statements. To their credit and the credit of all Danes, they refused to be cowed and, when no other practical alternative was possible, chose exile.

Arne Jacobsen (1902–1971), more than any other architect or designer, has come to be regarded as the innovator associated with the term "Danish modern." His career, in less dramatic terms, resembled that of such non-conformists as the fictional hero Howard Roark in the novel *The Fountainhead* by Ayn Rand, and, like the real-life figure of Frank Lloyd Wright, was an individualistic and superbly talented young architect who chose to struggle in obscurity rather than compromise his sense of integrity and personal vision.

Like them, Jacobsen had to fight to battle the public's accepted values and the official and traditional standards of his professional colleagues and the tabloid press to demonstrate what he believed was a superior and novel work of art. In so doing, he became Denmark's most influential 20th-century architect and designers and spread the concept of naturalism and Danish-Nordic design throughout the world. Jacobsen believed that the design of every component — down to the doorknobs — had to harmonious with the overall design and fit into the natural landscape. In the contracts he signed, he had a stipulation that "Professor Jacobsen should undertake as much as possible of the landscape design and the design of fixtures and fittings." His modernist classic chairs, known as the swan, egg and ant, have been duplicated and imitated in hundreds of hotels and office buildings.

Born in Copenhagen in 1902, Jacobsen began work from the ground up as an apprentice bricklayer and won a stipend to study architecture at the Royal Academy of the Arts in 1924. His humble beginning afforded him the first-hand feel and love of the materials he worked with. He began, like most architects, by designing private homes, fusing "rationalist simplicity" with classic elegance. This formula attracted the attention of larger clients and projects and Jacobsen was entrusted with major commissions such as an extension to the Nøvo pharmaceuticals factory and the Stelling Hus in Copenhagen. In both these projects, Jacobsen took pains to integrate the new buildings with their environmental surroundings.

In 1925, Jacobsen, while still a student, traveled to Paris for the Exposition Internationale des Arts Décoratifs, where he won a silver medal for a chair design. Before leaving the Academy, Jacobsen went to Berlin, where he was impressed by the rationalist architecture of Mies and Walter Groupius whose work influenced him greatly in his early Danish projects including a design for an art gallery which won him recognition and a gold medal upon graduation. Even a mundane gas station could be transformed by Jacobsen's innovative design and turned into an architectural attraction (Texaco Station, Skovshoved, Copenhagen suburb, 1936). By 1930, Jacobsen had established his own design office, which he headed until his death in 1971, and worked independently as an architect and interior, furniture, textile and ceramics designer.

Together with colleague Erik Møller, Jacobsen designed the Aarhus City Hall, inaugurated on June 2, 1941. It won considerable praise and made his name well known. It is one of the few city halls in the country that has been marked for preservation due to its unique architecture and is still consider "modern" by almost all foreign observers who encounter it and are unaware it was finished at the start of the second World War.

The war economy and Jacobsen's exposed Jewish identity brought a standstill to his career and in 1943, sensing the imminent threat of a much harder German policy towards the Danish Jews, he left the country, rowing across the Sound to Sweden in a small boat. Between 1943 and the end of the

German occupation of Denmark in May 1945, Jacobsen lived in exile in Sweden where he designed fabrics and wallpapers.

When he returned to his homeland in 1945, the country was in urgent need of both new residential housing and public buildings. Jacobsen's late 1940s houses and apartment blocks were, by necessity of postwar shortages, quite austere in design and hastily built but by the 1950s, he had become more experimental and less ready to compromise. His designs of the 1952 Allehusene housing complex, the 1955 Søholm houses, and the 1957 radical Round House for a local fish-smoking plant near Copenhagen all gained him notoriety.

As a Dane who spoke almost no English and seldom left his Copenhagen studio, his commission in 1958 to design a new college for Oxford University attracted immediate criticism. One letter to the editor of the *London Times* described his design as "the worst insult to British architecture since the 11th century when a Frenchman had been entrusted with the rebuilding of Canterbury Cathedral."

Unmoved by the critics, the Oxford dons gave Jacobsen their confidence and he went full speed ahead with the assumption that he had been given carte blanche on every detail. The result was hailed as "a completely coherent and perfectly proportioned campus."

Jacobsen became increasingly interested in product design and inspired by the work of the U.S. furniture designers, Charles and Ray Eames. From 1951 to 1955, he completed work on the ant chair, an intricately molded plywood seat on three spindly steel legs, followed by the hourglass form of the 1955 Series 7 chair. Both designs were considered ideal for modern living, being light, compact and easily stackable, and within a decade had achieved universal popularity as two of the most popular chairs of the late 20th century.

Jacobsen went on to put his theories of integrated design and architecture into practice by designing the SAS Air Terminal and Royal Hotel in Copenhagen in which every element of the building, down to the ceramic ashtrays and the stainless steel cutlery, were planned and overseen by him and was even featured in the science fiction film *2001: A Space Odyssey*. Jacobsen also designed another two

ARNE JACOBSEN 1902-1971

7.25
DANMARK
Torben Skov del./Lars Sjööblom sc.   2007   Strüwing fot.

Arne Jacobsen, the father of Danish design.

classic 20th-century chairs for the same hotel in 1957, called the swan and egg. In spite of what looks like a strange and awkward design for his egg and ant chairs, they are very comfortable to sit in. Other unique and very untraditional Jacobsen chairs are known as "the pot," resembling a flower petal and used in the bar, and "the drop," used as a dressing table chair in the guest rooms.

Jacobsen was easy to caricature. He smoked a long-stemmed pipe and frequently sported bowties, accentuating an air of intensive introspection and a bristly nature. Colleagues frequently described him as dictatorial, exacting and elitist, yet he often took jobs (line the hero Roark in *Fountainhead*) that some critics considered at the low end of their scale of prestige projects such as a fish smokehouse, a Texaco service station and even a hotdog stand. Regin Schwaen, a Danish architect at The School of Architecture & Urban Studies, had this to say of Jacobsen: "It's difficult for me to say exactly what it is that makes you feel so comfortable in his buildings. They have a clear structure that is very logical, but still everything is brought down to a human scale. Outside a building may be brick or marble, but inside the interiors were always warm and nice. The colors would usually be in the dark blue to green range — the colors you observe in Danish nature."

Reflecting on his career a few months before his death at the age of 69 in 1971, Arne Jacobsen concluded, "The fundamental factor is proportion. Proportion is precisely what makes the old Greek temples beautiful ... and when we look at some of the most admired buildings of the Renaissance or the Baroque, we notice that they are all well-proportioned. That is the essential thing."

Chapter 21

Tycho Brahe: Astronomer without a Telescope

Denmark has produced several world-class scientists, 20th-century physicists (father and son) Niels and Christian Bohr, the 19th-century chemist and physicist Hans Christian Ørsted who first observed and analyzed electromagnetism, and two 16- and 17th-century astronomers: Ole Rømer (1644–1710), who first accurately measured the speed of light, and Tycho Brahe (1547–1601), whose accurate and methodical observations of the stars, comets and the moon paved the way for the great intellectual breakthrough of his colleague, the German mathematician and co-worker, Johannes Kepler, and the Polish Nicolas Copernicus, which ultimately dethroned the old static earth-centered universe of Ptolemy and scientific philosophy of Aristotle.

That Brahe's work is less widely known is due to the fact that his observations, the most accurate and enduring for centuries to come, were all made with the naked eye before the widespread use of the telescope, a fact that defies the imagination today. How could he have done it? What makes Tycho Brahe so fascinating was his unorthodox character, quirky and eccentric behavior, and dedication to the task of painstaking observations, undertaken solely for the love of inquiry. As one of the richest men in the kingdom at the time, he did not spare his private wealth in zealously following his love of scientific observation.

In the end, he stopped just short of completely overthrowing the old geocentric model of the universe that reduced the earth to the reality of a third-rate planet revolving around a tenth-rate star drifting in an endless cosmic ocean. He and his student Kepler achieved unprecedented recognition that science must only follow one method — seeking confirmation of mathematical relations by verification through constant observation and calculations instead of speculation over the "essence" or "meaning" of phenomena. The procedure to follow if the observations did not support the procedure must therefore be to reject the theory and seek to establish a new one in harmony with the observations. This revolution led to the transition from the classical and medieval worlds to our present one.

Tyge (his original Danish name was Latinized to Tycho) Brahe was born on December 14, 1546, in the old Danish-ruled Skåne (today southern Sweden), the oldest son of Otto Brahe and Beatte Bille, both from noble families. His parents had made a deal with Otto Brahe's brother Jørgen to raise the child who was then surrendered to his paternal uncle and became his heir at the age of two. The young boy was sent to attend the universities of Copenhagen and Leipzig, travel through Germany, and continue his education at the universities of Wittenberg, Rostock, and Basel. At the University of Wittenberg, the young Tycho got into an absurd duel with Manderup Parsberg, a fellow Danish student, and lost the bridge and upper part of his nose. For the rest of his life he wore a metal insert attached by a paste and containing gold, silver and possibly copper that may have contributed to his death from metal poisoning. Was his silver nose a help in aiming his sharp eyesight to the night sky? Maybe!

The reason for the duel was ostensibly an argument about who was most skilled in mathematics. However, the hostility between Tycho and Parsberg did not endure, and Parsberg became one of Tycho's supporters under the Danish king, Christian IV.

The Supernova in Cassiopeia

Brahe returned to Denmark in 1570. He became fascinated with astronomy when he observed the explosion of a supernova in the constellation of Cassiopeia and immediately concluded that such an enormous disruption of the "celestial harmony" of the universe meant that the stars were not fixed for all time as believed by the ancient Greeks and accepted as dogma by the church.

A brilliant new star appeared in the sky in early November 1572, outshining all other stars in brightness and was even visible during daylight. It was observed by astronomers all around the world and eventually changed our understanding of the universe forever. Tycho Brahe was uniquely able to utilize precise measurements of the star's position and reported it in his book *Stella Nova*. He was also convinced (correctly) that the star was located far beyond the moon but at the time had no way of knowing that the distance was infinitely greater than any instrument of his time could measure. Sixteenth-century scientists did not know what kind of star they had observed. Only in 1940 was it concluded that it must have been a supernova — an explosion blasting apart a star at the end of its life.

This contradiction to the Aristotelian concept, that a change in the sky can only occur in the sublunar regime, ultimately led to the abandonment of the notion of the immutability of the heavens. In 1574 Brahe gave a course of lectures on astronomy at the University of Copenhagen and became convinced that the improvement of astronomy hinged on accurate observations.

Following another tour to Germany, he accepted an offer from King Frederick II to fund an observatory and was given the little island of Hven in the Sound between Copenhagen and the Swedish coast where his observatory, called Uraniborg after the Greek goddess of the sky, Urania, became the finest observatory in Europe and a veritable ivory tower for the great astronomer to gaze at the stars for the next twenty years.

Tycho designed and built new instruments, calibrated them, and instituted nightly observations. He also ran his own printing press. The observatory was visited by many scholars, and Tycho trained a generation of young astronomers and mathematicians.

After a disagreement with the new Danish King Christian IV, Tycho packed up his instruments and books in 1597 and left Denmark. He used his own considerable funds to travel again and settled in Prague in 1599 where he received the official appointment of "imperial mathematician" at the court of Emperor Rudolph II. He died there in 1601. At Prague, Tycho hired Johannes Kepler as an assistant to calculate planetary orbits from his observations. Kepler, with the subsequent enormous advantage of being able to use telescopes, published their findings, *Tabulae Rudolphina*, in 1627, twenty-six years after Tycho's death. Because of Tycho's accurate observations and Kepler's elliptical astronomy, these tables were much more accurate than all previous calculations. Johannes Kepler used them but they remained the property of Tycho's heirs.

Tycho Brahe's contributions to astronomy were enormous. He designed and built instruments, calibrated them and checked them periodically to ensure their accuracy. He thus revolutionized astronomical instrumentation and changed observational practice profoundly. Without the complete series of observations of unprecedented accuracy, Kepler could not have discovered that planets move in ellipses or the true shape of the planetary orbits. Tycho was the first astronomer to make corrections for atmospheric refraction.

The Tychonic Universe

Tycho himself was not to confirm the full heliocentric theory (all the planets revolve around the sun as postulated by Copernicus) due to the lack of suitable instruments to accurately measure the enormous distances to the stars, of a mathematical order infinitely greater than he supposed. After his death, Jesuit scholars supported Tycho's last effort to produce a compromise solution of the solar system for another two centuries. This system envisioned the best of both worlds by keeping the Earth in the center of the universe, so that he could retain Aristotelian physics in which the moon and sun revolved about the Earth, and the shell of the fixed stars was centered on the Earth but Mercury, Venus, Mars, Jupiter, and Saturn all revolved about the sun.

This Tychonic world system became popular early in the seventeenth century among those who felt forced to reject the Ptolmeic arrangement of the planets (in which the Earth was the center of all motions) but who, for various reasons, could not accept the Copernican alternative. Tycho gave several explanations why he was unable to accept the heliocentric theory. He was not restrained by Catholic dogma. Denmark had already thrown in its lot with the Protestant Reformation in 1536 at the decision of King Christian III.

Danish postage stamp issued on the occasion of the 400th anniversary of Tycho Brahe's observation of the supernova in the constellation of Cassiopeia leading to the conclusion that the universe was not eternally fixed.

The Reformation required two years of civil war in Denmark before the new victorious king could come to power and finally carry out the transition. Tycho was therefore not afraid to speak his mind like Galileo. He had honest doubts because of his inability to carry out the necessary experiments involving the parallax of the stars, the displacement or difference in the apparent position of an object viewed along two different lines of sight, measured by the angle of inclination between those two lines.

Family Life

Tycho with his noble title could not marry a commoner and legally have his heirs inherit the title. He had fallen in love with Kirsten Hansen, the daughter of a tavern keeper in his home village of Knudstrup.

Their union of a binding morganatic marriage after three years of cohabitation during which she wore the keys to the household meant that she remained a commoner but the children were legitimate. Nevertheless, they were not entitled to inherit their father's title and coat of arms. Together the couple had eight children, six of whom survived into adulthood, and remained married for almost thirty years until the time of Tycho's death. Tycho was extremely wealthy and often held large social gatherings in his castle on the island. He kept a dwarf named Jepp as a court jester who sat under the table during dinner.

Death

It is almost comical that with his experience of so many years of intensive stargazing, Tycho's death was caused by a urinary infection. While attending a banquet in Prague and having drunk a good deal of beer, he was unable to relieve himself. He died eleven days later, on 24 October 1601. According to Kepler's firsthand account, Tycho had refused to leave the banquet to relieve himself because it would have been a breach of etiquette. Before dying, he urged Kepler to finish his work and expressed the hope that he would do so by adopting Tycho's own planetary system, rather than Copernicus's.

Some accounts have suggested that he died from mercury poisoning. Authorities in the Czech government in Prague have recently allowed a further post-mortem examination of his remains. The body has been entombed since his death in the Old Town Square of Prague near the famous Prague Astronomical Clock.

While his observatory/palace at Uraniborg existed, it was both a center of research and a school for students of both astronomy and medicine. Two craters are named Tycho and Tycho Brahe — one on the moon and one on Mars. Tycho lived by the motto "Non videri sed esse" ("Not to be seen but to be"). During the prolonged fever he suffered before his death, Tycho muttered the Latin words, *"Ne frustra vixisse videar"* over and over signifying, "May I not have lived in vain!" I think we can conclude that he did not.

Chapter 22

Niels Bohr and the
Copenhagen Mystery

Niels Henrik David Bohr (1885–1962) was the most famous and internationally known of four Danes who had to flee from their homeland during World War II. The others were Piet Hein (chapter 14), Victor Borge (chapter 15), and Arne Jacobsen (chapter 20).

He was a Nobel Prize–winning physicist (1922) whose work in understanding atomic structure and quantum mechanics was groundbreaking and often mentioned in the same breath as Einstein's theory of relativity. Bohr has been described as one of the most influential physicists of the 20th century. He was part of the team working on the Manhattan Project that produced the atomic bomb and enabled the United States to decisively end Japanese resistance to bring an end to World War II in the Pacific theater. His portrait appears on the 500 kroner banknote, in a characteristic pose with one of his favorite pipes, as much a part of his persona as Sherlock Holmes's.

Other honors he received include the first ever Atoms for Peace Award in 1957, renaming of the Institute of Physics at the University of Copenhagen to the Niels Bohr Institute, the issuance of a Danish postage stamp in 1963 depicting Bohr, the hydrogen atom and the formula for the difference of any two hydrogen energy levels: $hv = \in_2 - \in_1$, the naming of the chemical element Bohrium

Niels Bohr on 500 kroner banknote. © Danmarks Nationalbank.

(atomic number 107), the naming of Asteroid 3948 Bohr after him, and a second Danish postage stamp in 1985 depicting Bohr with his wife Margrethe.

Bohr was born in Copenhagen in 1885, the son of Ellen Adler Bohr, from a wealthy Jewish family prominent in banking and parliamentary circles, and Christian, a devout Lutheran and professor of physiology at the University of Copenhagen. His brother Harald also achieved prominence as a mathematician and member of the Danish Olympic football team. Niels shared his brother's passion for football (soccer) and the two brothers played several games together with Niels as goaltender for the Copenhagen-based Akademisk Boldklub, popularly called by its initials, AB. The team, founded in 1885, is a professional Danish football club currently playing at the second highest level of domestic Danish football, the First Division.

Niels Bohr mentored and collaborated with many of the world's leading physicists of the 20th century at his institute in Copenhagen. He married Margrethe Nørlund, the daughter of Alfred Nørlund, a pharmacist from the town of Slagelse. She was an accomplished woman in many fields who had trained at a private girls' school where she studied nursing, physiology, hygiene and home economics. Nevertheless, Margrethe poured herself into Niels' work and acquired a considerable knowledge of physics. Throughout their lives, she acted not only as a charming hostess in their home but his intellectual sidekick who he used to bounce ideas off of. One of their sons, Aage Bohr, grew up as a chip off the old block to become a world-renowned physicist and also receive the Nobel prize for physics in 1985 (the only father and son winners).

Margrethe Nørlund and Niels Bohr met in 1909 through the agency of Poul and Niels Erik, her two brothers, who were his close friends, became engaged in 1910, and married in 1911 in a short civil ceremony. Both of them, although coming from different religious traditions, experienced a brief but intensive period of faith as teenagers, around the age of bar mitzvah/confirmation and then subsequently rejected a belief in God. She became his indispensable companion, intellectual sidekick, secretary and assistant, drafting notes and debating with him. She accompanied him on many of his travels and on one occasion saved his life by grabbing the steering wheel of their car after Niels had lost control. Bohr and his wife had six sons. Their oldest, Christian Alfred, tragically died in a boating accident. Another died from childhood meningitis. The others went on to lead successful lives.

Bohr began his academic career as an undergraduate at Copenhagen University studying mathematics and philosophy in 1905. Utilizing his father's laboratory, Niels ran a series of experiments to examine the properties of surface tension and his essay summarizing the procedure and results won a gold medal competition award sponsored by the Royal Danish Academy of Sciences and Letters, prompting him to give up his philosophy studies and adopt physics.

He received his Ph.D. in 1911 and went on to study under Sir Ernest Rutherford at the University of Manchester where, on the basis of Rutherford's theories, Bohr published his model of atomic structure in 1913, thus making widely known the theoretical structure of the atom we know so well today of electrons traveling in orbits around the nucleus of the atom and the table of elements illustrating their chemical properties as determined by the number of electrons in the outer orbits. Bohr also introduced the idea that an electron could drop from a higher energy orbit to a lower one, emitting a photon (light quantum) of discrete energy. This paved the way for the elaboration of quantum theory.

Those familiar with the significance of his scientific work abroad are generally unaware of the influence of Danish philosopher Søren Kierkegaard (chapter 18) on Bohr's work. In *The Making of the Atomic Bomb*, author Richard Rhodes argues that Bohr was influenced by Kierkegaard via the philosopher Harald Høffding, an old friend of Bohr's father. In 1909, Niels sent Kierkegaard's *Stages on Life's Way* as a birthday gift to his brother Harald and in the enclosed letter, wrote, "It is the only thing I have to send home; but I do not believe that it would be very easy to find anything better.... I even think it is one of the most delightful things I have ever read." Bohr enjoyed Kierkegaard's language and literary style, but mentioned that he had some "disagreement with Kierkegaard's ideas."

Bohr's merger of science and philosophy had to do with the principle of complementarity: that items could be separately analyzed as having several contradictory properties. For instance, physicists currently conclude that light behaves either as a wave or a stream of particles — two apparently mutually exclusive properties depending on how one carries on the investigation. It is precisely this point that has linked Bohr's science with the philosophy of Søren Kierkegaard (author of the essay *Either/Or*). Bohr found this had important philosophical applications. While Einstein preferred the determinism of classical physics over the probabilistic new quantum physics, he and Bohr had good-natured arguments over the truth of this principle throughout their lives.

The two scientists along with Max Planck were the founders of the original quantum theory and their "debates" are remembered because of their importance to the philosophy of science. Einstein believed that physics would tell him what was happening in the "real world behind the equations," while Bohr was primarily interested in the equations themselves and did not worry about an underlying reality.

In 1916, Niels Bohr became a professor of physics at the University of Copenhagen and, with the assistance of the Danish government and the Carlsberg Foundation, was appointed as Director of the Institute for Theoretical Physics in 1921. The institute served as served as a focal point for theoretical physicists in the 1920s and '30s. Most of the world's best known theoretical physicists of that period spent some time there.

Bohr achieved greater fame in the rapidly expanding field of nuclear physics and the theoretical foundations for the application of nuclear fission for energy, and of course, the bomb, although he originally envisioned this possibility as beyond the means of technical accomplishment (at least that was his view and that of his most famous student, Werner Heisenberg in 1939).

Relationship with Werner Heisenberg: What Happened at Their Meeting and the Play *Copenhagen*

The German physicist Werner Heisenberg worked as assistant to Bohr and university lecturer in Copenhagen from 1926 to 1927 and developed his uncertainty principle, while working on the mathematical foundations of quantum mechanics. Heisenberg later became head of the German atomic bomb project. Bohr was able to escape from Denmark just prior to the attempted round-up and deportation of Danish Jews (including individuals who like Bohr, were of part-Jewish ancestry). In October 1943, he reached Sweden and from there was flown to London where he was quickly asked again to join the British effort. On the flight from Stockholm to London in an unarmed De Havilland Mosquito, Bohr did not bother with putting on his oxygen equipment as instructed and passed out at high altitude.

It is likely he would have died had not the pilot responded immediately. Sensing that the lack of response from the Danish scientist was the result of loss of consciousness, the pilot immediately descended to a lower altitude for the remainder of the flight. As with his wife's rescue in their car when he lost control of the steering wheel, it appears that he had a guardian angel protecting the classic absent-minded scientist. Bohr commented when the plane landed in London that he had slept like a baby for the entire flight.

Both his role in the Manhattan Project and his relationship with Heisenberg became the controversial elements in Michael Fray's award-winning play *Copenhagen.*

Heisenberg made a famous visit to Bohr in September 1941 and discussed the question of the morality of scientists contributing towards the development of an ultimate weapon of destruction. This meeting and what followed became the subject of *Copenhagen*, which has been performed on Broadway in New York and in London, Rome, Geneva, Athens and Stockholm, exploring what might have happened at that 1941 meeting between Heisenberg and Bohr. The play is a dramatic masterpiece, featuring only three actors playing Niels and Margrethe Bohr and Heisenberg and the bare setting of a few chairs and a table, but it has held audiences spellbound.

Had Heisenberg come to confirm his own doubts about the feasibility of an atomic bomb project or was he attempting to squeeze information from Bohr to aid the Nazi development of such a weapon? Was Heisenberg honestly trying to convince his superiors that to invest in such a major undertaking would be a waste of time and resources? The possibilities leave many tantalizing questions and speculations.

In a correspondence to his wife, Heisenberg wrote of his final visit to Bohr in Copenhagen: "Today, I was once more with Weizsäcker [a colleague] at Bohr's. In many ways this was especially nice, the conversation revolved for a large part of the evening around purely human concerns, Bohr was reading aloud, I played a Mozart Sonata (A-Major)." Was this an honest trivial recollection or a camouflaged attempt to provide evidence that his visit was purely a friendly, social one with an old friend and esteemed mentor and colleague?

In 1957, Heisenberg wrote to author Robert Jungk, who was working on the book *Brighter Than a Thousand Suns*, explaining that his visit to Bohr had been motivated by his view that scientists on either side should help prevent development of the atomic bomb. During his life, Heisenberg had been a patriotic German and had been associated with nationalist and right-wing politics although he was not a Nazi. He and other German scientists who had worked with Jewish colleagues such as Bohr and Einstein were attacked in the press during the early years of the Nazi regime as "white Jews." Nevertheless, by 1939, he and many of these other scientists had reached a *modus vivendi* to remain at their posts and Heisenberg was appointed to be in charge of the German nuclear reactor program.

In New Mexico, while working on the Manhattan Project, Bohr acted as a consultant and was troubled by the moral issues of having to contribute to a nuclear arms rate. He believed that atomic secrets should be shared by the international scientific community. After meeting with Bohr, J. Robert Oppenheimer suggested he visit President Roosevelt to convince him that the atomic bomb developments should be shared with the Russians in the hope of speeding up its results. Roosevelt suggested Bohr return to the United Kingdom to try to win British approval but Churchill disagreed with the idea of openness towards the Russians and even suggested putting limitations on Bohr's ability to travel and influence other scientists. After the war Bohr returned to Copenhagen, advocating the peaceful use of nuclear energy. When awarded the prestigious Order of the Elephant by the Danish government, he designed his own coat of arms which featured the symbol of yin and yang and the Latin motto *contraria sunt*.

On October 24, 1957, the first Atoms for Peace Award was presented at the Geat Hall of the National Academy of Sciences in Washington, D.C. James Killian, president of M.I.T. and President Eisenhower's Special Assistant for Science and Technology, presented the award to Bohr and read the Award Citation:

> Niels Henrik David Bohr, in your chosen field of physics you have explored the structure of the atom and unlocked many of Nature's other secrets. You have given men the basis for greater understanding of matter and energy.... In your public pronouncements and through your world contacts, you have exerted great moral force in behalf of the utilization of atomic energy for peaceful purposes. In your profession, in your teaching, in your public life, you have shown that the domain of science and the domain of the humanities are in reality a single realm. In all your career you have exemplified the humility, the wisdom, the humaneness, the intellectual splendor which the Atoms for Peace Award would recognize.

Killian then presented the gold medal award and a check for $75,000 with a smiling President Eisenhower looking on. The president addressed Bohr, calling him "a great man whose mind has explored the mysteries of the inner structure of atoms and whose spirit has reached into the very heart of man." Neils Bohr was indeed a Great Dane.

Chapter 23

Karen Blixen: From Rungsted to Kenya and Back

"I had a farm in Africa, at the foot of the Ngong hills. The Equator runs across these highlands, a hundred miles to the North, and the farm lay at the altitude of over six thousand feet. In the daytime you felt that you had got high up, near to the sun, but the early mornings and evenings were limpid and restful, and the nights were cold."

Thus begin the famous opening lines of *Out of Africa*, one of the few really great books to have been turned into a magnificent Hollywood film, catapulting Karen Blixen into the rank of Denmark's most famous author after Hans Christian Andersen, but in many ways she was also his polar opposite. She was beautiful, involved in passionate affairs and came from an aristocratic cosmopolitan background while Andersen was ugly (the true ugly duckling), sexually repressed and from the lowest rank of the social and economic ladder in the small provincial town of Odense.

Her real name was Karen Christenze Dinesen (1885–1962), but she wrote at times under the three male pen names of Isak Dinesen, Osceola, and Pierre Andrézel. She wrote works both in her native Danish and in English and also translated between the two.

She is best known for Out of Africa and one of her stories, "Babette's Feast," probably the most successful Danish film to win high acclaim outside of Denmark. It is a gentle satire and parody on the humble tastes of rural, simple villagers who follow an extremely pious "inner mission" sect of Christianity and hold all luxuries of which they are completely ignorant in disdain. Two sisters, daughters of the local minister, have beautiful voices but under the stern watch of their father never allow themselves to train these talents and bring the gifts they possess to the outer world for the enjoyment of others. Babette, a French refugee from the chaos of the 1870 Paris commune, arrives in the village and gratefully serves them but never has the opportunity to prepare any of her magnificent cooking until the chance of a lottery win enables her to purchase of the necessary ingredients for her superb cooking. The villagers are treated to a meal fit for the most elegant tastes of the finest connoisseurs of French cooking. The experience exposes their hypocrisy and humanizes them, making them kinder and more forgiving of their neighbors' faults and foibles than all their stern faith.

A 2007 opinion poll in her native Denmark confirms Karen Blixen's standing as one of the most representative personalities in Danish history. She was twice nominated for the Nobel Prize in Literature and should have won it, according to Ernest Hemingway. She was in the final four for the 1957 prize and was the favorite two years later in 1959 but failed to receive it even though, according to documents from the Nobel Archive in Stockholm, she had the committee's majority support.

Blixen was in the running against 55 other authors from around the world, including Graham Greene, André Malraux and John Steinbeck, and, as now appears likely, she was denied it because of reverse discrimination. The Nobel Prize Committee based in Sweden and Norway had been accused by many writers as favoring Scandinavian authors. The Academy members were apparently scared to appear provincial and motivated to demonstrate that their intellectual horizon extended further than the Nordics.

She mastered English during the time she lived on a coffee farm in Kenya from 1914 to 1931. She married her second cousin, Baron Bror Blixen of Sweden, thereby acquiring the title Baroness. Following separation and divorce, she had a long love affair with the safari hunter Denys Finch Hatton, son of a titled English family. After losing the coffee farm in the Great Depression, Karen Blixen returned to Denmark and began a professional writing career that lasted until her death in 1962.

Her writing places emphasis on the story line rather than characters, and expresses a fascination with the role of fate. She believed that a person's response to the ups and downs of life offers a possibility for heroism and, ultimately, for immortality. What draws many readers to her work is the sense that one is listening to a storyteller. She wanted to revive a primitive love of mystery among her readers, the sense of myth and grandeur as if they were gathered around a campfire at her African plantation or listening to Homer, the Old Testament stories, the *Arabian Nights* or *Icelandic Sagas* (elements from all of which she skillfully wove into her stories).

She was the daughter of Wilhelm Dinesen, a writer, army officer, landowner and adventurer who had gone off to live among Indians in Wisconsin in 1872–73. She was born into a Unitarian upper-class family in Rungsted, north of Copenhagen, and educated in art in Copenhagen, Paris and Rome.

Her mother's strong Unitarian beliefs in a country where the state religion was Lutheranism undoubtedly influenced her individualism and approach to philosophy. She disapproved of any one-sided ideology and eagerly drew on the inspiration of the great works of Scandinavian and world literature including the Old and New Testaments.

Karen began writing at an early age and published her first stories when she was 22. She studied art in Copenhagen and had a major interest in painting. Her first major work, *Seven Gothic Tales*, appeared in America in 1934, where it was a literary sensation, immediately popular with both critics and public, yet the Danish critical reaction was cool.

She wrote fiction for various Danish periodicals in 1905 under the pseudonym of Osceola, the famous Seminole Indian chief, probably inspired by her father's connection with Native American Indians. Karen was born soon after her father's return to Denmark from Wisconsin. He hanged himself in 1895 when Karen was nine, after being diagnosed with syphilis. He was a retired soldier from a wealthy family and had written books of essays on hunting. Her mother, Ingeborg Westenholz, came from a family of shipowners. Both her parents grew up on country estates on Jutland and were connected to the royal circle, although not titled. Both sides of the family shared strong opinions on culture and ethics.

In 1938, *Out of Africa* was published and achieved notoriety with its nostalgic look and lyrical descriptions of a great love affair with safari hunter Denys Finch Hatton (played by Robert Redford in the film). The unusual situation of a Danish baroness amidst the wildlife, the elite upper class of British colonials, African tribes, and the dangers, drought, and disappointments of her coffee plantation in the Kenyan highlands fascinated American readers. Although she described Africans as individuals rather than the usual stereotypes, she was nevertheless criticized for the frank portrayal of power differences between whites and blacks in colonial Africa and her close ties to bohemian types.

Her family cottage home in Rungsted contains a Karen Blixen Museum. The house is called Rungstedlund, with personal memorabilia such as her tiny, well-worn 1918 Corona typewriter and last fountain pen (Blixen also wrote by hand in English, then wrote the Danish translation between the lines). The 400-year-old cottage originally was an inn for travelers along the coastal road between Copenhagen and Elsinore. Blixen was born here and returned sporadically during her 17 years in Africa. Before it opened as a museum in 1991, her home was used as a haven for writers who wanted to imitate her spirit. Visitors are limited to 10 at a time. This allows a leisurely and intimate self-guided tour. Blixen had pronounced aristocratic notions but even as a successful writer, she had to live under the tight restraints of an income that was far from meeting her tastes in fine things.

Karen Blixen on 50 kroner banknote. © Danmarks Nationalbank.

After returning to Denmark, she did readings of her work on Danish radio that were well received and made a successful visit to the United States, the home of her most enthusiastic reading public, where she spoke and read in her charming Danish-accented English in a sonorous voice (wonderfully copied by Meryl Streep in the *Out of Africa* film) to American audiences.

Her illnesses have been the subject of speculation and are touched on in the film. Karen Blixen herself attributed her symptoms to syphilis acquired from her husband. She was first diagnosed with syphilis at the age of 29, a year after she married, and was prescribed mercury and arsenic, the accepted treatment for the disease in her time. Her death from metal poisoning and progressive "anorexia" are attributed to the use of this deadly concoction. Heavy smoking also contributed to her ills.

At the age of 46, she returned to the Rungstedlund country manor where she was born, and she lived there as a writer until the end of her life, needing the continual support of her brother Thomas and sister Elle. The siblings and friends donated furniture and the scant income from her writings helped pay for clothes and a staff of workers including a live-in cook and secretary.

Karen Blixen had to appeal to the general public for contributions to protect her house and land. Fortunately, a successful campaign after her death led to the creation of the Rungstedlund Foundation, which now oversees the 40-acre property as a museum and bird reserve. In the second World War, she volunteered to help smuggle Jews out of German-occupied Denmark. She said she liked danger and had always considered herself someone brought up to defy authority. Her influence on Danish literature was especially strong in the 1950s when many young Danish writers found inspiration in her stories and through personal contacts.

Chapter 24

Queen Margrethe II

A popular tourist poster with cartoon figures of Denmark's monarch from Gorm the Old to Queen Margrethe II reads, "Once upon a time, there was a king of DENMARK named Gorm the Old. All through the years, his family has ruled the oldest kingdom of the world, and the present Quen Margrethe II is a descendent of the old king Gorm"; to be accurate there should be a qualifying statement like "more or less." She is very remotely related but certainly not a direct descendent of Old Gorm (the father of Harald Bluetooth and Canute the Great, see chapter 25), also called Gorm the Sleepy, who was king of Denmark from C. 900 to C. 940 or 950. Actually, he has always been considered the traditional ancestral "head" of the Danish monarchy, so the nickname "old" is not a reference to the fact that he lived to be between 50 or 60 but that he is regarded as the founder of the oldest royal dynasty in Europe still occupying a throne.

Margrethe (usually called Margeret in English) whose full name is Margrethe Alexandrine Thorhildur Ingrid was proclaimed queen by Prime Minister Jens Otto Krag from the balcony of Christiansborg Palace in Copenhagen on January 14, 1973. Her insignia and motto with the large initial M is "God's Help — the People's Love — Denmark's Strength." She became the first female monarch of Denmark since Margrethe I, ruler of the Scandinavian countries from 1388 to 1412 during the Kalmar Union. As a princess she was given an Icelandic name, *Þórhildur* = Thorhildur (spelled with the Icelandic thorn character, simplified as "th"), because at the time of her birth in 1940, Iceland was still under Danish rule (it declared its independence while Denmark was under German occupation in 1944 so the extra name has largely been forgotten).

Upon accession to the throne, the Queen's first step was to drop the long and anachronistic title of Danish monarchs: "The King (or Queen) of Denmark), the Wends and the Goths, Duke (or Duchess) of Schleswig, Holstein, Stormarn, Ditmarsken, Lauenborg and Oldenburg." All these titles of minor principalities were represented by symbols in the royal coat of arms that were also eliminated. Danes knew immediately that their new queen would be a forward-looking, progressive monarch. I once passed the queen walking along the main street in Aarhus accompanied by a sole bodyguard (as far as I could tell) and she gave me a pleasant smile. Like her parents, she and the royal family are known today as the least snobbish royals in Europe and have not been touched by a shred of scandal or extravagance.

At the time of her birth, only males could be heirs to the throne of Denmark as a result of the succession laws enacted in the 1850s when the Glücksburg branch was chosen to succeed. Since Margrethe had no brothers, it was assumed that her uncle Knud, the heir presumptive, would one day inherit the throne. As most people felt that Knud would not be suited to the role of king, a process of constitutional change started in 1947, when it became clear that Queen Ingrid would have no more children. With the increasing role of women in Danish life after World War II, sentiment overwhelmingly favored the proposed change that had to be passed by two Parliaments in succession and then by a referendum, which was held on 27 March 1953. The new act of succession allowed a woman to ascend to the throne only if she did not have a brother. Princess Margrethe therefore became the heiress presumptive.

She studied prehistoric archaeology at Cambridge in 1960–1961, then political science at the modern University of Aarhus in 1961–1962, in a move purposely designed to increase her popularity in the "provinces" away from

Portrait of Queen Margrethe II on Danish stamp from 1990.

the medieval University of Copenhagen, a stone's throw away from the royal palaces. She continued her education at the Sorbonne in 1963, and at the London School of Economics in 1965. Her knowledge of languages acquired through study and marriage includes fluency in English, French, and German, and good reading ability in Swedish, Norwegian and Icelandic. This is greater than the foreign language capabilities of every American president combined (and likely to remain so forever).

She married a French diplomat, Count Henri de Laborde de Monpezat, at the Naval Church of Copenhagen in 1971. The Count then received the Danish title of His

Royal Highness Prince Henrik of Denmark. The prince has had his portrait on numerous stamps and wears various uniforms, including that of an admiral, but everyone considers him to be harmless.

The queen is an accomplished painter and illustrator and could make a living as a professional artist in the opinion of all critics who have reviewed her work. She has held many art shows and her illustrations under the pen name of Ingahild Grathmer were used for the Danish edition of the *Lord of the Rings*, a work she also participated in by translating parts of it into Danish. Although an acknowledged chain smoker, the queen made a decision announced in the daily newspaper *B. T.* on November 23, 2006, that henceforth she would refrain from smoking in public.

The queen and the prince make it their duty to make frequent visits to the Faroe Islands and Greenland (see chapters 4 and 5) to emphasize the continued ties between these territories and Denmark as integral parts of the kingdom under the Danish crown.

Queen Margrethe II of Denmark is one of the few Western heads of state and certainly the only European monarch who has had the courage and frankness to warn her fellow countrymen not to tolerate certain behavior that some extremist immigrant Muslims display. She has done this without any euphemisms or the standard political correctness and expression of concern about "fear mongering" and "dangerous stereotypes" in criticizing Islam, so frequently displayed by Western leaders, most notably former President George W. Bush and Barack Obama.

In her 1984 annual New Year's speech, the queen cautioned the Danish people to remember to be kind and hospitable towards immigrants. The topics of tolerance, immigration and freedom of speech also featured in her 2006 speech yet nevertheless in her authorized biography (entitled *Margrethe,* 2005), she had this to say about Islam and its adherents: "We are being challenged by Islam these years. Globally as well as locally. There is something impressive about people for whom religion imbues their existence, from dusk to dawn, from cradle to grave. There are also Christians who feel this way. There is something endearing about people who give themselves up completely to their faith. But there is likewise something frightening about such a totality, which also is a feature of Islam. A counterbalance has to be found, and one has to, at times, run the risk of having unflattering labels placed on you. For there are some things for which one should display no tolerance. And when we are tolerant, we must know whether it is because of convenience or conviction."

There were none of the usual ifs, ands and buts and no attempt to distinguish Islam by adding the qualifying adjectives of political, extremist, radical or Islamist. As another Dane, Hans Christian Andersen, maintained, praising the emperor's clothes when he is naked is an illusion that only enriches unscrupulous tailors.

The monarch's two sons to the throne are the crown princes Frederik, the heir apparent, born 1968, and his younger brother (born 1969) Joachim. Joachim is fourth in line to the Danish throne, following crown prince and his two children. When Frederik does succeed to the throne, he will become King Frederik X of Denmark.

He studied political science at Harvard University from 1992 to 1993 under the name of Frederik Henriksen and took up a position for three months with the Danish UN mission in New York in 1994. He received a master's degree in political science from the University of Aarhus and was posted as first secretary to the Danish Embassy in Paris. He has since completed extensive military studies and training in all three services.

In 2003, Queen Margrethe gave her consent to the marriage of Crown Prince Frederick to Mary Elizabeth Dibaldson, an Australian marketing consultant whom the prince met while attending the 2000 Sydney Olympic Games. The Danish Folketing passed a special law giving Mary Dibaldson Danish citizenship upon her marriage, a standard procedure for new foreign members of the royal family. Formerly a Presbyterian, Mary became a Lutheran and member of the state church. On April 25, 2005, the Danish royal court announced that Crown Princess Mary was pregnant with the couple's first child, a son they named Christian and the heir apparent after Frederik assumes the throne. In October 2005, a second child was born, a girl, Princess Isabella. The monarchy seems assured for generations to come and continues to enjoy great popularity among the Danish people.

Chapter 25

Canute and the Danelaw in England

Denmark is the oldest monarchy and has the oldest flag in Europe. Its early unification as a state in the Middle Ages made it the most powerful nation on the European continent not dominated or threatened by Islam. Danes have every reason to feel a proud heritage in their more than a thousand years' history and legacy of nationhood. King Canute (ca. 990–1035), also known as Knut or Cnut Sweynsson, was a Viking king of England, Denmark, Norway and parts of Sweden. Although brief, the extension of Danish rule over areas bordering on the North Sea established Denmark as the major factor in West and North European affairs.

His political and military successes made him one of the greatest figures of medieval Europe and set the stage for Danish involvement in European matters. Had it not been for the victory of another branch of Scandinavian adventurers — the Normans who first raided then conquered and settled the northwestern coast of France (Normandy) and went on to conquer England in 1066 — Canute might have gone down in history as more important than Charlemagne in the formation of the modern European states.

One of Hans Christian Andersen's most beloved poems and the most often cited as a popular choice for a national anthem instead of the current two (one on royal occasions and another for other civic occasions), entitled, "*I Danmark er jeg født*" ("I Was Born in Denmark") expresses what has been a recurrent theme and dilemma in Danish self-identity — the knowledge that the present country's small size and modest power as a factor in international affairs masks a glorious past when

"du engang herre var I hele Norden, bød over England—nu du kaldes svag, et lille land,—og dog så vidt om jorden end høres danskens sang og mejselslag.
Du danske friske strand, plovjernet guldhorn finder. Gud giv dig fremtid, som han gav dig minder!" Dig elsker jeg! Danmark mit fædreland!

You once were master in all of the North, ruled over England — but now you are called weak, just a small country, yet nevertheless as wide across the world as wherever the Dane's song and chisel blow are heard.

You cheerful Danish beach, the plough finds the golden horn. May God give you a future as He gave you memories! I love you, Denmark, my homeland!

Du land, hvor jeg blev født, hvor jeg har hjemme, hvor jeg har rod, hvorfra min verden går, hvor sproget er min moders bløde stemme, og som en sød musik mit hjerte når! Du danske friske strand med vilde svaners rede, I grønne øer, mit hjertes hjem hernede, dig elsker jeg!— Danmark, mit fædreland!

The song continues by going from the great power status of the "Master in all of the North that once ruled over England" to the reasons Andersen loves his homeland even more than historical greatness or pride:

You land where I was born, where my home is, where I have my roots and from which my world extends, whose language is my mother's voice at home, I love you! Denmark my fatherland! You cheerful Danish beach with the wild swans' You green islands, my heart's home. I love you, Denmark, my homeland!

Throughout Danish history and most notably in the historical struggle with Germany over the Schleswig border, Danes have been torn by the two sources of love — the historical one of a thousand-year-old kingdom and flag that was the great power of the Middle Ages and united the shores of the North sea nations in contrast to the the much smaller and modest vision of mother's warm and comforting voice and home.

H.C. Andersen's song was written in 1850 during the Three Years' War (1848–50) against the Schleswig rebels with Prussian support who tried to detach the southern region of Jutland (Schleswig) and Holstein. It was printed for the first time in the newspaper *Fædrelandet* on March 5, 1850.

Starting in approximately the year 790, waves of Danish assaults on the coastlines of the British Isles for plunder were followed by settlers from Denmark. By 865, Danish chieftains wintered in East Anglia, moved north, and by 867 captured York, defeating various Saxon contenders and usurpers of the throne. The Danes placed a puppet Saxon Englishman on the throne and gradually extended considerable influence throughout the region of Northeast England north of the Humber River in an area that became known as the Danegeld. This Danish tax was tribute, simply blackmail paid to the Vikings to prevent a land from being plundered.

Most of the English kingdoms lay in turmoil and were unable to oppose the Vikings. A Danish Viking leader arrived in 870 at the head of a force called the Great Summer Army to overrun large areas of central and eastern England. The invading army then planned to move on to Wessex but was defeated on January 8, 871, at the Battle of Ashdown. By 878, an agreement was signed recognizing an autonomous Danish region in the Northeast of England known as the Danelaw. Viking chieftains agreed to respect the authority of the English king and to desist from further attempts at expansion beyond a fixed boundary line.

The Danish-controlled area lasted for approximately two centuries. It was formalized between King Alfred the Great of England and the Danish ruler Guthrum the Old. The border ran roughly north of a line drawn in London trending to the northwest to Chester. Five fortified towns became particularly important in the region: Leicester, Nottingham, Derby, Stamford and Lincoln, today referred to as the East Midlands.

The Saxon King Alfred managed to keep the Danes out of his country, repulse the invaders and even retake York. The Danish leader Guthrum died in 890 but adopted Christianity in what must have been an attempt to make himself more respectable and acceptable as a candidate for eventual rule over all of England. A wave of Norwegian Vikings then appeared to aid their Danish cousins in England in 947 when Erik Bloodaxe recaptured York. The English-Saxon king on the throne in 980 was the 12-year-old Ethelred, a great-great-grandson of Alfred the Great. Early historians judge him to have lacked *ræd* ("counsel" in Anglo-Saxon), so he became known as Ethelred the Unready. Certainly his advisors proved helpless to offer any advice beyond bribing the marauding Danes.

In 991, the English crown started to "buy peace" by making regular protection payments. Events soon proved the truth of Kipling's famous couplet on appeasement: "If once you pay him the Danegeld, you never get rid of the Dane." In Great Britain, Danegeld has acquired the meaning of any coercive payment, whether in money or kind. For example, as mentioned in the British House of Commons during the debate on the Belfast Agreement: "I feared that the Belfast agreement might be built on sand, but I hoped otherwise. But as we have seen, Danegeld has been paid, and the thing about Danegeld is that one keeps on having to pay it. Concession after concession has been made. What will be the next one?" To emphasize the point, the phrase was widely used by critics of the Munich Agreement at the time of Chamberlain's appeasement policy towards Hitler over the Sudeten question.

Objectively, however, the reign of the Danish King Canute the Great (1016–1035) brought stability with his proclamation of a joint monarchy embracing Denmark and England (1018). His grandfather was Harald Blaatand (Bluetooth), who had been the first acknowledged king of a united and Christianized Denmark embracing Jutland, the islands and southern Sweden.

What brought him to England and the ambition to rule not only over the Danelaw but establish a united kingdom embracing the British Isles and Denmark was the desire for revenge. The Saxon King Ethelred plundered parts of the Danelaw and the Isle of Man in the year 1000 thus violating the old treaty and border. It was an apparent first step to evicting the Danes from all of Britain. In 1002, Ethelred married Emma, a sister of Duke Richard of Normandy.

With a powerful ally at his back, Ethelred ordered the massacre of all Danish men in England. The massacre provoked Canute's father, Sven, to vow revenge for the death of several close relatives. He carried out several raids on the region of East Anglia in 1003 and 1004 but withdrew to Denmark in 1005 due to famine conditions throughout much of England.

Subsequent raids and threats enabled Sven to extract large amounts of Danegeld from the English but in 1013 he made up his mind to regain lost territory in England and took his son Canute with him. They proclaimed their intent was to rescue the remaining Danes in the Danelaw and went on to conquer a large part of the country, forcing Ethelred to flee to Normandy. Sven died in 1014, setting the stage for a confrontation between Ethelred and Canute.

On the death of his father Sven, who had ruled as Danish King of England for only five weeks, Canute was proclaimed king by the Danish army in England. However, Canute's brother Harald was in line for succession and became Denmark's actual king instead. The English nobility opposed the invading Danes and recalled their leader King Ethelred from Normandy to lead an army against Canute. Canute then retreated back to Denmark and proposed a shared rule with his older brother in a joint kingship. Harald rejected this proposal but offered Canute command of his forces for another invasion of England, on the condition he did not continue to press his rival claim.

Canute managed to assemble a large fleet to launch another invasion of England with the help of Polish and Swedish allies, relatives of his mother. In the summer of 1015, Canute's fleet sailed to England with an invading Danish army of 10,000 in 200 long ships with many Vikings from Nor-

Roskilde Cathedral, where the Danish kings are buried, and a Viking ship. The Viking Ship Museum in Roskilde offers a permanent exhibition that features the best preserved ship and an exhibition of seafaring and maritime adventure during the Viking Age when Denmark ruled a trans–North Sea kingdom under King Canute that included the east of England and parts of Ireland and Scotland.

way and Sweden. The invasion force battled the English in a grisly campaign for the next fourteen months. Practically all of the battles were fought against Ethelred the Unready's son, Edmund Ironside. A passage from a contemporary document, *Encomium Emmae Reginae*, paints a vivid picture of Canute's fleet. Moreover, the description of the social and economic character of the Danish force is illuminating.

> There were so many kinds of shields, that you could have believed that troops of all nations were present.... Gold shone on the prows, silver also flashed on the variously shaped ships.... For who could look upon the lions of the foe, terrible with the brightness of gold, who upon the men of metal, menacing with golden face, ... who upon the bulls on the ships threatening death, their horns shining with gold, without feeling any fear for the king of such a force? Furthermore, in this great expedition there was present no slave, no man freed from slavery, no low-born man, no man weakened by age; for all were noble, all strong with the might of mature age, all sufficiently fit for any type of fighting, all of such great fleetness, that they scorned the speed of horsemen.

Canute's army crossed the Thames early in 1016, causing the English army to disband and leaving London unprotected. Canute was then accepted as king of all England in November 1016. At its height, the Danish kingdom exerted its rule over much of England and turned the North Sea into a "Danish lake."

Following the Danish victory at the Battle of Ashingdon over Edmund Ironside, Canute and Edmund drew up the Treaty of Olney, which allotted the Danelaw and the English midlands to Canute, while Edmund retained control of southern England. This essentially repeated the agreements of the 870s between King Alfred the Great of Wessex and the Vikings. Edmund died shortly after this treaty, leaving Canute as the first Danish-Viking king of all England. To seal his victory and claims, Canute married Ethelred's widow Emma in 1017 but her two sons by her first marriage remained in Normandy (their heirs were the invading Norman force that conquered all of England in 1066).

Canute held power by uniting Danes and Englishmen aided by a period of tranquility, wealth, law and custom, rather than sheer brutality. After a decade of conflict against rivals in Norway he also claimed the Norwegian crown in Trondheim in 1028 and took Sweden's capital and had coins struck that refer to him as king. A description of Canute can be found within the 13th-century Knytlinga saga:

> Knut was exceptionally tall and strong, and the handsomest of men, all except for his nose, that was thin, high-set, and rather hooked. He had a fair complexion none-the-less, and a fine, thick head of hair. His eyes were better than those of other men, both the handsomer and the keener of their sight.

Canute extended his authority across the Irish Sea and won the promise of loyalty from Irish chieftains as his vassals in Dublin. His possession of the archdioceses of England and Denmark gave him considerable influence within the Church so as to allow him to gain concessions on the tolls his people had to pay on the way to Rome. He also gained a share of the price of the *pallium* his bishops had to acquire. The *pallium* (derived from the Roman *pallium* or *palla*, a woolen cloak) was an ecclesiastical robe in the Roman Catholic Church, originally worn only by the pope, but subsequently awarded by him to bishops, as a symbol of the jurisdiction delegated to them by the Holy See.

After his 1026 victory against Norway and Sweden and on his way to Rome for the coronation, Canute proclaimed himself "King of all England and Denmark and the Norwegians and of some of the Swedes." The term *Danevæld* refers to the great trans–North Sea and Baltic Danish-dominated state comprising Denmark, much of England, part of Ireland, and southern Sweden.

During the more than two centuries of distinctive Danish presence in England, Anglo-Saxon speech was influence by its contact with Danish in the direction of simplification especially with regard to the conjugation of verbs. Danish dropped the cumbersome case endings (as in Latin) that were still current in Anglo-Saxon and moreover had only one form for verbs in the present and the past tenses, whereas Anglo-Saxon, like old Germanic and Latin tongues, had distinctive forms for each person. Another feature of cultural borrowing by English speakers from Danish took place in areas of vocabulary and spelling. Compare, for example, the Danish terms closely resembling English such as *kniv (knife)* and *vindue (window)* with the German equivalents of *messer* and *fenster*.

Why bother with so much ancient history and geography? Most Danes today probably can't recall a great deal about the medieval kings and their intrigues but they do retain a sense of historical continuity as a great nation and grasp that terms like *Danegeld* and *Danelaw* reflect an honored and important tradition their ancestors played in the fortunes of Scandinavia and the British isles. Even abroad, many educated people who know little about Canute or Denmark have heard the legendary story of the great king who pretended to command the tide to stop before the water reached his feet.

"Let all men know how empty and worthless is the power of kings. For there is none worthy of the name but God, whom heaven, earth and sea obey." This is the legendary remark Canute is supposed to have spoken while seated on his throne on the seashore with the waves lapping round his feet. The story relates that flattering court followers claimed that his power was so great he could command the sea. The king played along and had his throne carried to the seashore and sat on it as the tide came in, commanding the waves to advance no further. When they did not stop, he had made his point — though the deeds of kings might appear great in the minds of men, they were as nothing in the face of God's power. Canute died in 1035 at the age of perhaps 40 and his great *Danevæld* survived him by only a few years as neither of his sons proved capable of holding it together.

One of the most beautiful of Danish poems set to music speaks of the enduring love of the people for their "Danmark i tusind aar, hjemstavn og bøndegaard ... og fri mands arv" ("Denmark through a thousand years, our native soil and farmsteads, ... and the legacy of free men"). The Danes, like much older peoples such as the Jews and Greeks, have had the capacity to carry recognition of their long history as a psychological element of stability through great epochs in the past, full of many trials, tribulations, achievements, adventures and celebrations that enrich their everyday lives.

Chapter 26

The German-Danish Border Question, 1815–1919

Denmark is today divided over the question of how best to absorb a new immigrant population from Asia, Africa and Latin America who differ significantly from the native majority in culture, language, religion and race. Sixty-five years ago, the Danish government had the opportunity to annex South Slesvig, a region that had been part of the Danish kingdom for centuries, and reabsorb that part of the Danish people who had been separated and alienated from their original homeland by German rule. The fear that a completely culturally homogeneous population was an absolute necessity for the maintenance of national identity resulted in the unwillingness of the Danish government to assume the responsibility to take on this task. Ironically, since then, the Danish minority in Germany has thrived under the new conditions of tolerance and mutual respect for cultural diversity and even succeeded partially to "integrate" and absorb members of the German majority.

The border region between Germany and Denmark known as "Slesvig" in Danish ("Schleswig" in German) is one of several historical European disputes that has been subjected to a vigorous competition for the hearts and minds of communities regarding the loyalty its inhabitants. From the end of the Napoleonic Wars until 1864, the Schleswig-Holstein question bedeviled the foreign ministries of the European powers.

For the remainder of the chapters on the border question, I will use both the Danish nomenclature *Slesvig* as a matter of convenience when dealing with the movement to preserve or recover the territory for Denmark and *Schleswig* when writing about circumstances that engaged German interests.

The settlement reached under the provisions of the Treaty of Versailles ending World War I was considered by most observers to be the fairest of all the boundary changes but was nevertheless challenged by the German minority in Denmark between the two world wars, but not by the Nazi regime under Hitler. In the immediate post-war years 1945–48, what had been assumed to be one of the most stable border regions in Europe was shaken to its core by an unexpected reborn Danish national sentiment in South Slesvig. In spite of what appeared to be a solid majority of local sentiment demanding an eventual plebiscite to determine the issue of a return to Danish sovereignty, the Danish government refused the opportunity to jump on the bandwagon and claim the "right of self-determination" it had always espoused as the most important factor in determining where a boundary should be fixed.

The border conflict over the entire southern portion of the Jutland penin-sula (called "Sønderjylland" in Danish, meaning "South Jutland"), comprising both North and South Schleswig (see map), is of particular interest for two noteworthy reasons:

1. It demonstrates that national and ethnic identity are not necessarily the same thing and not all national conflicts are destined to endure as the result of unchangeable inherited ethnic traits. This contrasts with the popular view that the population of a border region unequivocally "belongs" to either one nationality or another if given the opportunity to express their opinion.

   Nationality is often perceived as an inherited set of discrete characteristics including a distinctive language, religion, race or view of history that regards the disputed territory as one's own sacred heritage.

   The history of Slesvig offers considerable insight into the processes of how Danish ethnic origin was not sufficient to prevent the Germanization of a sub-stantial part of the population over several centuries. Ethnic Danes in much of the region first adopted German as the principal language of education, administration, the church and polite society while still retaining many other identifiable Nordic-Danish aspects of behavior, culture and tradition. The lin-guistic shift was not synonymous with national feeling and loyalty. Today, the Danish minority in Germany is predominantly German speaking.

2. The resolution of the border issue in 1945–55 culminating in agreements between the Danish and West German governments was firmly based on the principles of mutual respect for minority rights and free choice and associa-tion. This contrasts with the more usual pattern of "ethnic cleansing" and wholesale exchanges of population which have been the prevalent method of dealing with recalcitrant or hostile minorities elsewhere. Denmark foreswore the opportunity to change the border in its favor following World War II and make good its historical claim to former Danish territory.

The two duchies of Schleswig and Holstein had been joined together in the person of King Christian I in the Middle Ages. His successors were simul-taneously king of Demark and duke of Schleswig-Holstein. This polite fiction was shattered in 1863 when the rising tide of German nationalism used the excuse that the legal succession to the duchies had come to an end with the termination of the House of Oldenburg in Denmark.

The election of a new ruling house for the kingdom of Denmark could not be imposed on the duchies. The dynastic problems had become so convoluted from the remnants of medieval arrangements and marriages that it provoked Lord Palmerston, British Prime Minister (1855–65), to quip that only three people knew how to explain the problem — Prince Albert (consort of Queen Victoria whom he tried to influence with his pro-German sentiments) who had died in 1863, a Danish statesman who had gone crazy, and Palmerston himself who had already forgotten it due to more pressing problems.

The spirit of pan-German nationalism had been fanned by the revolutions throughout Europe in 1848 and cynically manipulated by Prussian ambitions to work towards unification of a large German state. By 1863, the crisis brought about by the absence of a male heir to the Danish throne (the eventual monarch who succeeded to the throne was the nephew of the deceased king's sister) was seized upon by Bismarck to advance the pan–German cause.

On one hand, Prussia used legalistic arguments based solely on the archaic medieval arrangements that had produced the original agreement of the fifteenth century, when the king of Denmark inherited the title of Duke of Schleswig-Holstein and the two provinces were solemnly declared to be inseparable. Prussian intervention was, however, the first major step on the road to forge a united German nation-state by fostering nationalist sentiment in Slesvig (ethnically and linguistically mixed) and Holstein (wholly German in character and not a cause of contention). The dispute was portrayed by Bismarck as a legal matter rather than a German nationalist cause, a charade that did not escape British notice.

Concerned as always by factors of naval strength (Denmark still had a powerful navy) and the balance of power, the British had traditionally sought to preserve Denmark's territorial integrity but were too involved with affairs elsewhere, notably:

1. Concern about a possible confrontation with the United States over the issue of protecting its trade in cotton with the American South (and eventual hopes for full secession of the Southern states and the independence of the Confederacy), and
2. Retaining control of India that had been shaken by the great Sepoy uprising of 1857.

The Three Years' War, 1848–1850 (The First Dano-German War)

The European revolutions of 1830 and 1848 brought a new spirit of constitutionalism and republicanism, liberalism and a wave of nationalism throughout Europe. Only Russia and England were largely untouched. As a result, many German principalities granted their subjects more rights and representation as well as freedom of the press. Denmark, having been defeated in the Napoleonic Wars, suffered bankruptcy and economic instability. At the Congress of Vienna that redrew the map of Europe, it was forced to cede Norway, a Danish possession for more than four hundred years, to arch-rival Sweden.

These events provoked serious calls for reform but the country had the great misfortune to have been ruled by an out-of-touch monarch, King Frederick VI. He had ruled Denmark for 55 years (first as prince regent, and then as king) until his death in 1839. Resentment towards the throne and association with Denmark prevailed in thoroughly German-minded and -speaking Holstein, in the university city of Kiel, and among the Frisian population along the west coast who had never experienced the type of feudalism that prevailed in most of Denmark and Germany.

The Problem of Succession to the Throne

Frederick VI left no sons and a successor had to be chosen. A young German-reared cousin was the candidate who became Christian VIII (ruled 1839–1848). Like his predecessor, the new king was reluctant to grant concessions or real reforms. The cause of the duchies evoked considerable sentiment in Prussia as the focus of a greater German fatherland while in North Slesvig, local Danish speakers began to fear that a drift towards involvement in a German confederation would be detrimental and promote the already privileged position of the German-speaking aristocrats, merchants and bureaucrats.

The new king began by ordering a more favored use of the Danish language in schools and churches but was forced under pressure to withdraw his proposal that Danish should be in official use where there was a preponderant population of monolingual Danish speakers throughout Slesvig. The king was sarcastically referred to in the German press as "*Der König von dem Inselreich*" ("King of the Island Kingdom"), a term of ridicule contrasting Denmark's geographical situation with the mighty continental dimensions of Prussia) and seditious papers were circulated denying the right of the new Danish line to maintain the joint title as dukes of Schleswig and Holstein where the Salic Law (prohibiting succession through the female line) had prevailed since medieval times.

Christian VIII died in 1848 and was succeeded by his son Frederick VII (ruled 1848–1863) who sought to avoid the crisis by separating Slesvig and integrating it within the kingdom, renouncing any claim to Holstein, and proclaiming a new liberal constitution. This provided an expansionist and militarist Prussia, under the thumb of the skillful and cunning leadership of Otto Von Bismarck, the opportunity to plan the first of a series of steps that led inevitably to the unification of Germany.

Though it was truly the victim, Denmark was portrayed as "a shameless little dwarf state" and the ethnic German conspirators in Schleswig-Holstein, who were bent on secession, were cast in the role of an "oppressed people" yearning to participate in the wave of liberal revolutions against the tyranny that was, at the time, sweeping Europe. The events also played on latent feelings of Danish inferiority. Two wars (1848–50 and 1864), followed by Prussian intervention, resulted in an initial Danish victory due to a favorable constellation of European power interests on the part of the foreign ministries of czarist Russia and Great Britain. Unfortunately for Denmark, the victory would only to be followed by a massive defeat at the hands of a joint Prussian-Austrian assault in alliance with the rebellious duchies.

The 1864 Second Dano-German War

The Danes had pinned their hopes on continued support of the great powers. However, their strategic interests were diverted by other priorities; the Russians in Poland, support for the declining Ottoman Empire in the Balkans, British fear of confrontation with the United States over their sympathy for the Confederacy, and worries about an invasion of Canada. Prussia undertook to support the rebels in Schleswig-Holstein oblivious to all Danish attempts to placate national feeling by ceding Holstein outright to the German confederation and Austria tagged along so as not to leave the field of German nationalism entirely to Prussia.

Denmark had in the past relied on the *Dannevirke*, a line of earthwork ramparts that had initially been erected in the tenth century and reinforced periodically, enabling Denmark to prevent an invasion of the Jutland peninsula from the south since the days of Charlemagne and the Holy Roman Empire. Danish resistance was crushed in a final assault preceded by a massive artillery bombardment at Dybbøl mill near Sønderborg on the island of Als where 37,000 Prussian troops opposed an outnumbered Danish force of 11,000 equipped with inferior, out-of-date muskets.

Following their victory — Prussia and Austria divided the spoils — Schleswig was annexed by Prussia and Holstein by Austria. This proved to be the prelude to the Seven Weeks' War in 1867, in which Prussia decisively defeated Austria, took Holstein and used the fruits of victory to seduce many of the small German principalities to get on the bandwagon of a great German empire. The war cemented the leading role of Kaiser Wilhelm and Bismarck as masters of the new German empire (the Second Reich; Charlemagne had created the First, and Hitler would lay claim to the Third). The various claimants to the duchies by princes of the Augustenburg dynasty that had sought to advocate their feudal rights to replace the Danish Royal House as the legal rulers were pushed aside and forgotten.

A popular German poem at the time captured the spirit of the events of 1864–67 by exclaiming "*Was ist das deutsche Vaterland?*" ("What is the German Fatherland?") and answered "*Schleswig-Holstein Meer umschlungen!*" ("It is Schleswig-Holstein surrounded by the sea!")

The Language Issue

Throughout the seventeenth and eighteenth centuries, the German-speaking nobility and wealthy merchants dominated the cultural life of Schleswig as well as Holstein and played an increasingly important role in church and school affairs. Previously they had not regarded their language and culture as barriers to their official status as subjects of the Danish king and citizens in his realm. Some of them even wrote poems in the German language extolling the kingdom of Denmark and the royal house. Their attitude was it was more proper to use the language of "high culture," German, rather than what they regarded as a crude peasant tongue, Danish. The diaries of several pastors stationed in Slesvig in the 18th century reveal the contempt for those Danish-speaking peasants ignorant of German as if their language implied a lack of morality.

One of them, Christopher Heinrich Fischer from Saxony, was installed in 1730 as a pastor of the local community in Hyrup (Hörup) in Angel, about 15 kilometers south of Flensborg (Flensburg). By 1738, Pastor Fischer confided that his congregation "had no morals and spoke no German." He wrote that his parishioners included many elderly people who were unable to understand German and so "had no sense at all for true Christianity in theory or in practice."

The same year, Fischer was visited by his son, a student from Kiel. The two of them became involved in harsh words with several parishioners who gave them a beating and officially protested to church authorities over the irresponsible and arrogant behavior of their pastor. Fischer actually left behind a record of his church sermon held on the First Trinity Sunday which was later cited in court proceedings held against him (he was finally dismissed in 1750) and is worth quoting at some length to indicate the social gap between the two classes and language users well into the late eighteenth century.

When I came home and took off my boots in the study room, a great deal of
blood ran out of them due to the many blows I had received which struck an
artery. Ach!, you thieves and robbers of the church, what pains I have had with
this congregation. Oh God, You have sent me to hell where there lives a devil in
almost every house of my congregation. It would have been better to serve the
devil as a swineherd than to be the shepherd of souls for such Christians. You
pack of devils and hell-raisers, have I not sought to teach you German? But to
no avail when this devilish riff-raff continues to speak its stupid Danish tongue
throughout, even with children and servants.... What can please the Devil more
than that you cannot say the Lord's Prayer, cannot pray God's commandments or
even sing a song when the service and all the actions designed to save the soul
occur by means of the German language.

It was only during the 18th century after German had largely displaced
Danish from much of South and Middle Schleswig that the language divide
came to play a major role in defining the newly established national movements. The oft-repeated and automatic assumption in many nationalist rivalries that language is the most distinguishing marker and the easiest
recognizable component of identity is not borne out in the case of Schleswig/
Slesvig or Alsace-Lorraine or Switzerland. Even a thorough guidebook (*Guide
to the Peoples of Europe,* edited by Felipe Fernandez-Armesto, Times Books,
London, 1997, pages 29–33) devoted to the peoples and cultures of Europe
has made the mistake of identifying "national minorities" on both sides of the
present Danish-German border in terms of language.

An ironic expression of the deeply embedded Danish folk character and
newly acquired German nationalist sentiment in Schleswig-Holstein was
revealed by none other than the poet Hoffman von Fallersleben, the author
of *Deutschland, Deutschland über Alles,* in 1845 when he arrived in the city of
Schleswig to meet with and congratulate the leadership of his "fellow German
tribesmen brothers" for their resistance to the Danish crown and wound up
noting in his diary that "it turned into a depressing meeting. These
Schleswigers have almost nothing in common with us other than our language.
The Danish soul is deeply embedded within them and emerges at every opportunity."

The achievements of Germany's philosophers, musicians, composers, scientists and writers, the appeal of a modern sense of nationalism, the problems of an orderly succession to the Danish throne and the attraction of a
rising, powerful Prussia all conspired to make the Schleswigers look south-
ward. Danish continued to be spoken primarily by those classes who had the
least influence among small farmers and an urban proletariat in the few big
cities.

In the more prosperous areas facing the Baltic (known as Angel) south
of the line of the Sli estuary–Dannevirke–Trene River, the local dialect variety

of Danish (Sønderjysk) was replaced by German as a result of a socially ambitious class of farmers cultivating German to improve their economic ties with the much greater market opportunities of the German empire.

It became the language spoken in the home to give children a social advantage in school, the church and "fine society." The wealthiest farmers who raised cattle driven to sale in northern German along the cattle market trail known as the *haervej* more readily and easily adopted German as the language of commerce and then at home. In contrast, the poorer farmers near the North Sea coast retained Danish longer, until the mid-nineteenth century. The population on the smaller islands in the Little Belt was more closely tied to the bishop residing in Odense on Fünen and preserved Danish language ties and associations even after the annexation of all of Slesvig by Prussia.

British Assessment of the Loss of Schleswig-Holstein

The 1864 war had immeasurable consequences for the balance of power in Europe. It led directly to the unification of a great German empire and a powerful naval rival of Great Britain in the Baltic, North Sea and North Atlantic. It was perfect timing for Bismarck. Such a development was inimical to the long-term interests of not only Great Britain but also of Russia, France and the United States, none of which were able or willing to lift a finger to stop German aggression.

British interests in the Baltic and traditional balance-of-power considerations would normally have encouraged a stronger British response but the complexity of the feudal-medieval issue of succession to the throne and archaic arrangements linking Slesvig with Holstein left much public opinion abroad unsympathetic to Denmark's plight. The image of an "oppressed" German and Frisian population in a conflict with the outmoded monarchy in Denmark made the Schleswig-Holstein rebels into an underdog.

Any British hope of enlisting French support was frustrated by the antagonism of Napoleon III who had sent a French army to install Maximillian, an archduke of Austria on the throne of Mexico while the United States was still engaged in the Civil War. American interest in foreign affairs during the Civil War was limited to the question of avoiding British or French support or intervention on behalf of the Confederacy but the issue of the secession of the Danish duchies in January 1864 did elicit modest public sympathy for the plight of Denmark. Napoleon III had felt betrayed by the British refusal to intervene a year earlier in 1863 when czarist Russia crushed Polish independence. The czar was also alarmed by the new Danish king's proclamation of a liberal constitution and feared that such ideas might spread from Denmark to his own realm. He preferred the disputed provinces under the control of an autocratic ruler like himself.

Lord Russell, who served as prime minister during the Three Years' War and later as foreign secretary (1861–65), could do no more than request that Prussia and Austria honor their previous "guarantees" to respect the "territorial integrity of the Danish monarchy." When it became clear that this was a vain hope, both Russell and his prime minister, Palmerston, threatened intervention but it was an empty bluff. Sweden was sympathetic to the point of allowing several hundred Swedish and Norwegian volunteers to join the Danes but stopped far short of risking a confrontation with Prussia.

It would have served both the British and Danes well on the eve of World War II and the trust they placed in the Munich Agreement, portioning Czechoslovakia, and the Non-Aggression Pact, signed by Denmark and Nazi Germany in May 1939 (another scrap of paper) to have recalled the prophetic and apocryphal words of Lord Robert Cecil, later prime minister of Great Britain, who, in the *Quarterly Review* of April 1864 at the end of the war wrote:

> The crisis has at last come. The concessions upon which England has insisted have proved futile. The independence upon which she professed to value so highly is at an end. The people whom she affected to befriend are in danger of being swept away. One of the most wanton and unblushing spoilations which history records is on the point of being consummated. But as far as effective aid goes, England stands aloof.... Her pledges and threats are gone with last year's snow, and she is content to watch with cynical philosophy the destruction of those who trusted to the one, and the triumph of those who were wise enough to spurn the other.

The *Dannevirke* had been repaired and strengthened at the outset of the first war in 1848 but left without adequate rail connections or modern barracks. Nevertheless, Denmark's naval power and the threatened intervention of Great Britain resulted in a Danish victory in 1850, putting down the insurrection and ending Prussian intervention. Unfortunately, this brief respite created the illusion among many Danes that the *Dannevirke* was a kind of 19th-century impregnable "Maginot Line" (which of course was also outflanked and proven to be useless in 1940). In the 1864 war, it was abandoned without a shot during the extremely cold winter that enabled the Prussian Army to outflank it across the frozen Sli River to the east and marshes to the west.

Attempts by the British to support a compromise peace in 1864 during a cease-fire establishing a defense line across Jutland following the *Dannevirke* and Sli River were too late. The utility of such a boundary that also closely followed what had been the original line of demarcation between languages and ethnic groups of the Middle Ages was demonstrated to have no value in modern warfare. The harsh peace terms imposed on Denmark resulted in the loss of all of Slesvig including the *Dannevirke*, the historic city of Flensborg, an area of 19,000 square kilometers and a total population of 600,000. The end result was that indeed Denmark was reduced to the dimensions of a true "dwarf state" (from a pre-war size of 58,000 square kilometers to a new one of only 39,000 and a pre-war population of 2,500,000 to only 1,700,000).

The new boundary left behind a large population of ethnic Danes who were now German citizens and doomed to forced participation in four more wars to come (against Austria in 1866, against France in 1870 and in the two world wars against the Allies). These losses came hard on the heels of the loss of Norway in 1815, and the loss of the southern region of Sweden (Skåne) in the 1660s. Many Danes developed an inferiority complex that their shrinking nation was doomed to one failure after another and could perhaps just manage to survive if it refrained from any policy likely to antagonize any of the great powers. Hans Christian Andersen even wondered if any of his works would survive and if anyone would speak Danish in a hundred years' time (see chapter 17).

The lesson of 1864 cast a long shadow into the 20th century. Danish forces had been badly outnumbered, outgunned and without allies. The alternative to Denmark's shrinking geography and keeping one's head in the sand was that military preparedness and strong, dependable allies had to be the means to prevent further aggression and disaster. A large majority of the Danish public at first accepted the lesson taught by the "ostriches" on the political left that led directly to the humiliating capitulation to the German invasion of 1940. By 1949, enough Danes had realized their folly by switching to the other view and approving Denmark's full membership in NATO.

German Treatment of the Danish Minority, 1864–1920

Germany raised a great war memorial to the fallen heroes of their war of liberation — a gigantic 45-meter-high granite tower at Knivsbjerg near Åbenrå (Apenrade). At the foot of the tower stood the inscription of the Schleswig-Holstein uprising in Plattdeutsch "*Jungs holt fast*" ("Hang on, boys!") At the top stood an inscription with Bismarck's words from a speech to the Reichstag: "*Wir Deutsche fürchen Gott und sonst nicht auf der Welt*" ("We Germans fear God but nothing else in the world."

The German element of Schleswig's population known as *hjemmetyskere* ("home Germans") in Danish were the native born in contrast to those Germans who now moved into Schleswig from Holstein or other parts of Germany to work as civil servants, new landowners and those in the liberal professions after Prussia's outright annexation of Schleswig in 1867. Well aware of the resentment among the pro-Danish Slesvigers, the *hjemmetyskere* strove to preserve their status and supported measures designed to increase the German identity of North Schleswig where they were still a minority.

Their lobby organization, *Deutscher Verein für das Nordliche Schleswig,* was established in 1890 and, following the completion of the mammoth Bismarck German Victory Memorial at Knivsbjerg in 1897, they held annual celebrations there. Their local periodical, *Schleswiger Grenzpost,* received subsidies from the German government and followed a line of constant attack against what they called the "Danish separatist movement."

By contrast, the Danes in North Schleswig, who had long suffered from an inferiority complex with regard to German culture, cultivated a new ingrained pride and patience that "right makes might." They took their cue from the great Danish clergyman and philosopher N.F.S. Grundtvig (see chapter 16) who had pictured the Danish people as a decidedly feminine nation like the Nordic goddess Freja waiting for her husband's return or like the widow in the New Testament who, through the power of her faith in Christ, receives her dead son back:

> As Jesus approached the city of Nain, "there was a dead man carried out, the only son of his mother, and she was a widow, and many people of the city were with her" (Luke 7:12). Because of her son's death, no one was left to care for her. When the Lord saw her, He "had compassion on her, and said unto her, Weep not. And he came and touched the bier; and they that bore him sat still. And he said, Young man, I say unto thee, Arise. And he that was dead sat up, and began to speak. And he delivered him to his mother" [Luke 13–15].

After North Schleswig's return to Denmark in 1920, the most frequent motif used in status, memorials, and paintings was of a daughter returning to the bosom of her mother. Grundtvig inspired the Danish will to resist and taught that coercion could never triumph over freedom.

In the formulation of the Peace Treaty ending the Second Dano-German War signed in Prague in 1866, Prussia agreed to hold an "eventual" plebiscite to decide on a border rectification according to the principle of self-determination. It held out the remote prospect of the Danish majority in North Slesvig eventually being reunited with Denmark. This provision, known as Paragraph 5, was simply abrogated in 1879 (with the approval of Austria) as one more scrap of paper.

The completion of the Kiel Canal in 1895 linking the Baltic with the North Sea made German determination to become a world naval power a top priority and reinforced the determination to hold on to North Slesvig. Some high-ranking naval staff were so anxious to promote the reach of the German navy that they advanced the idea of a return of part of North Slesvig to Denmark in exchange for the Danish West Indies (eventually sold by Denmark to the U.S. in 1917 — see chapter 6).

German rule set out to enforce assimilation, promote emigration, impose military conscription and limit or suppress any expression of Danish culture and sympathies toward Denmark. By 1888, Danish was abolished as the language of instruction in public schools except for a few hours of "religious instruction" in rural areas.

Due to these policies, North Schleswig under German rule lost nearly one-third of its population by the turn of the century through emigration. More than 60,000 Slesvigers, the great majority of whom were decidedly pro-Danish in their sympathies, emigrated to the United States (see chapter 11).

During the period of occupation of North Slesvig, the Danish minority managed to send an average of one delegate to the Reichstag and two representatives to the Prussian Assembly. German police and intelligence agents gathered evidence of any manifestation of Danish sympathies such as illegally flying the *Dannebrog* (Danish flag), and even the use of red and white (the Danish flag's colors) bricks in the construction of houses or even sheds and barns. In 1908, the use of Danish at public political meetings was forbidden. For the rest of the world, the Danish-German border and the Schleswig-Holstein question has been "resolved." Much to their surprise in 1920 and again in 1945–48, the issue reemerged as a result of two German defeats in war.

The Danish National Character, ca. 1900

The loss of North Slesvig produced an introspective national character as both a cause and a consequence of the confrontation with Germany. In connection with the Paris World Fair of 1900, two well known Danes, the theologian Hans Olrick and the philosopher C. N. Starcke, produced an evaluation of Denmark's development as a homogeneous national state since the 1864 catastrophe. The book *Danmarks Kultur ved Aar 1900 som Slutning af et Hundredaars Udvikling* (*Denmark's Culture in 1900 at the End of a Century's Development*) was published in both Danish and French and gave outsiders a firsthand look at how Danes perceived themselves. The chapter entitled "Træk af Nationalkarakteren" ("National Characteristics") paints a picture of a people in harmony with their surroundings, a homogeneous society, and self-restrained, phlegmatic individuals, light-hearted but with a certain melancholy and fondness for understatement, dry humor, and irony, whose natural instinct is to shy away from any dramatic confrontation. Great expectations and risk-taking are viewed suspiciously and to be avoided — a clear reaction to the disastrous policies of 1848–64 which were undertaken without any adequate preparation after centuries of apathy, neglect and reliance on the grandiose and worthless promises of others (the British and the Swedes).

There is an idealization of the banal everyday and the mediocre which is elevated into the quality of dependability and steadfastness. It is the origin of what is known as *jenteloven* (see chapter 12 on *hygge*), a term used to disparage anyone who is seeking to excel because it would violate norms of "solidarity." This outlook came to shape much of Danish social attitudes, literature, art and foreign policy. It also drove away those Danes who felt their life perspectives were curtailed at every step and only emigration to America would give them a fresh chance to develop their own unique ambitions.

According to Olrick and Starcke, "Our literature's strength lies in the finely tuned poem and the unembellished story but we cannot master imposing drama. Our music is harmonious and beautiful but never stormy or wild (leave that to the Russians or Spaniards). Our science is methodical but we don't set the world on fire. We know our limitations and whoever seeks to sever his bonds will rarely be rewarded."

The prevalence of such attitudes was a formidable barrier to all those who sought to rally the people on behalf of a credible defense policy, or promote a socialist revolution or, following World War II, take the initiative and "seize the day" to regain South Slesvig. All these policies were regarded for several generations by a majority of Danes as rocking the boat.

Chapter 27

The Danish–German Border
Question, 1920 to the Present

The Plebiscite

Following Germany's defeat in World War I, a plebiscite was held to decide the political future of Slesvig in 1920. It was divided into two zones. The results appeared to be clear cut with a majority of 75 percent in the northern Zone 1 voting to become part of the kingdom of Denmark while in the southern Zone 2, an even larger majority of 80 percent elected to remain within Germany. Flensborg still had a Danish-speaking majority before its incorporation into Germany and most Danish speakers were workers in the city's northern district who constituted the most active members of the Social Democratic party at the outbreak of World War I. Their adoption of Marxism made them doubly suspicious elements as far as the German national authorities were concerned.

By the outbreak of war in 1939, the active and visible Danish minority among the indigenous population in southern Schleswig had been reduced from 20 percent to less than 10 percent of the electorate and by 1945 it probably stood at less than 5 percent, yet, in the 1947 communal elections, more than half the native-born population in South Schleswig identified with the Danish political movement agitating for a new plebiscite and seeking to enjoy the cultural rights established for the Danish minority.

How and why did so many Slesvigers in the south remain loyal to Germany after World War I, provide a large measure of support for the Nazi Party's accession to power in 1933, only grudgingly accord the small Danish-minded population their right to cultural autonomy from 1933–39, yet massively transfer their loyalties during 1945–47? The easy answer is, of course, opportunism. However, a closer look provides insights into the component elements of ethnic identity, culture, language, religion, class, political loyalties,

The 1920 plebiscite and boundary changes in Jutland. Courtesy of The IBRU, University of Durham.

economic interests, education and the prevailing power relations between Germany and Denmark, and how these were evaluated differently over time.

They also put into sharp relief two opposing principles on which boundary disputes have been settled and reveal that sometimes the individual may be split between heart and mind. For the Nazis, the issue of loyalty was decided by the rubric of "blood and soil" (Blut und Boden). Hitler summed it up by writing: "A Chinese does not become German because he begins to speak German and votes for a German party." In the Danish view exemplified by Denmark's great clergyman-poet-philosopher-theologian Grundtvig, "All belong to a people who so regard themselves."

The Aftermath of World War I and the Nazi Regime

More than 5,000 Danish-minded Schleswigers fell in German uniform in 1914–18 for a war that was viewed with little or no enthusiasm. Most supporters of the social democratic opposition in the northern districts of Flensburg, who were still identifiably Danish in their sympathies, were nevertheless swayed by the opportunity to be a part of what they hoped would be a democratic republican industrial Germany rather than by the opportunity to be reunited within an enlarged but monarchist and still largely agrarian Denmark. It was a decision they came to rue.

During the years of the Nazi regime prior to the outbreak of World War II, the Danish-minded minority was repeatedly labeled by the German authorities as a front for social democratic and Marxist elements hiding their dissatisfaction with the new regime behind the guise of national minority rights. In fact, just the opposite was the case. The large "German" majority in plebiscite Zone 2 in 1920, especially in the city of Flensburg itself, was the result of the Marxist sympathies of social democrats who regarded themselves as Danish Slesvigers but voted for their class interests rather than ethnicity.

Many Danish-minded workers in South Schleswig became increasingly aware of their mistake in having voted to remain part of Germany out of Marxist theoretical principles. Their close proximity to Denmark and cross-border contacts made them aware of how far the Danish working class progressed economically and socially under a democratic system opposed to militarism, and committed to the fostering of humanitarian values and the spread of adult education on a massive scale. Germany's war of aggression against Denmark in 1940 and the agitation of many German-minded North Schleswigers who had been Danish citizens for two decades but enthusiastically supported the Nazi Party program and agitated to rejoin Germany was a doubly bitter pill to swallow.

During the interwar years Denmark made social and economic strides on behalf of the working class which had been held responsible for the high pro-German vote in 1920 due to the mistaken belief that these objectives would be more easily realized in Germany. In the 1933–45 period the organized minority Danish community in South Slesvig (SSF —*Sydslesvig Forening*— the South Schleswig Association) stood fast against the Nazi juggernaut and maintained its own schools, libraries, welfare assistance and the only non–Nazi newspaper in Germany, *Flensborg Avis*. This was due to their courage in the face of constant Nazi harassment and official German government policy, which necessitated the formal respect of commitments based on the reciprocity of the Danish government toward the German-minded minority in North Slesvig.

In 1936, a book entitled *Dansk Grænselære* (*Danish Border Lesson*), by a young student, Claus Eskildsen, looked at the border conflict and national dispute in Schleswig over the generations. Eskildsen contrasted the two principles and explained how the 1920 border dividing Schleswig into north and south between Denmark and Germany respectively had utilized self-determination on the basis of a freely held plebiscite as the fairest method of leaving behind the smallest national minorities. He then examined a host of characteristics which are handed down through inheritance and have left their physical mark on the landscape or in the popular subconscious of the native population: place-names, house and farm and barnyard construction, architecture, personal family names, customs, manners, work habits, myths, beliefs, superstitions, nursery rhymes, clothing, and food. From this Eskildsen argued that South Slesvig clearly revealed its origin as part of the Danish folk territory, albeit one which had been subject to generations of German influence. This had laid down a veneer of German acculturation, primarily in terms of language, but had left the old Schleswig folk character still in tune with its close Danish and Nordic antecedents.

Critics argued that Eskildsen's book had been written largely as a tongue-in-cheek critique of the Nazi regime and its evidence of a Danish presence in the landscape and among the habits of local Slesvigers was anecdotal and "belonged in a museum." The book gave considerable moral encouragement to the hard-pressed Danish minority in Nazi Germany and later played a considerable role in the postwar debate on the future political identity of the area when tens of thousands of German refugees from areas annexed by Poland and Czechoslovakia poured into Schleswig. South Slesvigers were then able to feel as well as intellectually appreciate how much closer to the Danes than to other Germans they were in the popular subconscious aspects of their identity. A majority then translated this feeling into a conscious rejection of their identity as German Schleswigers and voted for the SSW political party —

(*Südschleswigschen Wählweverbandes*, called *Den Sydslesvig Vælgerforening* in Danish (South Schleswig Voters' Association) — a new organization in political alliance with the umbrella organization representing the Danish minority (SSF — *Sydslesvig Forening*).

The Postwar Pro-Danish Movement in South Slesvig

By 1947, an absolute majority of native-born South Slesvigers subscribed to support the SSW's program of an administrative separation from Holstein, removal of all German refugees who had fled to Slesvig from other areas lost to Poland and Czechoslovakia, a mandate administration under the UN and an eventual plebiscite on reunification with Denmark. What had been denounced as objects and attitudes "fit only for a museum" had become part of a new self-identity. Petitions were presented by local South Schleswigers to the British authorities urging an eventual mandate with their pledge to become loyal Danish citizens.

Following Hitler's death, the Nazi high command was transferred to Admiral Doenitz in Flensburg. As a result the city was subjected to further destruction in April–May 1945. This was another irony — the city with the most significant non–Nazi community in Germany held out and endured further Allied attack as a result of its strategic location as the last stronghold of the Nazi regime. Its collapse, Germany's overwhelming defeat, the revelation of the crimes against humanity carried out in the name of the German people, the economic ruin and chaos at the end of the war in 1945 and the arrival of a wave of refugees provided the inhabitants of South Schleswig with a new vantage point to view the preceding centuries of national ferment. It also led to a re-emergence of the long suppressed local social democrats in Flensburg who had endured the Nazi regime in silent opposition and had been too intimidated to openly identify with the Danish minority. Many of them now sought to identify with their Danish roots and colleagues as an independent, local, Danish-oriented Slesvig party rather than continuing as an essentially German one.

Denmark faced a crisis and dilemma of the first magnitude. Its own declaration forswearing any demand for border changes was made immediately following German surrender in May 1945 and did not envision the mass popular wave of support for the tiny minority's organization which would come to embrace a majority of the population. Nor did it foresee the massive immigration of German refugees which more than doubled the population of Schleswig and threatened to permanently change the ethnic balance in the area.

Danish politicians had come to judge the strength of the Danish minority in South Schleswig on the basis of the last free communal election before 1933 when approximately 4,700 votes were cast for the Danish minority's party and 100,000 for the Nazis, amidst a total electorate of 185,000. This was the basis for the Danish statement against any territorial revision. The Danish government could not have expected that centuries of gradual Germanization in Schleswig could be wiped out by a landslide of Danish sympathies in the course of a few years. By June 1945, a petition with close to 13,000 signatures appealed to the British occupation authorities to let the local population seek a closer association including reincorporation into Denmark.

On this basis, *Südschleswigsche Vereiningun* (SSV) was established with the declared object of working in cooperation with the existing veteran Danish minority organization SSF. In 1946–47, membership in the SSV/SSF increased more than twenty-fold. Careful monitoring was undertaken to prevent membership by opportunists. Membership was limited to those born in South Schleswig or Denmark and their spouses, provided that they had not been members of the Nazi party (apart from those obligatory organizations for teenagers such as the *Hitlerjugend*—Hitler Youth).

Danish nationalists argued that it would be a repeat of the mistake of 1920 not to demand the incorporation of all Slesvig but they met with the powerful resistance of the Danish social democratic party, anxious to lead the country into renewed prosperity. Its leaders aspired to work closely with the sister social democratic party in the new Federal Republic of West Germany. The hesitation and subsequent refusal of the Danish government to press the British administration of South Schleswig for adoption of this program made it obvious to the local population that the area would remain under German sovereignty, albeit with new safeguards to ensure the full cultural autonomy of the German and Danish minorities on both sides of the border.

Nationalist circles in Denmark saw the cause and effect of SSW's vote decline since the highpoint in 1947 of an absolute majority of the native-born population in opposite terms. They believed it was precisely the Danish refusal to seek an alteration in the border which gravely wounded the incipient expansive movement of the postwar years. It meant that South Schleswig's original character had been severely distorted by the presence of a new non-native German refugee population whose hostility towards "fellow-countrymen" seeking to "surrender" their new refuge to a foreign power could only be expected to intensify as Germany emerged from the trauma of defeat.

The view of the spokesman for the federal legislature in Kiel, the capital of the state of Schleswig-Holstein, that supporters of the SSF were "Germans who risked turning their backs on their own people" gave a clear indication of the further recriminations that would surely follow continued agitation.

This point of view also colored the attitude of the British occupation authorities who were reluctant to antagonize German feelings as the Cold War increased in intensity and both Denmark and West Germany became allies in NATO.

New SSF members were labeled "pork-fat Danes" because for a brief time they were eligible to receive food parcels distributed by the Danish Minority Organization with help from a special Danish Food Aid Fund. This special help was ended in February 1946 and did not account for the second great wave of membership in the Danish minority organization. Denmark's failure to seek any change in the border resulted in a major governmental crisis which settled the issue of a boundary change. The question of South Schleswig's future political status caused a grave crisis and new election to the Folketing in October 1947. This toppled the government that had been led by Knud Kristensen of *Venstre* (liberal party), prime minister of Denmark from November 1945 to November 1947 in the first elected government after the occupation, who, in an emotional moment had stated: "Let us hope that our folk family will one day stand before the judgment of history with the verdict.... 'They did what they could, they left behind a Denmark larger and richer than they had received.'"

Although *Venstre* increased its representation significantly, its additional support was largely taken from other small parties sympathetic to incorporating South Schleswig. A new minority government under social democratic leadership with support from other left-wing groups followed a policy of reconciliation and rejected regaining South Schleswig as potentially too risky. It avoided any demand to change the status of South Schleswig and steered the government through the next few years. Full cultural rights accorded to both minority groups were worked out between the Danish and West German governments in 1949 and 1955 (the Kiel and Bonn Accords).

The subsequent decline in support for the SSW in communal elections (from its high point of 99,000 votes in 1947 to 66,000 in 1951, 42,000 in 1954 and 24,000 in 1967) has been used by most Danish politicians to justify their decision to react to what critics say was a wise and coolheaded decision not to be swept along by emotions. In the last state elections to the Schleswig-Holstein State Assembly (*Landtag*) in August 2009, the SSW increased its vote to 70,000, won 4 seats out of a total of 69 and got about 4.2 percent of the popular vote. If Holstein is eliminated, the SSW share of the vote in the land of Schleswig alone is about 10 percent, with almost a 20 percent share of the popular vote in the city of Flensburg.

German defenders of South Schleswig's cultural identity and political status regarded the SSW as the subject of Danish manipulation and rank opportunism. Supporters of South Schleswig's status within Germany have argued that Schleswig's "German high culture" could not be replaced except by the import of a "foreign-state Danish culture" rather than an indigenous cultural development. Other German-minded Schleswigers in the revived social democratic party saw the events of 1945–48 as an indication that something was indeed lacking and to be distrusted in the postulated German high culture that primarily spoke to a privileged class.

The Great Powers and Their Non-Involvement in the Postwar Danish-German Border Dispute

The incipient pro-Danish movement was nipped in the bud due to a combination of Cold War considerations and global factors. No one on the Allied side had anticipated any territorial demand against the vanquished Germany from a West European state. The old Schleswig-Holstein dispute of the 19th century and the Versailles Treaty and partition of Slesvig in 1920 had all been resigned to the history books. World events such as the withdrawal of the British from India, the partition of Palestine, the Greek Civil War, the Berlin Blockade, the communist coup in Czechoslovakia and the communist victory in China all dwarfed the pro-Danish movement and its renewed campaign for a referendum or special minority rights.

The official statement by Danish Prime Minster Buhl a few days after the surrender of Nazi Germany that "the border with Germany remains firm" ("*Grænsen ligger fast*") sealed the issue for the big four major occupying powers (the USA, the UK, the USSR and France, each with their respective zones of occupation) with an interest in postwar reorganization of a conquered and occupied Germany.

The USSR was reluctant to support a Danish separatist movement that could well be perceived as antagonistic to German nationalism. The Russians were busy cultivating their new communist puppet state, the DDR, and had already acted to detach and transfer huge prewar German territories in Silesia, Pomerania and East Prussia to itself and its Polish and Czech allies in the Eastern Bloc. Within West Germany, a reborn Communist party, like the social democrats, considered the Danish separatists as direct competitors for gaining influence in Schleswig-Holstein.

Under President Truman's leadership, American foreign policy put its trust in the new declaration of human rights and protection of minorities proclaimed by the United Nations rather than new territorial adjustments. Neither Norway or Sweden, which had previously shown sympathy for the Danish minority in South Slesvig, supported any renewed unrest along the Danish-German border.

In the face of opposition from the Danish and German governments, the German and Danish social democratic parties, the British occupation authorities, the USSR, Norway, Sweden and the United States interested in ensuring the adhesion of both West Germany and Denmark to NATO, the Danish Minority Organization and its political party faced insurmountable opposition. Many of the "new Danes" among the local population in South Slesvig sought to reintegrate into German society in the face of hostility from friends and neighbors who were now certain that the region would remain under German sovereignty. The British authorities placed obstacles in the way of the Danish minority organization and censored its political propaganda to avoid the possibility of encouraging a separatist movement and an eventual referendum.

Some Personal Accounts

There are many touching personal accounts told in 1945–48 and revealed in the memoirs of South Slesvigers that repeat such expressions as (in Danish) *"Jeg er Flensborger og ikke Ostpreusse"* ("I'm a Flensburger and not some kind of East Prussian.") and (in German) *"Weil wir so belogen wurden"* ("We were so lied to"), *"Ich vil von Duetschland ab"* ("I'm completely through with Germany"), and *"Es ist der einzige Weg aus dem deutschen Chaos herauszukomen"* ("It's the only way out of the German chaos!").

The following story is worth repeating for its honesty and poignancy. It is the life story of Christian Ruge, born in South Schleswig in 1915, the child of mixed Danish and German ancestors and educated at the teacher's training college in Kiel. A visitor to Denmark in the prewar period, Ruge admitted that he felt the people there enjoyed a sense of personal freedom which was missing in Nazi Germany and he immediately noticed upon passing the border at Kruså but that did not turn him against the regime. In his own words:

> I was never a member of the Party but it would be dishonest to say that I had come untouched through seven years of intensive Nazi influence in my school and public life. The main responsibility in our not being able to fathom Nazism's dangerous and immoral nature must lie with our college and high school teachers. They were sources of authority for us due to their scientific idealistic education.... I had these doubts about German society many years earlier but had suppressed them until they reappeared and became a frightful certainty that I had stood on the wrong side as a result of an experience I had in Goerlitz (Silesia) in March 1945. It was when a friend of mine told me the truth he had seen with his own eyes of the hell of Auschwitz, the death camp in Upper Silesia. That night, I lost my faith in Germany and everything German. For indeed all of these horrors had been committed by Germans in the name of the German people. The mask had been ripped away from the face of the rigid construction

of German great power status and this has revealed its deformation and horrible immorality. My entire life's building on a German foundation what collapsed that night like a pack of cards and what was left was simply a terrible void. It was clear to me that I and other young men in our native region had been persecuted, misused and shamed by German power politics and its misdeeds [quoted in J. P. Noack, *Det Sydslesvigske Graænsespørgsmål, 1945–1947*, vol. 1. pp. 225–226].

A number of leaders of the postwar pro-Danish wing of the Social Democrat party in Schleswig that split from the main body over the issue of promoting an eventual referendum on reunification with Denmark in the period 1945–47 rationalized their decision by explaining that the high hopes and expectations they had anticipated for Germany's future had been dashed and that the only remaining prospect for the Slesvig region was to draw nearer Denmark.

It is pointless to argue what might have happened had Denmark demanded incorporation of Slesvig in its entirety in 1920, or responded to the movement seeking a border revision in 1947. What is clear, with the benefit of hindsight, is that most South Slesvigers underwent a change in self-identity from Danish to German (1700–1850) to Danish (1945–47) to German again (1948–1965) or maintain a "Schleswig first" outlook today.

The core Danish minority population today in South Schleswig is much stronger than in 1920 and 1939 and in recent local elections the SSW has increased its share of the vote to regain strength and even attracted some voters who are the descendants of German refugees from the lost areas in the east that were annexed by Poland and Czechoslovakia after 1945. They identify with the Danish minority and feel that the program of the Danish

John Bull as a butcher about to chop off part of Schleswig for Mother Denmark. 1947.

minority organization and the SSW speaks more closely to their social and economic interests than the German political parties. Both the German and Danish governments signed solemn agreements regarding their respective minorities, guaranteeing them free rights to organize socially, culturally and politically and that their own self-identity could not be questioned, challenged or "tested." Even the descendants of the refugee population who entered the *lände* from other areas are aware of its special border area character as distinct from Holstein. A closer examination of other conflicts may reveal similar ambivalence and changes in self-image under conflicting pressures and fluctuating circumstances. In the end, it was Grundtvig's definition and not Hitler's that was accepted by both sides.

The Border in Danish Literature

The struggle to preserve Danish identity in Slesvig became a major theme in literature. Prior to 1864, Danish literary circles were under the influence of the cosmopolitan critic Georg Brandes who preached imitating the lofty cosmopolitan mainstream of German, French and English writers who were concerned with social problems. Starting with Holger Drachmann in 1877 who compared the stand of the Danish Army at Dybbøl to Thermopolae, a host of writers and poets took up similar themes. In Karl Gjellerup's novel *Germanernes Lærling* (*The Germans' Apprentice*), 1882, the tough *Sønderjyde* (South Jutlander) is idealized as a John Wayne type, silent and courageous, who will outlast the Germans. P.F. Rist's *En Rekrut fra Fire og Tris* (*A Recruit from Sixty-Four*) describes a typical Danish farmer-recruit — the opposite of the well disciplined spit-and-polish Prussian soldier, who nevertheless has a deep sense of devotion to his duty against overwhelming odds. Wilhelm Dinesen (Karen Blixen's father) praises the same qualities in *Fra Ottende Brigade* (*From the Eighth Brigade*).

After 1920, however, the theme of *danskheden* in South Jutland exercised little appeal as most Danes became convinced that the national struggle had achieved its goal with the return of North Slesvig. Few Danish language writers of any standing remained behind the new border in South Slesvig apart from Willy August-Linneman (1914–1985) from a Flensborg suburb. His novels recount the experiences and feelings of abandonment and helplessness of the Danish minority in Nazi Germany. He never properly received the recognition of the modern Danish literary establishment and his work embarrassed those in Denmark who felt he was pointing a finger at them for having turned a blind eye to the plight of their countrymen.

His debut novel, *Sangen om de Lyse Næetter* (*The Song of the Light Nights,*

1939), is a socially realistic account of people's lives during the mass unemployment, rampant inflation, oppression and war preparations under the Nazi regime in his native Flensborg. His *Natten før Freden* (*The Night Before Peace*) tells the story of a South Jutland fighter for liberation from the German yoke and takes a position in favor of Denmark's recovery of all South Slesvig.

Chapter 28

The Yellow Star Legend and Kings Christian X and Boris III

Denial of the Holocaust has been fittingly demolished by all sober and serious historians and the legal case won by Deborah Lipstadt and Penguin Books in a London court against the charge of libel gained world attention. The result should be a clarion call to ensure a rigorous examination in determining what is historical fact or fiction. During the trial, an English court found that David Irving was an "active Holocaust denier," as well as an anti–Semite and racist and that he "associates with right-wing extremists who promote neo-Nazism." The judge also ruled that Irving had "for his own ideological reasons persistently and deliberately misrepresented and manipulated historical evidence." He was convicted of "glorifying and identifying with the German Nazi Party," which is a crime in Austria under the Verbotsgesetz Law, and he served a prison sentence from February to December 2006 on the charges.

Lost amid the absurd denial of the Holocaust, however, is a widely believed myth due largely to Hollywood, Leon Uris (author of the best-selling novel *Exodus*), minor Danish diplomatic personnel, wishful thinking, and the BBC's research methods as well as to several prominent historians who have written widely about the Holocaust.

It is the story of the rescue of the Danish Jews and their safe passage to Sweden in October 1943, proclaiming that the Danish king, Christian X (grandfather of the present Queen Margrethe II), in an act of solidarity with his Jewish subjects, actually put on the yellow-star armband (or volunteered to do so) when the German occupation authorities issued such an order.

He never did so. The German occupation authorities never ordered the Jews in Denmark to wear the yellow armband. Very few readers bothered to read Uris's remarks in the foreword to the book *Exodus*; "Most (i.e., not all) of the events in *Exodus* are a matter of history and fact. Many of the scenes were created around historical incidents for the purpose of fiction."

The Bulgarian king, Boris III, has largely been ignored and forgotten. He paid with his life after heroically resisting Hitler's demands to deport Bulgaria's Jewish population (eight times larger than Denmark's 6,000) and use his country as a launching pad to wage war against the Soviet Union. The stories of the Danish and Bulgarian kings demonstrate the susceptibility and readiness of the public to be swayed by the power of the mass media to invent and deny facts.

From May 5–9, 1995, the 50th anniversary of V-E Day was celebrated all over the world with a fabulous four-day extravaganza of events culminating in London with a gala reception at the Guild Hall attended by over fifty heads of state. British and world television had considerable time to prepare for this event and do any required research. Yet, BBC presenter Vivian White, in his live commentary accompanying the entry into the Guild Hall of the assembled heads of state, remarked that Danish Princess Benedikte (the queen's sister who attended the event because the queen was unable to do so) "was, as we all know, the granddaughter of King Christian X, who together with his entire family, put on the Yellow Star in an act of Solidarity with his Jewish subjects."

I was living in London at the time and his words knocked me out of my chair. The reason was I had had several previous confrontations with Jewish friends and acquaintances who simply refused to accept a denial of this story. I had lived and worked in Denmark for seven years (1978–84) and was vice-chairman of the Danish-Israeli Friendship Society in Aarhus. On one occasion, we gave a reception for the visiting mayor of Beersheba who began his after-dinner talk in English by expressing the admiration of all ordinary Israelis for the "heroic action of King Christian ... who put on the yellow-star to save his Jewish fellow countrymen." I politely informed the mayor after observing the cringing faces of the assembled Danish audience in a whisper in Hebrew that the story was a myth and got an explosive reaction (in Hebrew), "Of course it's true; we all know this in Israel!"

So the BBC is certainly not alone but when I informed them of their error in a letter, what was the reaction? I noted the queen's autobiography, the pamphlet in English issued by the Danish Foreign Ministry and the Museum of the Danish Resistance (October 1943, *The Rescue of the Danish Jews From Annihilation*) and asked that they simply contact the Danish Embassy in London for one minute to enquire about the validity of what they had just televised and broadcast around the world to an audience numbering several hundred million viewers. Did they accept this suggestion? No!

The reply, dated November 30, 1995, thanked me for my critical letter. The text from their "Accountability Assistant," reads as follows:

King Christian X on a daily round of horseback riding through the streets of Copenhagen to boost popular morale shortly after the German Invasion of Denmark in 1940.

As this is a specialist area of knowledge, I have consulted Professor Cesarini of Manchester University and he has commented that it was a myth that the Danish Royal Family wore the Star of David during the occupation of their country by the Nazis…. Thus, although we accept that the reference to wearing the Star of David was inaccurate we would not agree that an on-air correction would be appropriate…. I will nevertheless ensure that a copy of my letter is sent to our News Information Library for their records. Thank you for writing.

Yours sincerely,
Carol Deakin,
Accountability Assistant,
BBC, London

I received a letter the following week from noted British Jewish historian Sir Martin Gilbert, an authority on the Holocaust, who wrote: "I fully share your anguish at the perpetuation of the Danish King Yellow Star myth and at the refusal of the BBC to correct it. I also share your feelings about the importance of the Bulgarian experience being better known."

For the BBC, errors on the order of "King Christian X and his entire family wore the yellow star" are simply "inaccurate," though it is disheartening that they feel no compulsion to correct their errors in an effective manner, i.e., through the broadcast medium.

It was simply a matter of the casual ignorance and elementary wrong assumptions stemming from the fact that in news organizations, routine checking is left to a hired staff with little sense of what is required to substantiate information, which may require searching primary sources in the original languages (eyewitnesses, ear-witnesses, diaries, newspapers, radio broadcasts, and government archives). The fact is that mistakes are repeated over and over again simply because they appear in print in books even by "distinguished authors" and other experts who do not have the requisite knowledge of original sources in the key language to verify a particular claim. Footnotes in these works simply cite another author who has quoted another secondary source.

Queen Margrethe II has been thanked so many times by guests for her grandfather's supposed action that she has written in her autobiography that this mistaken belief has caused her considerable embarrassment. King Christian was a puppet king with no real power. Unlike European other monarchs, such as the queen of Holland and the king of Norway, he did not choose to flee to England and help in the establishment of a government in exile. During the first three years of the occupation, he warned his fellow countrymen not to participate in acts of sabotage against the German occupation forces.

This was the government line which he adhered to and which also guar-

anteed Denmark a special relatively mild status, including no harsh discriminatory measures against the Danish Jews (until the planned deportation in
October 1943).

The king was certainly a decent man placed in a difficult situation. In
1942, he wrote a letter to Marcus Melchior, the Chief Rabbi, expressing
"relief" that a fire at the synagogue in Copenhagen did not cause extensive
damage. He and the queen had attended special services at the 100th anniversary celebration of the synagogue in 1933. A photo of their presence on that
occasion was published in several American popular weekly magazines in 1943,
ten years later, without an indication of the actual date, thus leading to the
common perception among many Americans that the king was demonstrating
public criticism of German anti–Semitism.

Both the king and cabinet ministers expressed their views on several
occasions during the early years of the occupation that there was no need to
adopt any legislation affecting Jewish citizens because "there is no Jewish
problem in Denmark." The armband myth in the Leon Uris book thus fell
on fertile ground.

Even before the publication of *Exodus*, the story of the yellow armband
existed, as did the total fabrication spread by the staff of Danish ambassador
Henrik Kaufmann that the Danish Jews so loved the royal family that they
were willing to voluntarily be interned by the German occupation authorities.

The reasons for this was the embarrassment of Kaufmann and other Danish diplomatic personnel that the government and king had decided to cooperate with the German occupation authorities and the very bad publicity
Denmark had received due to its disgraceful surrender within four hours after
German troops crossed the border. The king and the government even refused
the proposal of the Danish commander-in-chief, William Prior, to destroy
the Danish military airfields to prevent them from being used by the Germans
in their coordinated attack on Norway.

Kaufmann refused to follow the dictates of the Danish government and
signed agreements with the American and British governments to defend the
overseas Danish territories of Greenland and the Faroe Islands respectively.

For this, he was censured and dismissed by the puppet Danish authorities
in Copenhagen. He and his overly eager staff wished to create an image of
Denmark as a fighting ally and not a defeated and humiliated collaborator of
the Nazis (as the Quisling government in Norway). They seized upon the
Jewish angle as a way to win sympathy among Americans for a Denmark that
in reality opposed the Nazis and did everything to frustrate their evil inten-
tions.

Another widespread contribution to the myth followed the death of King

Christian in 1947. His Head Librarian of the Royal Judaica Collection (the largest in Europe) stated in an interview (in Danish) that the king had told him shortly before his death that if the German authorities had instituted the yellow star armband in Denmark he might have considered wearing it himself. This purely hypothetical "might have" situation was translated into English by several over eager journalists as the simple "he did."

As if *Exodus* were not enough, another novel, *A Night of Watching* by Elliot Arnold (Pan Books, London, 1967), puts these words into the mouth of a Jewish protagonist: "There is the King, the most wonderful man in Denmark and our friend.... He gave his word that nothing would ever happen to us" (p. 75).

What accounts then for the Danish myth cited in countless versions in serious and popular literary and historical works and repeated by various pundits and most recently on the television show *The View* by the staff of commentators anxious to demonstrate their sophisticated knowledge about this brave act of solidarity.

The yellow star myth stems from the novel (and film) *Exodus*. Its persistence is no doubt due to the difficulty of many people abroad in believing that such a heroic action stemmed from the determination of ordinary citizens, the same ones who had agreed that the government had done the wise and expedient thing by not resisting the German invasion of 1940. On the other hand, under Bulgaria's communist regime, the efforts of both the king and the Bulgarian Orthodox church were targets of constant invective, slander and "revisionism" so that his very real role in the rescue of Bulgaria's Jews has been erased or minimized. Why such ignorance and willful amnesia about the actions of King Boris III?

The answers are a product of the Cold War, cultural biases, ignorance of geography and perhaps unconscious prejudices. Documents revealing the role of the monarchy and the church in saving the country's Jews were suppressed by the communist party while the role of the party and its leaders at the time were elevated to the role of heroic saviors. In this regard, hard-core Jewish communists, including the editors of the Sofia-based Jewish communist newspaper *Evreiski Vesti*, loyally repeated the party line. The great majority of Bulgarian Jews (almost 95 percent) were allowed to emigrate to Israel in 1948–51 and were aware of the truth.

Michael Bar-Zohar is an Israeli historian of Bulgarian origin. He arrived in Israel in 1948 with his family, was a member of the Israeli Knesset, and has told the full story of the Bulgarian rescue and the role of King Boris III in his gripping book *Beyond Hitler's Grasp: The Heroic Rescue of Bulgaria's Jews* (Adams Media, Holbrooke, Massachusetts, 1998). His conclusion regarding the king needs to be shouted from the rooftops to shake up Jewish ignorance in America: "The final responsibility was the king's and his decision saved the Jews of Bulgaria. The Bulgarian Jews became the only Jewish community in the Nazi sphere of influence whose number increased during World War II" (p. 268).

In contrast to the Danish armband myth, Bulgarian Jews in their thousands did actually wear armbands with the portraits of King Boris and the royal family as a sign of loyalty, devotion and gratitude. The Bulgarian authorities as allies of the German government required Bulgarian Jews to wear armbands with tiny Jewish stars but most Jews did not bother to wear them and suffered no repercussions. Those who did wear them were frequently assured by their fellow Christian Bulgarians of sympathy and support.

The *numerus clausis* introduced to ensure that Jews constituted only a limited participation in business and medicine, was set at a higher proportion than that of the Jews in the general overall population. It reflected the much higher Jewish urban population rate. "Conversions" to Christianity were accepted by the Orthodox authorities with a minimum of embarrassment and, no matter how perfunctory, were guaranteed by the church as authentic.

The king and Bulgarian cabinet ministers (excluding the representatives of an anti–Semitic party eager to demonstrated complete loyalty to the Nazi racial ideology) all informed the German representatives in their country that the measures undertaken, as limited as they were, "completely solved" the Jewish problem and that deportation was out of the question. The Chief Rabbi of Sofia was hidden by one of the leaders of the Bulgarian Orthodox church, the Metropolitan Stephan, who declared publicly that "God had determined the Jewish fate and men had no right to torture Jews or persecute them."

Boris delayed and misled the Germans and acted to revoke deportation orders. Queen Giovanna (a daughter of Italian King Victor Emanuel) persuaded the Italian ambassador to issue Italian passports and transit visas to Jews of foreign nationality or who were stranded in Bulgaria. German documents and the personal memoirs of Monsignor Angelo Roncalli (later Pope John XXIII) reveal the role of the king and the Bulgarian Orthodox church in protecting his Jewish subjects. King Boris also managed to help Jewish refugees from Slovakia to be sent throughout Bulgaria and receive transit visas to Palestine.

The king failed only in extending his protection over areas temporarily occupied by Bulgaria (Greek Thrace and Yugoslav Macedonia), but not under his direct authority. Bulgaria had been maneuvered into the war as an ally of Nazi Germany primarily to recover these regions, part of Bulgaria before World War I and a cause of great resentment among Bulgarian nationalists.

The Jews of Thrace and Macedonia were deported to Auschwitz and murdered, a fact that became known in Bulgaria and caused revulsion.

Boris died under mysterious circumstances on August 28, 1943, and was likely murdered by agents of the Gestapo. This occurred shortly after his return from a meeting with Hitler in Berlin when he adamantly refused to change his policies on the Jewish question and join the war against the USSR. In many Jewish circles, there is a profound distrust and antipathy toward the peoples of Eastern Europe, to their virulent anti–Semitism and extreme nationalism as well as their state churches. The considerable degree of collaboration among many Poles, Ukrainians, Lithuanians and Romanians with the German occupation forces has resulted in Eastern Europe long being regarded as a single bloc. The inclusion of all Eastern Europe into the Communist East bloc under Soviet leadership during the Cold War reinforced this perception. The fact that the Bulgarian experience was so totally different confounds those who find it easier to maintain stereotypes.

On the other hand, the stereotype of handsome, fair-haired, blue-eyed Danes who appear more Aryan than the Germans or the Slavic Bulgarians apparently lends them a special distinction and appeal, especially when it comes to having rejected the savage doctrines of anti–Semitism.

The great majority of the Danish people did not act heroically during the greater part of the war; approximately 8,000 Danes volunteered for service in the SS organized *Frikorps Danmark* to fight with German troops on the Eastern front. Although some were members of the German minority in the South Jutland border area, many were ethnic Danes.

This compares with about 800 active saboteurs at the height of the resistance and the 4,800 volunteers in the *Danforce Brigade* which assembled in Sweden and trained to participate in an invasion force to liberate Denmark. Many Danish seamen on merchant and fishing vessels also refused to obey the orders issued by their government in the days following the German invasion on April 9, 1940, to head towards "neutral" (pro-Axis) Italian and Spanish ports, but instead volunteered to serve in the Allied cause. Almost 1,500 of them lost their lives in German submarine attacks.

By contrast, only a handful of Bulgarian volunteers aided the Axis cause by serving with the German forces in the campaign against the USSR and Bulgaria, like Finland, switched sides late in the war.

This is not to castigate the Danes. The myth of the yellow star armband detracts from the vital participation of thousands of Danes from every walk of life who did help their Jewish countrymen at a moment's notice to assemble and flee, guarded their property and welcomed them back at the end of the war. The real story is much more inspiring and a tribute to traditional Danish values of concern for human rights than the myth of the king.

Nothing better illustrates this than the most popular Danish television drama *Matador* (the equivalent of our Monopoly game) that traces the fortunes of several families in the provincial town of Korsebæk located several hours' rail or car journey from Copenhagen. Maude is married to Hans Christian Varnæs, the director of the local bank, and is a model of an upper-class Danish traditional housewife who is constantly concerned about looking her best and avoiding any unpleasantness. She often suffers from extreme emotional stress over the smallest inconvenience or problem in the management of the household or her children's minor escapades.

The bank's chief assistant is the affable Herr Stein, a Jew who, on occasion, visits the Varnæs home on business. When he is given the information that the Germans are about to deport the entire Jewish population of the country, he is stranded and out of touch with developments in Copenhagen and arrives at the Varnaes home in desperation.

Only Maude is home but she unrepentantly seizes the opportunity to call upon others in her circle of relatives, friends, and her husband's employees to extend all possible help. Due to her quick presence of mind and initiative, a refuge and escape route is found for Herr Stein.

This series in 24 hour-long episodes has been shown and shown again many times on Danish television and is the nostalgic favorite of many older viewers who lived through the war. No other television series has been so popular. It speaks to the viewers of the realities that the generation of the 1930s–1940s experienced and the unexpected strength that many of them found in times of adversity.

The Danish and Bulgarian peoples and their churches both have a right to take pride in their wartime record. The actions of both also stand in contrast to the generally dismal record of other European peoples, nationalist regimes and state churches. With respect to the "Tale of Two Kings," Boris III was a martyr whose personal example influenced history. Christian X was a decent man and a patriot but a weak king whom history and circumstances cast in a heroic mold because he wore the crown.

Chapter 29

The "Jewish Question" and the Danish Minority in Nazi Germany

As an American Jew who lived in both Israel and Denmark for many years, I had ample opportunity to observe and contrast how a large segment of the younger generation in all three countries lacks the richly deserved pride their parents inherited from the past. This pride is derived from strong religious values, democratic political beliefs and a deep cultural heritage that enabled the greatest generation to confront World War II and the Holocaust. In doing research on a book about the border dispute between Germany and Denmark, I came across a fascinating and unexpected example of how the Danish minority in southern Schleswig, subject to intense Nazi pressure to conform, resolutely resisted by asserting its own values and proved to be an inspiration to the local disheartened Jews. The latter had gone from believing they were loyal and patriotic Germans to a despised outcast group of social pariahs. This story deserves to be told and made more widely known in our own chaotic world, so lacking in moral constancy and opportunistically seeking only the most expedient way out of difficult situations.

Denmark has won an honored place among many Jews for its famous rescue of almost the entire community in October 1943, a brave humanitarian operation that has become a legend. Wholly unknown is another no less courageous gesture by ethnic Danes residing in South Schleswig, reduced to a minority under constant pressure and subject to harassment and intimidation by the Nazi regime. The Danish minority's situation in Nazi Germany is of interest because it represents the only non–German community that the German government could not simply capriciously ignore or mistreat with impunity (as it did towards the Jews, Poles, Lithuanians, Frisians and Sorbs) but had to try to accommodate in some degree in order to ensure good relations with Denmark, a policy which German foreign policy sought to promote. The Danish minority, whatever the views of its individual members towards the Nazis' racist ideology and in spite of sympathy towards Denmark in the face of naked German aggression in 1940, had to obey German law and fulfill all their duties as German citizens, including military service.

In 1920, a plebiscite divided the border region of Schleswig between Germany and Denmark. Approximately 6,000 North Schleswigers (the overwhelming majority Danish-minded) fell in German uniform between 1914 and 1918 for a war that they viewed with little or no enthusiasm in contrast to the German-minded population's vision of even greater national aggrandizement. In proportion to North Schleswig's population, war fatalities were higher than the national German average. Several hundred Danish-minded North Slesvigers took advantage of nearby Denmark to flee across the border and either avoid conscription or desert. Most supporters of the social democratic opposition in the northern districts of Flensburg, several other larger towns (Schleswig, Husum) and among day laborers who were still identifiably Danish in their sympathies were nevertheless swayed by the opportunity to be a part of what they hoped would be a democratic republican industrial Germany. This seemed more attractive to the urban working class than an enlarged but monarchist and still largely agrarian Denmark.

It was a decision they came to rue. Additionally, many of them were swayed to vote for Germany in the plebiscite by the threats of employers, especially at the largest workplaces in Flensburg — the naval base, shipyards, railway yards, paper mill, glass factory, rum distillery and breweries — that production and many jobs would be moved to Germany proper if Flensburg were to be allotted to Denmark. Most Jews in the border area lived in Flensburg. By and large, this was a young community unfamiliar with previous Danish rule (from the Middle Ages until 1864 when the areas of Schleswig and Holstein were ceded to Prussia), of no more than 100 individuals in 1933. Most were reform minded, favored assimilation and were non–Zionist. Almost no Jews lived in the northern part of Schleswig, which was predominantly rural and had been returned to Denmark in 1920.

Older and larger Jewish communities were found in South Schleswig in the university town of Kiel, Altona (a suburb of Hamburg) and Friedrichstadt, which had the only synagogue in the region. They had historically identified with the German majority. By 1914, the adoption of Marxism made many workers in Schleswig who still identified with their Danish heritage doubly suspicious elements (potential Danish sympathizers and anti-imperialists opposed to a war of aggrandizement or colonial expansion). Even before the war, the German social democratic party had on occasion argued for a policy of reconciliation between German and Danish workers.

Their close proximity to Denmark and cross-border contacts made many workers who had voted for Germany in the 1920 plebiscite realize how far the working class progressed economically and socially in Denmark under a system opposed to militarism, the fostering of humanitarian values and the spread of adult education on a massive scale. The progress made in Denmark during the interwar years resulted in higher living and educational standards for the working class. Much of the pro-German vote in 1920 had been due to the mistaken belief that these objectives would be more easily realized in Germany.

In South Schleswig, the minority community organized cultural activity promoted increased knowledge of Danish, open libraries, youth and scout movements, sports, education, and credit facilities to protect Danish-owned farms and offer church and welfare services for the minority community. A difficult problem between the minority and the government which worsened under the Nazis was the fact that a majority of supporters of the Danish Minority Organization — *Slesvigske Forening* (SF) — were workers sympathetic to or former members of the social democratic party.

A clear majority of the votes cast for the Danish list were to be found in the working-class districts of Flensburg leading to charges that "subversive Marxist elements were hiding behind a mask of an ethnic community." Quite a few of these individuals were indeed reluctant to bear the economic burdens imposed by membership in the official minority organization and the social ostracism they would have to endure as "traitors" from their comrades. Although the rank and file of the Danish minority organization came from a socialist background, the political work was led by individuals who had a conservative, Christian-democratic and even anti-socialist background.

When a German-dominated European organization of national minorities proposed a conference in Bern, Switzerland, in 1933, the choice of Jacob Kronika as the Danish "observer" was sharply opposed and considered an "unfriendly act." Kronika had been editor of the German language newspaper "*Der Schleswiger*," and Germans considered it totally inappropriate for a spokesman of the Danish minority to have edited a propaganda organ to "win souls" from the German majority in South Schleswig. Moreover, the congress was not attended by ethnic German representatives from North Schleswig, apparently to smooth the way for some perfunctory Danish participation. The German-dominated congress was so biased that no Jewish groups saw fit to send representatives and even the Swiss press characterized the congress as a pro-German charade.

Nazi policy regarding national minorities was contradictory in spite of their fervent nationalism and support for an irredentist policy to reclaim the areas lost in World War I, although the local Schleswig-Holstein Nazi Party assumed that this meant a return to the Kongeåen — i.e., a restoration of the pre-war boundary with Denmark. The German Foreign Ministry and various national Nazi Party spokesmen were careful to omit North Schleswig in their comments on future boundary revisions. Moreover, Hitler made several public speeches, most notably on May 17, 1933, in which he clearly defined Nazi attitudes towards the nationality question as being based on free will and these remarks were given prominence in the Nazi newspaper *Völkische Beobachter*.

Of course, this policy did not apply towards the Jews who were automatically to be excluded from German citizenship and defined by "race and blood." Expressions of friendship towards Denmark as part of a friendly Nordic community of nations were made in German propaganda literature but revisionist circles in Schleswig-Holstein launched a new campaign in the spring of 1933 attacking the 1920 boundary, making it clear to the Danish community that the new regime posed a dire threat (chapter 27).

One of the first casualties of the new policy was the close alliance in the Reichstag between the Danish and Polish minority communities whose representatives had worked in harmony. A protest over a new electoral law promulgating a minimum of 60,000 signatures to qualify for participation in a national election split the Danish minority organization's leadership, which felt that too close an identification with the Polish minority party might rebound to their detriment. German opposition to the boundary with Poland was intense and the Danish foreign ministry, through their consul in Flensburg, made it known that it would be unwise to link the Danish and Polish communities in the public mind.

For some, however, this was a clear sign of opportunism and disloyalty since the officially recognized Polish minority community was more than ten times larger and had provided the backbone for the other much smaller minorities. Nevertheless, an important consideration was to stress that Danish-minded Slesvigers believed in the principal of self-determination rather than the grandiose claims of both Germans and Poles who stressed "blood, language and soil."

Shortly after the Nazis assumed power, discussions within the Ministry of the Interior led to proposals of a new citizenship law that would distinguish between formal "state citizenship" and a soon-to-be-created "participatory citizenship" that could only be acquired through service to the state in such Nazi organizations as the NSDAP, SA, SS, and *Deutsche Arbeitsfront* (DAF) — a Nazi-run union which would by definition exclude non–Germans. Severe measures had already been taken to eliminate Jews from all positions of importance and curtail their rights as German citizens under special legislation. Attempts by the Danish minority organization to clarify this matter with the Ministry of the Interior received only answers indicating the necessity of distinguishing "Aryans" from "non–Aryans" in the determination of what was called *Reichsangehörigkeit* ("belonging to the state"). The constant threat of deprivation of their rights as German citizens hung over the Danish minority throughout the Nazi regime.

The only way for the Danish community to react was an editorial in the Danish language newspaper *Flensborg Avis* warning of the possible consequences of such an action upon ethnic German minorities in other countries. One ironic consequence of the Nazi racist ideology to prove their Aryan (i.e., non–Jewish) ancestry was the rediscovery of some Schleswigers that the marriage or baptismal certificates of their grandparents or great-grandparents were in Danish or that family memorabilia such as diaries and letters revealed that in previous generations some individuals felt that their need to learn German and imitate the Germans to fully integrate within German society were impositions.

The ability of the organized Danish minority community in South Schleswig to stand steadfast against the Nazi juggernaut and maintain its own cultural life, schools, libraries, welfare assistance and the only non–Nazi newspaper in Germany from 1933–45 was due to their courage and tenacity in the face of constant harassment as well as official German government policy. This policy made necessary the formal respect of commitments based on the reciprocity of the Danish government toward the German-minded minority in North Schleswig. An unintended consequence was that a tiny Jewish community in Flensburg, the major city of North Schlewig and only a few kilometers from the Danish border, was able to take heart and prepare and organize for emigration or flight to Palestine or Denmark.

Aware of their tenuous position walking a tightrope, the Danish minority could not openly express the opposition of the overwhelming majority of its members to the regime's anti–Semitic policies. The editorial line of Flensborg *Avis* remained as it had been under the Weimar Republic that it did "not interfere in internal German matters." The paper went further in asserting that it aimed to serve as a bridge between Germany and Denmark, a view which the editors felt even more essential after the Nazis came to power and in spite of frequent criticism from the press and left-wing parties in Denmark. No one, however, of any standing in the SF or *Avis* openly or behind closed doors approved of the Nazi Party's race laws, boycott of Jewish shops, anti-miscegenation laws, exclusion of Jews from public life, and deprivation of all civil rights culminating in the mass violence on *Kristallnacht* (Night of the Broken Glass) in 1938, by which time almost all Jews had left Flensburg.

It must be remembered that although the Nazis were the largest party in Germany on the eve of their assumption of power, the combined electoral strength of the social democrat and communist parties in many areas was greater. This was true in Schleswig-Holstein where the Nazi Party had won overwhelming support from the rural population and many small farmers threatened with bankruptcy, while the social democrats and communists were strong in the larger towns (Kiel, Schleswig and Husum) and strongest of all in Flensburg, where their combined strength and that of the Danish minority presented the Nazis with more of an obstacle than elsewhere to their usual smooth sailing over potential opposition.

A few local Jews were department store owners and shopkeepers with a tradition of excellent relations with the Danish minority. One of them, Herr Rath, was a faithful advertiser in Flensborg *Avis* and, after being forced to leave Flensburg in 1935, expressed appreciation in a paid public notice appearing in the newspaper, thanking the community for its excellent treatment of him and his business. A Nazi-sponsored anti–Jewish boycott in Flensburg in April 1933 ended with little effect as the Jewish shopkeepers retained almost all their customers (from both the Danish and German communities) who were quite unsympathetic to Nazi appeals to boycott Jewish-owned shops that offered them credit at a time when few others were willing to do so.

During the blockade of Jewish-owned shops, patrolled by uniformed S.A. guards carrying signs with cartoons of Jewish stereotypes denouncing, "Germans who buy at Jewish shops are Traitors!," an unruly crowd of Flensborgers broke through the picket line to carry on doing business, a sensational news item carried only in the *Avis*. It is unlikely that any similar event occurred throughout Nazi Germany. Needless to say, the rival German majority-owned newspaper, *Flensburger Nachrichten*, downplayed the incident and enthusiastically supported the boycott.

From 1930 to 1938, Jews in Flensburg made use of a rented room for social events and meetings in the building of the Danish community center. Although sympathetic, there were clearly limits beyond which the Danish community could not openly express offers of assistance. Requests by Jewish parents whose children had been expelled from the German public school system were refused permission to transfer them to the Danish minority school. From 1934 to 1938, a *Hechalutz* ("Pioneer"), socialist-Zionist training farm, operated in a Jägerslust, a country estate on the outskirts of Flensburg.

Good relations formed with local Danish-minded farmers were later utilized in helping German-Jewish teenagers reach Denmark and carry on their agricultural training in 1939–40. All of these boys and girls either reached Palestine (possible by traveling through Russia and Turkey until the German invasion of the USSR in June 1941) or else fled to Sweden along with almost the entire Danish Jewish community in 1943. Alexander Wolff, the owner of Jägerslust who had made his estate available for the Zionist training program, managed to emigrate to the United States. Wolff later received compensation and a monthly pension after the war from the federal state of Schleswig-Holstein, was an invited guest of the Flensburg City Hall in 1966, and was interviewed by *Flensborg Avis*.

Flensborg Avis was conspicuous among newspapers in Germany by its avoidance of editorial comment on Nazi anti–Semitism. It faithfully reported the anti–Jewish legislation without comment except for a few occasions when it dryly noted that these measures were designed by the government to uphold the "German sense of honor and racial purity." It must be also be borne in mind that the Danish government and its representative at the Danish consulate in Flensburg had warned the SF leadership and *Flensborg Avis* not to openly antagonize the Nazi regime or express sympathy on a community-wide level for Jews, social democrats, and communists who had been forced out of public positions or had fled to Denmark.

This became even more acute after the Nazi prohibition against *Flensborg Avis's* German language daily supplement, *Der Schleswiger*, as a result of accusations that the paper had been openly circulated among groups of "disgruntled communist workers in Hamburg's harbor" who then had distributed it to "unscrupulous elements" and bookshops throughout Germany, representing the anti–Nazi "Confessional Church" (led by the Rev. Martin Niemöller until his arrest together with more than 800 pastors in July 1937). The Danish minority community in South Schleswig had thus been branded as an ally of the regime's opponents by some local Nazi politicians and revisionist circles anxious to recover North Schleswig. With the accusation of aid to communists, social democrats and the Christian opposition hanging over their heads, it is understandable that the Danish minority community could not risk further charges of open collaboration with the Jews.

Stamp commemorating the signing of Copenhagen-Bonn Declaration of 1955 guaranteeing minority cultural rights in both Denmark and West Germany. The stamp was issued in an identical format (apart from the languages) in both West Germany and Denmark. The dots represent minority schools.

The ability of the South Schleswig Danes to withstand constant harassment was a product of their ethnic pride and tenacious Christian or socialist values. It was also made possible by official German government policy that, at times, contradicted rabid local Nazi party members, intent on recovering "lost North Schleswig" as an irredenta. Hitler was anxious not to offend public opinion throughout Scandinavia by putting undue pressure on Denmark. His foreign policy was based on the reciprocity of the Danish government toward the German-minded minority in North Schleswig.

The unintended effect was that the local Jews had before them an inspiring example of their proud Danish neighbors who refused to bow to Nazi power and submerge their ethnic identity and strong Socialist or Christian values. The challenge of today is that we are in danger of becoming totally absorbed by the problems of the moment. Only by maintaining our moral compass and remembering and teaching those values and traditions that have been an inspiration throughout our history can we resist the present threats to our civilization from fundamentalist Islam and its advocates.

As in 1943, most Danes do not seek a confrontation with powerful forces unable to accept and coexist with Danish tolerance and democratic values. Shock and disbelief followed the constant mob violence in Muslim countries in 2006 over the so called "Muhammad cartoons," resulting in hysterical attacks of hatred on Danish embassies and the repeated burning of Danish flags (Europe's oldest national flag). Expediency and the desire to avoid such a confrontation has led to support for apologies by the editor of *Jyllands-Posten* and even Danish Prime Minister Fogh, but as the violence continues, there has been a growing realization that, like 1943 when ordinary Danes did what they could to aid their Jewish fellow citizens, Danes cannot escape their proud heritage — even if against their initial hopes for avoiding confrontations. Like Andersen's story of the steadfast, one-legged tin soldier in the fiery furnace, they must stand true to their values.

Chapter 30

The Danish-Swedish
Sibling Rivalry

Scandinavia and Iberia are the two maritime peninsulas fronting on the Atlantic Ocean and respectively guarding the entrances to Europe's two great inland seas — the Baltic and the Mediterranean. Each of these regions has witnessed both a struggle between a unifying cultural-linguistic and religious heritage, and a bitter national envy and rivalry that for a time encompassed union and threatened absorption of the "lesser" (Portugal and Denmark) siblings. This was followed by a renewed independence and sense of distinct identity and the identification of the "greater" rival (Spain and Sweden) with imperialist ambitions, and indelibly stamped as an arrogant and hypocritical usurper. In both peninsulas, the originally ascendant powers of Denmark and Portugal achieved independence as a distinct nation-state, regional hegemony and a far flung overseas empire — only to lose out and suffer a long period of hurt feelings of inferiority vis-à-vis the newly dominant rival "big brothers" (Sweden and Spain).

Denmark and Portugal increasingly relied upon their Atlantic coasts and overseas orientation to establish vast colonial empires in the mid–Atlantic (the Azores, Madeira, Brazil) and the North Atlantic (the Faroes, Iceland and Greenland, and the Virgin Islands), and even further in Africa, India and Asia. One of the most fascinating and as yet incomplete studies of an episode in the history of exploration is the brief but fertile period of Portuguese-Danish cooperation (1425–1476).

Few neighboring countries were at war so often with each other from the Middle Ages until the end of the Protestant reformation as Sweden and Denmark — in much the same way as France and Germany from Napoleonic times until World War II. For most Americans this comes as a surprise, since both countries along with the rest of Scandinavia enjoy a modern image of peaceful states that enjoyed neutrality throughout most major modern European conflicts. The many similarities in culture, language, religion, the common reputation as welfare states with advanced social legislation and a social security net to prevent outright deprivation have obscured much of the same differences in outlook that distinguish Americans and Brits in spite of a long common history and shared institutions.

Like the differences that led to the American Revolution and the final separation from England in spite of the presence of a large contingent of loyalists who remained true to their king and oath of allegiance, Danes and Swedes could not agree on the form of the union between them. The differences separating them did not constitute an ocean but a common land boundary and narrow stretches of water. What we call southern Sweden today is known by the regional name of Skåne (with its own flag). It was both in terms of physical geography, landscape, soils, vegetation and climate a part of the Danish kingdom from the earliest appearance of a state embracing Jutland (Jylland), Skåne across the Øresund and the main Danish islands of Fünen (Fyn) and Zealand (Sjæland), lying amidst the two "Belts" in the Kattegat.

Norway, originally an independent nation and largely responsible for the early Viking explorations that led to the discovery of Iceland, Greenland and America, suffered the loss of almost one-third of its population due to the Black Death and was so devastated that it found a union with Denmark as the only reasonable solution to avoid the total dissolution of society. Sweden also felt that the advantages offered by a union with Denmark, the function of which was called a "loving bond" under a united crown offered it strategic advantages. This union in 1497, under the Danish Queen Margrethe I, was a political move designed to be a union of equals.

Like the case of the English governors and the American colonial houses of representation, the Swedish and Danish nobility were diverse sources of power. Growing resentment of the Union led to the desire for renewed Swedish independence and the eviction of the Danes from Skåne, a move that would award Sweden a share in the control of the narrow straits, through which European maritime traffic passed from the North Sea and the Baltic. It also meant the end of Danish monopoly. With two such contrasting visions of their future and status, the union collapsed and war followed war from 1434 until 1720. Even with Denmark's ability to mobilize allies, most notably the Russians, the results were almost continuously successful for Sweden, and a terrific blow to Denmark's prestige and image as the leading Scandinavian power.

The result was also a strong national enmity that built upon existing resentments. A final blow was dealt when Sweden picked the winner in the Napoleonic wars and Denmark was forced to cede control of Norway to its bitter enemy, adding a final humiliation and promoting Sweden to the undisputed position as the big brother. This diplomatic victory was bitterly resented in both Denmark and Norway as an example of Swedish imperialism, prompting the great Danish clergyman N. F. S. Grundtvig (chapter 16) to publish a pamphlet in 1813 denouncing the aggressive spirit that "now dominates Sweden" and acted as "the servant of evil." The Danes were convinced that they and the Norwegians had after several centuries of sharing a common homeland, acted wisely, justly and in respect for Norway's individuality. The Norwegians of course wanted to regain their independence and had to wait until 1905, when a wiser Swedish government realized that to deny these aspirations would poison relations among the Scandinavian brothers.

Although Denmark proper (Jutland, Fünen and Zealand) was never conquered by Sweden, it too suffered humiliation by its archrival as a result of constant military defeats that eclipsed its early domination of the Baltic. This ignominy served as a cause of irredentist hopes for centuries and prolonged the hatred between the two countries. To this day, the Danish royal anthem sings of a naval victory of their King Christian IV over the Swedish fleet in 1644. By contrast, the Swedish anthem never even mentions the name of the country but exclaims, "I will live and die in 'Norden'" (a term, like Scandinavia, referring to the entire region).

World War II added a modern chapter when Denmark and Norway fell to a German invasion, while Sweden maintained a profitable neutrality and allowed transport of both German troops and German-controlled Norwegian and Finnish raw materials across its territory issues, which created an additional layer of resentment, rivalry and competitiveness.

The Danes have always had a reputation among their Scandinavian colleagues as being much more European, especially because of French influence, and therefore are regarded as somewhat decadent, less puritanical, lackadaisical, sloppy, and more interested in good food and pursuing beautiful women than the aloof, industrious, neat, well-groomed, rational (the Danes would add "arrogant") Swedes — or the athletic, honest, and nature-loving Norwegians. Of course, like all stereotypes, there is both exaggeration and enough of a grain of truth in these images to convince observers to look for confirmation.

Anthropologist Thomas Hylland Eriksen tells the following joke about the mutual Scandinavian stereotypes that accentuate their sense of individuality and nationhood. A Swede, Dane and Norwegian have been arguing all day. They have been shipwrecked on a deserted island. A genie appears out of thin air and tells them he can grant each one wish.

The Swede immediately says, "I want to go home to my comfortable bungalow with my Volvo, video recorder and slick IKEA furniture." His wish is granted and he disappears. The Dane then says, "I want to go back to my cozy apartment in Copenhagen, to sit on the sofa with my feet on the table next to my sexy girlfriend and a six-pack of beer." And off he flies. The Norwegian, after discovering he is alone and giving the problem some thought tells the genie, "I am so lonely, I wish my two friends would come back."

The popular press, especially the mass circulation tabloids, delights in playful teasing and taunting the older brother rival that sometimes reaches grotesque proportions. Although educated people regard this pandering to old prejudices as the cheapest form of sensationalism, its continued emotional long-term appeal cannot be doubted. A favorite part of this teasing are the double meanings employed in manipulating the two closely related languages. Danes and Swedes will often prefer to converse in English rather than speak their own languages with each other. The written form is sufficiently similar so that the general meaning of texts can usually be understood but differences in intonation, pronunciation and the distinct different meanings of closely sounding words provide an endless form of humor. Swedes have a special "Sj" sound and most Danes use a pronounced glottal stop that is difficult for non-natives to imitate.

In 1944, a Dane and a Swede, Ellen Hartmann and Valfrid Palmgren Munch-Petersen, wrote a special dictionary titled *Farlige ord og lumske ligheder i dansk og svensk* (*Dangerous Words and Awkward Similarities in Danish and Swedish*) that should be read by anyone needing to master the neighboring language and avoid embarrassing mistakes. One can imagine the reaction of an American woman to an expression like: "I came by yesterday to knock you up but nobody was home." For an Englishman until circa 1970 this simply meant: "I came by and knocked on the door to see if you were home."

All this may seem like making a mountain out of a molehill for many foreign observers who imagine that the Scandinavian peoples are so similar they should have long ago buried the hatchet. Indeed, all the Scandinavian states remain among the most stable in the world politically. They cooperate in many economic and social areas such as the joint SAS airline and are culturally, socially and linguistically similar, but maintain a distinct sense of political separateness.

History and especially geography has determined much of their foreign policy and prevented them from following a common one or joining in an alliance. Norway and Denmark joined NATO due to their inability to maintain their neutrality in World War II, while Sweden continues to be neutral. All three jealously guard their independence. Denmark's close proximity and border conflict over Schleswig (Slesvig) prevented Norway and Sweden from considering a Scandinavian alliance before the world wars with their prospect of German expansionism and revenge. Finland, bordering the Soviet Union and with territorial losses sustained in 1940, made it difficult for the other

Scandinavian states to join an alliance that would endanger them in order to protect that country.

The Case of Sweden (*Tilfældet Sverige*) by the Danish journalist Mogen Berendt became a popular best-seller in Denmark during the 1980s. He analyzed renewed Danish-Swedish policies and popular prejudices that have contributed to irritating albeit minor disagreements. These included the proximity of the Swedish nuclear power plant in Barsebeck facing the Danish coast of Zealand and Copenhagen, Swedish import regulations affecting the sale of Danish pork products, differences in policies over taxation, the sale of alcoholic beverages, differences in adoption laws and a border dispute over the island of Hesselø, an island with a handful of inhabitants.

The Swedes are often the target of jokes and satire that picture them as arrogant, snobbish, overly formal and fond of titles. A victory by the Danish team over its Swedish rival in international competition is still considered the most emotionally satisfying for Danish football fans. Well known Danish psychologist Per Christensen, commenting on the underlying reasons for the appeal of the book, had this to say:

> The Swedes have typical narcissistic traits. They feed on an ingrown imaginary greatness. The Swedes are full of megalomaniac impressions and are clearly tied to their own traits and achievements. The Danes, can on the other hand, be described as chronic depressives with a lack of self-confidence and a tendency to exaggerated skepticism of highflying plans and ideas. The Swedish attitude towards Denmark easily becomes commandeering, arrogant and nonchalant.

Ekstra Bladet, the leading Danish tabloid daily, had this to say in 1983 following a number of mass protests in Denmark against Sweden's nuclear reactor: "It is of no consequence that the Swedes regard themselves as the 'big brother' of the North, which, as we know, consists of five independent nations. We in Denmark hardly wish Swedish conditions where everything is forbidden and nothing permitted."

For the Swedes, the term "Danish conditions" is meant to assume the opposite — an exaggerated permissiveness and lack of organization. The Swedes' image of themselves, however, received a major shock following the unsolved murder of Prime Minister Olaf Palme in 1994.

Fortunately, the rivalry takes on its most aggressive forms during international football matches between the two national teams. The earliest matches were overwhelming Danish victories 8–0 and 10–0 in 1913. Apparently the Danes were much more familiar with the game due to close relations and many previous matches with Germany and Britain, but it did not take long for the Swedes to catch up. In 1916, they shut out Denmark 4–0, prompting national jubilation — a major news event to lighten the news for the two neutral nations weary of the depressing news of catastrophic loss of human life in a war tearing the rest of Europe apart. From the early 1960s until the mid–1970s, Swedish football clearly excelled and Sweden remained undefeated on home ground for thirty-nine years — until a Danish team ended the streak with a 2–1 victory, causing serious politicians and newspapers in Denmark to proclaim the date May 11 as a national holiday and suggesting that children receive the day off in the future.

Of course, much of these attitudes are taken with a grain of salt and there are strong personal human connections and a sense of solidarity and brotherhood among the Scandinavian nations, as well as countless examples of friendships and cooperation. Several thousand Norwegians and Swedes volunteered for service in Denmark's cause in the 1864 war when the Prussians and Austrians invaded the country. Many hundreds of Swedes, Norwegians and Danes also overcame the official neutrality of their governments to volunteer for aid to the beleaguered Finns who faced similar overwhelming odds in the face of the Soviet invasion during the Winter War of 1940. Like the relations among siblings, a lot of good-natured kidding exists alongside deep emotional bonds.

Robert A. Heinlein's best-selling novel *Job* is a remarkably astute observation by an outsider of the inter–Scandinavian rivalry between Denmark and Sweden. The plot involves the adventures of Alec, a salesman from Kansas, and Margrethe, a Danish stewardess, who meet on board a cruise ship. They are suddenly and unpredictably carried off to a parallel universe where the geography is the same but history is a bit different. Their startled reactions provide a source of amusement as they rush to a library after learning their fate to find out what has happened in their new world. Alec explains:

> I had looked up American history while Marga checked up on Danish history.... I found out that [William Jennings] Bryan had been elected in 1896 but had died in office ... and that was all I needed to know; I then simply raced through presidents and wars I had never heard of.
>
> Margrethe had finished her line of investigation with her nose twitching with indignation... I asked her what was troubling her....
>
> "I'm glad this isn't my world! Alec, in this world, *Denmark is part of Sweden.* Isn't that terrible?"
>
> Truthfully I did not understand her upset. Both countries are Scandinavian, pretty much alike — or so it seemed to me....
>
> "And that silly book says that Stockholm is the capital and that Carl the Sixteenth is king. Alec, he isn't even a royal! And now they tell me he is *my* king!"
>
> "But sweetheart, he's not your king. This isn't even your world.".....
>
> She sighed. "I don't want to be a Swede."
>
> I kept quiet. There were some things I couldn't help her with.

Bibliography

Albaek, Erik. *Crisis, Miracles and Beyond: Negotiated Adoption of the Danish Welfare State.* Aarhus: Aarhus University Press, 2008.

Arneson, B. A. "Occupied Denmark Holds a General Election." *American Political Science Review* (October 1943).

Bar-Zohar, Michael. *Beyond Hitler's Grasp: The Heroic Rescue of Bulgaria's Jews.* Holbrook, MA: Adams Media, 1998.

Berdichevsky, Norman. *The Danish-German Border Dispute: Aspects of Cultural and Demographic Politics, 1815–2001.* London: Academica Press, 2002.

_____. "The German-Danish Border: A Successful Resolution of an Age Old Conflict or Its Redefinition." *International Boundaries Research Unit: Boundary and Territory Briefing* 2.7 (1999).

_____. "The German Speaking Danish Minority in South Schleswig." In *Nations, Language and Citizenship,* edited by Norman Berdichevsky, pp. 191–198. Jefferson, NC: McFarland & Company, 2004.

_____. "Gågade, the Danish Pedestrian Shopping Street." In *Landscape Journal: Design, Planning and the Management of Land* 3, no. 1 (Spring 1984): 15–23.

Bidstrup, Knud. *Danmark dit og mit Dansk Byplanlaboratoriums Skriftserie 15: En Aktuel Geografi.* Copenhagen: Dansk Byplanboratorium, 1977.

Blixen, Karen. *Out of Africa.* New York: Penguin, 2001.

Boolsen, Vibeka. "En, to, mange ... Invandrestatistik og dansk-jødisk historieskrivning om Faaborgs jøder." Faaborg, Denmark: Faaborg Folkebibliotek. 2006.

Borschenius, Poul, and Werner Keller. *Spredt blandt folkslagene,* vol. 4: *Historien om de danske jøder.* Copenhagen: Fremad, 1968.

Branner, Hans. *Den 9ende April — Et Politisk Lærestykke?* Copenhagen: Dansk Udenrigspolitisk Institut, 1987.

Buckser, Andrew. "Keeping Kosher: Eating and Social Identity among the Jews of Denmark." *Ethnology,* 38, no. 3 (Summer 1999): 191–209.

Bugge, K. E. *Skolen for livet: Studier over N.F.S. Grundtvigs pædogogiske tanker.* Copenhagen: Gads Forlag, 1965.

Carr, W. *Schleswig-Holstein, 1815–48.* Manchester: Manchester University Press, 1962.

Cassidy, David C. "A Historical Perspective on *Copenhagen.*" *CUNY,* http://web.gc.cuny.edu/ashp/nml/copenhagen/Cassidy.htm.

Christianson, John Robert. *On Tycho's Island: Tycho Brahe, Science and Culture in the Sixteenth Century.* Cambridge: Cambridge University Press, 2002.

Davidsen-Nielsen, Niels, Erik Hansen, and Pia Jarvad. "Engelsk eller ikke Engelsk — That Is the Question." *Engelsk Indfyldelse på Dansk, Dansk Sprognævns skrifter,* 28. Copenhagen: Gyldendal, 1999.

Djursaa, Malene. "Denmark." In *Fascism in Europe*, edited by S. J. Woolf, pp. 237–256. London and New York: Methuen, 1981.

Eilstrup, Per, and Niels Eric Boesgaard. *Fjernt fra Danmark: Billeder fra vore Tropekolonier, Slavehandel og Kinafart Lademanns Forlags aktieselskab.* Copenhagen: Lademanns Forlagsselskab, 1974.

Eriksen, Thomas Hylland. "The Nation as a Human Being—A Metaphor in Mid-Life Crisis?" In *Siting Culture*, The Shifting anthropological Object edited by Kirsten Hastrup and Karen Fog Olwig. New York: Routledge, 1997.

Eskildsen, Claus. *Dansk Grænselære*, 7 editions, edited by C. A. Reitzels Forlag. Denmark: 1936–1946.

Eyck, Erich. *Bismarck and the German Empire*. London: George Allen & Unwin, 1950.

Ferguson, Robert. *The Vikings: A History*. New York: Viking Adult, 2009.

Frank, Diana Crone, and Jeffrey Frank. *The Stories of Hans Christian Andersen: A New Translation from the Danish, Including the Original Illustrations of Vilhelm Pedersen and Lorenz Frølich.* London: Grants Books, 2004.

Fray, Michael. *Copenhagen*. London: Drama Methuen, 1998.

"The Geographer: The Denmark-German Boundary." *International Boundary Study*, 81. Washington, D.C.: Bureau of Intelligence and Research, 1968.

Goldschmidt, Salomon, and Lisa Karen. *A Guide to Jewish Denmark: 5th Congress of the European Association for Jewish Studies.* Copenhagen: C. A. Reitsels Forlag, 1994.

Goldsmith, Juliet, "Tak for Mad" in Scandinavian Review, 1975, pp. 62–68.

Hæstrup, Jørgen. *Dengang i Danmark: Jødisk ungdom på træk, 1932–1945.* Odense: Odense Universitetsforlag, 1982.

Hammerich, Paul. *Skindet på næsen*, vol. 1: *En Danmarkskrønike 1945–72.* Copenhagen: Gyldendal, 1983.

Hansen, Stig. *The Viking Chef: Cooking Danish—A Taste of Denmark.* Copenhagen: self-published, 2007.

Harck, Ole. "'Dänische sprache ... eine Stunde wöehentlich'? Die Juden im dänisch-deutschen Grenzland." In *Menorah und Hakenkreutz*, pp. 141–146. Wacholtz Verlag, 1998.

Helmer Pederson, Eric. *Drømmen om Amerika Politikens Danmarks Historie.* Copenhagen: A/S, 1985.

Herb, G. H. *Under the Map of Germany: Nationalism and Propaganda, 1918–1945.* London and New York: Routledge, 1997.

Hornby, Ove. *Kolonierne i Vestindien Danmarks Historie.* Copenhagen: Politikens Forlag, 1980.

Hunks, A. R. "The Slesvig Plebiscite and the Danish-German Boundary." *Geographical Journal* 55 (1920): 127–138.

Jensen McDonald, Julie. *Delectably Danish: Recipes and Reflections.* Iowa City, IA: Penfield Press, 1984.

Jones, Glyn. *Denmark: A Modern History.* London: Croom Helm, 1986.

Jürgensen, Kurt. *Die Britische Südschleswig-Holsteinische Politik nach dem Zweiten Weltkrieg: Zeitschrit für Schleswig-Holsteinisch Gechichte*, Bd. III. Oeversee, Germany: Akadamie Sankelmark, 1986.

Kaiser, Niels-Jørgen. *Smilet er den korteste afstand: Erindringer fortalt til Niels Jørgen Kaiser.* Copenhagen: Gyldendal, 2001 [biography of Victor Borge].

Kirchoff, Hans. "Denmark, a Light in the Darkness of the Holocaust? A Reply to Gunnar S. Paulsen." *Journal of Contemporary History* 30, no. 3 (July 1995): 465–479.

Kirmmse, Bruce. *Kierkegaard in Golden Age Denmark* (Indiana Series in the Philosophy of Religion). Indianapolis: Indiana University Press, 1990.

Klatt, Martin, and Jørgen Kühl. *SSW—Mindretals og regionalparti I Sydslesvig.* Flensburg: Dansk Centralbibliotek, 1999.

Koefoed, H.A. *Teach Yourself Danish*. London: English Universities Press, 1966.

Krimmse, Bruce (ed.). *Encounters with Kierkegaard: A Life Seen by His Contemporaries*. Princeton: Princeton University Press, 1996.

Lauring, Palle, et al., eds. *Verdens Nyheder: Verdens Historie i dagblad form*. Copenhagen: Skrifola, 1958.

Lifson, Thomas. "Denmark Under Siege." *The American Thinker*, http://www.american thinker.com/2006/02/denmark_under_siege.html.

Lindeberg, Lars. *Arvefjenden: Dansk-svenske landskampe pa slågsmarker og fodboldbaner fra sågntid til nutid*. Copenhagen: Lademanns Forlagsasktieselskab, 1985.

_____. *De så det ske Danmark under I verdenskrig og genforeningen 1920*. Copenhagen: Forlaget Union, 1965.

Lundbæk, Henrik. *Staten staerk og folket frit: Dansk Samling mellem fascism og modstandskamp*. Copenhagen: Tusculanums Forlag, 2001 [on Arne Sørensen and Danish Unity Party].

Lundgreen-Nielsen, Flemming (ed.). *På sporet af dansk identitet*. Copenhagen: Spektrum, 1992.

MacKaye, David L. "Grundtvig and Kold." *American-Scandinavian Review* (Autumn 1942).

Mead, William E. *An Historical Geography of Scandinavia*. London: Academic Press, 1981.

Merkle, Benjamin. *The White Horse King: The Life of Alfred the Great*. Thomas Nelson, Nashville, TN. 2009.

Mogensen, Caresten. *Dansk under Hagekorsets Skygge*. Flensburg: Dansk Centralbibliotek, 1981 [on the Danish minority in Germany under the Nazi regime].

Møllehave, Johannes. *Mit Eventyr—12 samtaler om H.C. Andersen*. Copenhagen: Forlaget Bindslev, 2005.

Neal, Harry Edward, "Danish Legacy in America," *Scandinavian Review*, March, 1976, pp. 55–63.

Noack, J. P. *Det sydslesviske grænsespørgsmål 1945–47*, 2 vols. Aabenraa, Denmark: Insitut for Grænseregionsforskning, 1991.

Olwig, Kenneth. *Nature's Ideological Landscape: A Literary and Geographic Perspective on its Development and Preservation on Denmark's Jutland Heath* (The London Research Series in Geography 5). London: George Allen & Unwin, 1984.

Ottaviani, Jim. *Suspended in Language: Niels Bohr's Life, Discoveries, and the Century He Shaped*. Ann Arbor, MI: G.T. Labs, 2004.

Paulsen, Gunnar S. "The Bridge over the Øresund: The Historiography of the Expulsion of the Jews from Nazi-occupied Denmark." *Journal of Contemporary History* 30, no. 3 (July 1995): 431–464.

Pedersen, Karen Margrethe. "To Be Danish and to Have Danish as a Second Language." *Sprogforum* 19 (2001).

Petersen, Peter. *The Danes in America* (In America Books Series). Minneapolis: Lerner Publishing Group, 1988.

Rasmussen, Eric. *Danmarks Historie, vol. 13 Velfærdstaten på vej, 1913–1939*. Copenhagen: Politikens Forlag, 1965.

Reissz, Matthew. "Europe's Jewish Quarters." In *Copenhagen*, edited by Matthew Reisz, pp. 114–123. New York: Simon & Schuster, 1991.

Rerup, Lorenz. *Grænsen. Fra grænsekamp til sameksistens*. Copenhagen: Det Udenrigspolitiske Selskab og Det Danske Forlag, 1969.

_____. *Slesvig og Holstein efter 1830*. In the series *Danmarks Historie uden for Danmark*. Copenhagen: Politikens Forlag, 1964.

Rossel, Sven Hakon. *Hans Christian Andersen: Danish Writer and Citizen of the World*. Seattle: University of Washington Press, 1996.

_____. "Hans Christian Andersen: Writer for All Ages and Nations," *Scandinavian Review*, Summer, 1986. pp. 88–96.

_____. *A History of Danish Literature* (Histories of Scandinavian Literature). Lincoln: University of Nebraska Press, 1993.

Roussel, Aage. *The Museum of the Danish Resistance Movement: A Short Guide.* Copenhagen: The National Museum, 1989.

Rying, Bent. *Denmark — The South and the North.* 2 vols. Copenhagen: Royal Danish Ministry of Foreign Affairs, 1989.

Sandiford, K. A. *Great Britain and the Schleswig-Holstein Question, 1848–1864.* Toronto: University of Toronto Press, 1975.

Savalastoga, Kaare, and Preben Wolf. *En by ved grænsen: Gyldendals Ugleboger.* Copenhagen: Nordisk Forlag, 1961.

Schmidt, Jørgen W. *Oh, du Zion i Vest; Den danske Mormon Emigration, 1850–1900.* Copenhagen: Rosenkilde og Bagger, 1965.

Seaver, Kirsten. *Frozen Echo: Greenland and the Exploration of North America, ca. 1000–1500.* Stanford: Stanford University Press, 1997.

Skaale, Sjurdur (ed.). *The Right to Self-Determination: The Faroe Islands and Greenland* (Nijhoff Law Specials). Leiden, the Netherlands: Hotei Publishing, 2005.

Sondergaard, Bent. "The Fight for Survival: Danish as a Living Minority Language South of the German Border." In *Minority Languages Today: A Selection from the Papers Read at the First International Conference on Minority Languages held at Glasgow University,* pp. 138–143. Edinburgh: Edinburgh Free Press, 1980.

Starcke, C. N., Hans Olrik, and J. Varlsen. "Danmarks Kultur ved aar 1900 som Slutning af et hundredaars Udvikling." Publication for the Paris World's Fair, 1900. Cited in *På sporet af dansk identitet.* Edited by Flemming Lundgreen-Nielsen. Copenhagen: Spektrum. 1992.

Stræde, Therkel. *Royal Danish Ministry of Foreign Affairs and the Museum of the Danish Resistance October 1943: The Rescue of the Danish Jews from Annihiliation.* Copenhagen: Royal Danish Ministry of Foreign Affairs. 1993.

Thau, Carsten, and Kjeld Bindum. *Arne Jacobsen.* Copenhagen: Arkitektens Forlag, 1998.

Thurman, Judith Isak Dinesen. *The Life of a Storyteller.* New York: Picador, 1995 [biography of Karen Blixen].

Vilhjálmur, Örn Vilhjálmsson, and Bent Blüdnikow. "Rescue, Expulsion and Collaboration: Denmark's Difficulties with Its World War II Past." *Jewish Political Studies Review* 18 (Fall 2006): 3–4. Jerusalem Center for Public Affairs website.

Wendt, Frantz. *Danmarks Historie, 1939–1965, Politikens Danmarks Historie,* vol. 14. Copenhagen: Politikens Forlag, 1966.

Willumsen, Anne-Mette (ed.). *Droning Margrethe II — et livsvaerk.* Copenhagen: Skovgaard Museet, 2010 [biography of Queen Margrethe II].

Woofenden, Ian. *Wind Power for Dummies.* Hoboken, N.J.: Wiley, 2009.

Wullschlager, Jackie. *Hans Christian Andersen: The Life of a Storyteller.* Chicago: University of Chicago Press, 2002.

Yahil, Leni. *The Rescue of Danish Jewry: Test of a Democracy.* Philadelphia: Jewish Publication Society of America, 1969.

Index